BRIDGING
THE ATLANTIC

BRIDGING
THE ATLANTIC

*ANGLO-AMERICAN FELLOWSHIP AS
THE WAY TO WORLD PEACE*

A Survey from Both Sides
Edited by

PHILIP GIBBS

Essay Index Reprint Series

BOOKS FOR LIBRARIES PRESS
FREEPORT, NEW YORK

INTERNATIONAL STANDARD BOOK NUMBER:
0-8369-1928-9

LIBRARY OF CONGRESS CATALOG CARD NUMBER:
78-128245

PRINTED IN THE UNITED STATES OF AMERICA

CONTENTS

BRIDGING THE ATLANTIC

Bridging the Atlantic is a discussion of Anglo-American unity as a way to world peace. Distinguished contributors from both sides of the Atlantic offer their views on this pressing problem.

The reader is made abundantly aware of the obstacles to Anglo-American unity of action—economic, political, historical, prejudicial—and is also shown the instruments for overcoming these obstacles, which must be pushed aside in order to achieve world peace and stability. The issues are faced squarely and discussed frankly by all of the contributors, and the total of what they have to say constitutes a book of international importance.

The people who have written it have been drawn from various fields of interest: statesmen, journalists, novelists, soldiers, economists, and social workers; but their common purpose, the center toward which their different viewpoints are turned, supplies the unity of the book.

Sir Philip Gibbs has edited this book on a subject with which he has long been identified: American-British understanding and unity. He is well known in both England and America, not only for his many novels, but for his thorough knowledge of both countries and his efforts to explain them to each other.

I THE COMMON IDEAL

By Sir Archibald Sinclair

---

1. The Spirit of Democracy

THIS IS an important book and it deserves the careful attention of all liberal-minded citizens on both sides of the Atlantic. Covering as they do the broad field of the common liberal faith of the two great democratic nations, the chapters of this book emphasize not only the ideals which are shared by the two countries but the support and stimulus which each derives from the other.

George Washington, more than 150 years ago, paid tribute to "the Benign Parent of the human race" who had wonderfully preserved the American colonists and had destined their Revolution to be one of the great liberating influences in the history of the world. In those distant years of the 1770's the youthful Republic of America was painfully cutting the ties which bound it to England. During the century and a half which has passed since then, the Republic of the United States and the Kingdom of Great Britain have forged new ties of friendship, understanding and a common idealism. In the immortal words of Burke, "These are ties which, though light as air, are as strong as links of iron."

Washington's confidence in the protection of the Benign Parent of the human race has been shared by generations of American statesmen even down to the present day. They have never failed to emphasize the Christian ideals of service and love for others on which the policies and ideals of progressive parties in the United States have always been firmly founded. So it has been with the long and illustrious history of liberal thought in Britain. Men of many creeds and races have been attracted to it because of the simple foundation of its teaching on a belief, not only in justice for all men, but in equality for all men whatever the power of their individual wealth may be, and whatever the power and influence of the class to which they belong may happen to be. These truths, which were hammered home to the English people by Gladstone, have remained an essential part of the democratic ideal ever since. We who follow this ideal do, therefore, claim that we share with the Americans a common tradition and a common foundation for our political faith.

More than that, we can also claim that our immediate objectives are identical with those of the leaders of progressive thought in America. We are both striving with all the strength and resources we possess for the speedy overthrow of the evil and tyrannical forces of the Axis—whether they owe allegiance to the crooked cross of Germany or to the rising sun of Japan. It is doubtful if this common objective was ever better expressed, or if indeed the war aims of the Allies were put into more simple yet stimulating language than when President Roosevelt said last October, "The objective of to-day is clear and realistic. It is to destroy completely the military power of Germany, Italy and Japan to such good purpose that their threat against us and all other United Nations cannot be revived a generation hence. We are united in seeking the kind of victory that will guarantee that our grandchildren can grow up and, under God, may live their lives free from the constant threat of invasion, destruction, slavery and violent death." That programme—simply stated but difficult, engrossing and all absorbing—is the cardinal policy of every liberal-minded person both in Great Britain and the United States. In the old days of the Reform Bill our democratic forbears used to cry, "The Bill, the whole Bill and nothing but the Bill." We of to-day might well take for our slogan, "Victory, total Victory and nothing short of Victory."

II. The Essential Problem

While that remains the immediate objective, people in both countries are beginning to look ahead to the distant scene; naturally enough, their minds are beginning to peer forward through the smoke of battle to the world after the war. From the unity which is engendered by war and is imperative for its successful prosecution, people are beginning to look ahead to politics after the war. Plotting the shape of things to come is a pleasant pastime, though it is one in which wishful thinking is apt to guide the plotter's hand. From much that is vague and uncertain one thing emerges clearly and certainly—the need for progressive thought will never have been greater than it will be after the war. In the long eventful history of mankind there will never have been a greater necessity for a broad, tolerant and radical outlook than there will be after this war. We must not allow victory to be emasculated by outworn theories of economic self-sufficiency. Equally, we must not allow victory to mean the enthronement of reaction. These are real dangers, and we must guard against them.

In this connection, one of the most encouraging and hopeful portents is the extent to which liberal doctrines are being evolved in the United States, and to the extent to which practical liberalism is being preached by the most prominent statesmen of America. The influence of such opinions—backed by such potent authority—may well prove decisive after the war.

The essential problem which a modern democracy has to solve is how to combine public welfare with private liberty—how to combine the good of all with the good of each. The first effort towards solving this problem was undoubtedly made by the great British Liberal Government of 1906. The Americans have shown us how to continue the effort. In America during the last ten years, where private enterprise has been needed, it has been given fair play; when plans were needed, Americans have shown that they can outplan the planners. Democracy can therefore with particular force echo that quotation used with such telling effect by the Prime Minister, "Westward look, the land is bright."

Readers of this book cannot fail to realize the extent to which true democracy is being preached. To us who are progressives this is a highly significant and encouraging fact, but it is also a fact which bodes well for the future of nations and for the future of mankind. Some recent speeches by Mr. Henry Wallace—the Vice-President of the U.S.A.— illustrate this point, and they are quoted here not because they are isolated examples but because they are representative ones. Speaking last October of the world after the war, he said:

"There must be an international bank and an international T.V.A. (Tennessee Valley Authority) based on projects which are self-liquidating at low rates of interest . . . The new democracy by definition abhors imperialism. But by definition also it is internationally minded and supremely interested in raising productivity and therefore the standard of living of all peoples in the world."

Speaking on the same subject last December, he said:

"The aim should be to preserve the liberty, equality, security and unity of the United Nations—liberty in the political sense, equality of opportunity in international trade, security against war and business depression due to international causes, and unity of purpose in promoting the world's general welfare."

In the same speech Mr. Wallace touched on the subject of international trade:

"We can be decently human and really hard-headed if we exchange our post-war surplus for goods, for peace, for improving the standard of living of so-called backward peoples. We can get more for our surplus production in this way than by any high tariff, penny pinching isolationist policies . . ."

What liberal-minded person could deny the force and truth of these sentiments?

In a book of this kind the reader is reminded at almost every line of the ties which bind Great Britain with the U.S.A. Their value as a stabilizing and soothing influence in a distracted world is incalculable. The two nations are bound together by a common language and literature, and by common religious and political beliefs. Both peoples have the same faith in individualism, both have what Lincoln called "a patient confidence in the ultimate justice of the people."

In the history of mankind this common idealism between the two nations is a factor of immense significance. All progressive thinkers, since they are not hide-bound by class consciousness and are not wedded to powerful vested interests, can claim a special affinity with the prevailing opinions of American statesmen. We, too, must strive for the same international ideals and the same reforming but genial spirit at home. This book will do a splendid work in making the political ideals of our allies better known to us, in reminding us that our kinsmen have not been idle in working for liberal and progressive politics.

In both countries liberal and democratic traditions are no recent growth. Both the American and the Englishman love freedom and love liberty because they have experienced them, because they know them at first hand. This idea was well expressed by that sagacious Liberal,

Edward Grey, when discussing the two nations with Theodore Roosevelt. He wrote, "Some generations of freedom on both sides have evolved a type of man and mind that looks at things from a kindred point of view, and a majority that has a hatred for what is not just and free."

II THE AMERICAN PEOPLE

By Sir Philip Gibbs

---

1. DIVERSITIES OF CHARACTER

I THINK I may claim to know the American people fairly well, as far as one may know a big people in a big country with many diversities of character in their forty-eight States, living in different conditions of climate and geography, and having many foreign strains among them not yet wholly assimilated into the Melting Pot.

The vastness of the United States is not realized by people in these little islands unless they have been "over there" and travelled by train or car or aeroplane for thousands of miles this way and that. Texas is larger than France. Many single States are bigger than the British Isles. The difference between, say, New England and California in climate, geography, and their way of life is as much as between Norway and the French Riviera.

Our people are apt to regard the Americans as all the same—"the Yanks"—and certainly they all have a definitely American quality of mind and outlook, but the New Englander or the man of Vermont may be sharply distinguished in character as well as accent from his fellow-countryman in Virginia or Kentucky, just as the Scot differs from the Yorkshireman or the South country English.

I have met most of these American types in all sections of their social "set up" as they call it. I have sat on high stools in the drug stores of small towns drinking a friendly "coke" and talking to the fellow next to me. I have talked to the inhabitants of Main Street in many cities. I have been into many American homes—very lovely, some of them—and

6

become friends with cultured and charming people; I have had un-forgettable conversations with small shopkeepers, garage hands, coffee-shop girls, factory hands, the floor ladies of great hotels, innumerable women of high idealism and a social conscience, great numbers of ordinary business men, travelling salesmen or drummers as they are called; and I have become on friendly terms with darkey porters called red caps, shoe-shine boys, taxi-cab drivers, high school students, uni-versity men, newspaper men, big and small industrialists, local judges, Congressmen and Senators, Red Indians and coloured folk. I have visited the ranches of Texas, the horse farms of Kentucky and the country houses of Virginia. I have sat among the intellectuals in Green-wich Village, New York, and had exciting conversation in little restau-rants of many nationalities in that great city.

Outside New York itself, so restless, so nervy, so swarming with harried lives and yet so rich in intellectual adventure, I have found every-where a shrewd, kindly, good-natured hospitable folk who have made a pretty good job of life with a standard of comfort and social well-being higher than ours, on the whole, and with a sense of humour illuminating their speech and mind, and giving a sparkle to their most trivial conversation. I have not seen the black patches in their industrial conditions nor come into close touch with the distress, the tragedy, the vice and the crime which seem inevitable in all forms of civilization. My mental picture of the American people is that of a rather happy, vital and dynamic country with a habit of "getting together" in small groups or masses, and with an eagerness in their minds for some form of uplift making for mental and social advancement.

There are many social distinctions in the United States, mostly of wealth. Taking the nation as a whole, I find it has a more truly demo-cratic spirit than we have attained. My brother's hired man in Massa-chusetts, a tough old New Englander, talks about him by his Christian name; and of another brother of mine he used to ask, "How's old Cosmo? He's a great fellow." This handy-man invited me to go to the movies with him, put on his best clothes, polished up his Tin Lizzie and was ready to treat me on level terms, without the need of subservience on his side or condescension on mine.

A tall and dignified old man in a small town of Massachusetts kept a tiny shop for the sale of tobacco and newsprint, to which I used to go to buy papers and cigarettes. He was not puffed up because his brother is a Judge. I am sure the Judge does not feel humiliated because his brother is a small shopkeeper. It goes like that in the United States, though here and there one may find the same snobbishness as in England, our national curse, now being broken down.

II. AMERICAN EDUCATION

I was in America recently for nine months, before and after Pearl Harbour. I had not been there for some years and I saw—or thought I saw—certain changes. The people seemed to me to have lost some of their rough edges. They had better manners, I thought, in the humbler sections of society. They were more sure of themselves and therefore had lost the inferiority complex which used to make them boast to strangers. They had become, in the mass, better educated. I do truly believe that the nation is reaping the first fruits of a fine educational system and wonderful educational opportunities which we are only just beginning to plan in this country of ours. There are private schools and snob schools in the United States catering for the very rich (who will no longer be very rich) and privately endowed schools for various religious and social ideals—some of them very good indeed—but the mass of American people go to the same preparatory schools and high schools where they are well taught in fine school-houses. I had a look at some of their school books. They are beautifully produced and delightfully illustrated, far beyond the standard of our own in elementary schools. After the high school great numbers of young Americans go on to their State universities. In all material and equipment they are marvellous. The colleges are nobly built, the "Campus" is generally a fine park with playing-fields and this background must have a good effect upon young minds, lifting them up a little.

University education in the States does not go so deep or so high as our own—though it turns out very fine scholars and scientists—but the usual swarm of undergraduates skim superficially and in an elementary way over wide sweeps of knowledge. They will "do" the whole history of European art in six months. They will get a bird's-eye view of world history in a term or two. They will take easy degrees in psychology or philosophy. Not very profound all this, except for men and women who are earnest in scholarship. Is it much different in our own universities? But there is just this difference and, to my mind, it is of great importance to the general intelligence of a nation. It is much more widely spread, this university experience. Millions of young Americans have had it. It is accessible to the multitude because of low fees—sometimes earned out of term time by students who serve in restaurants or garages, or paid for by working mothers who stint and scrape for their boys and girls. It seemed to me that these young people who had been to college had a better address to life than the previous generation. It has raised the tone of the social code.

Years ago I visited the University of Michigan at Ann Arbour, never heard of over here. Most of the young men there were the sons of farmers. I was inducted into one of their Greek letter fraternities, representing the arts and professions. Several young men made speeches to me with great dignity and gravity. My son, who had just been to Oxford, was very much impressed, as I was too, for there was something very good in all this if manners maketh man.

With this university background young Americans of to-day—great numbers of them in many States—keep on reading such publications as the *Reader's Digest* and a variety of magazines which at least keep their minds lively and interested in the affairs of life.

I was particularly struck by the coffee-shop girls, corresponding somewhat to our A.B.C. but on a better scale of catering with a wider programme of "eats" and drinks. They used to talk to me because they had seen me announced to lecture in their city.

"Just out from England?"

"Yes."

"You must have had a terrible time. What's it really like over there?"

They were nice to look at. They had charming manners. Some of them had read such books as Shirer's *Berlin Diary* and Ambassador Davies's book on Russia. They had, of course, all read *Gone With the Wind*. They could talk knowledgeably about the war. The only person I met in the United States who prophesied correctly about Japan was one of these coffee-shop girls. I had had a conversation with a very high officer of the United States Army who had an utter disbelief in the Japs daring to attack his country. But this girl whispered to me over the breakfast-table:

"I have an idea that the Japs will attack us suddenly without warning or any declaration of war. It's the kind of thing they would do. And I don't believe we're prepared."

It would be foolish to pretend that the American people are highly cultured in all sections of society. They are not. But what I did see very clearly was an average intelligence, an alertness of mind, an ability of expressing ideas and an elementary education much wider spread than in Great Britain.

I told this to a taxi-cab driver in Chicago, who asked what differences I saw since my last visit.

"You're wrong," he said. "They're all half-wits and degenerates; I ought to know. I drive thousands of 'em about. Why, when I talk to them about history or economics they don't understand the words I'm using."

He was very critical and very amusing. After a conversation in traffic blocks—when he twisted his head sideways from his wheel—he got down from his cab at journey's end, shook me warmly by the hand and said, "I'm a 'Roumanian Irishman.'" Perhaps that accounted for his critical opinion of his fellow-citizens.

III. REACHING FOR THE STARS

A very high percentage of Americans—especially the women—do not stop their education or end their desire for knowledge after school age. On the contrary, the white-haired ladies and the middle-aged mothers are tremendously active in attending lectures at their clubs and other institutions. They go in great crowds to "conventions" on this, that, or the other pursuit of political and social ideals. Their husbands and sons laugh at their high and constant idealism. This reaching for the stars is a social habit or an intellectual exercise which does not perhaps produce practical results, but keeps them all merry and bright, satisfies their social conscience, saves them from boredom, and is very good for conversation at the family table.

"Say, Ma," says young John, "you just wallow in idealism. What's the good of it anyhow?"

To young John I would answer that his mother's idealism in recent history has sent vast quantities of Bundles for Britain to mothers and children bombed from their homes, generous gifts to British hospitals heavily burdened during and after the "Blitz," and, as in past history, has collected many gifts for stricken peoples. I am grateful for this idealism—not merely a gush of sentimentality but put to the test of hard work.

In many cities like Cleveland, Ohio, and San Francisco to which I went on my last tour, I found committees of American women—before Pearl Harbour—making and collecting garments for England's bombed cities; several hundreds of them in each city, doing hard drudgery because of pity and admiration for our civilians.

IV. REMOTE FROM THE WAR

Some months before Pearl Harbour, when I flew by Clipper out to the United States and began my journeys from one State to another, I was aware in my own mind of a growing sense of remoteness from the war in Europe. In Ohio and Texas and Kentucky and Kansas and Nebraska, it seemed enormously far away, as indeed it was, but also far away in mind as well as space.

I had just come from a besieged island. I had been through many air raids in London. I had walked through its ruins day by day. I had heard the constant drone of enemy aircraft after black-out time, night after night, over my own chimney-pots, for many months of nights. I had heard the explosions of many bombs and seen the sky alight with ruddy fires. Yet even to me, with that recent experience in my mind, there was gradually a kind of disbelief that this country of the U.S.A. could ever be touched by the war.

It was still the Land of Abundance. Every kind of food was plentiful, and much of it was wasted so that after lean rations in England it seemed to me shocking. I remember the heavy spread of juicy steaks in Murphy's Restaurant, Los Angeles. The heartiest American appetite could not tackle more than half. The meat was removed. Before the end of dinner a little cardboard box was placed on each table. On it was printed, "Murphy loves dogs too."

Here was peace and plenty. Why should they ever be disturbed by Adolf Hitler? It seems to me, even now, astonishing that President Roosevelt, that amazing man, could lead public opinion as far as he did, step by step, in his policy of Aid to Britain as the last defenders of democratic liberty, from Cash and Carry to Lend-Lease, from the making of munitions to "Shoot at sight" in the naval warfare. How could he overcome that sense of remoteness and lack of self-interest in the American mind?

V. THE UNKNOWN BRITISH

What is Britain to the vast mass of Americans? What ties of sentiment are there among those descended recently from Germans, Italians,

Swedes, Hungarians, and other races not particularly in love with us? They have never even seen an Englishman.

"Do many English come here?" I asked a one-armed fellow selling newspapers outside a hotel in Fort Worth, Texas. We had had a very good conversation and I had found him a most interesting fellow.

"You're the first specimen I've seen," he told me; and then he eyed me up and down with a friendly glint before he added, "And I must say I ain't dissatisfied." I was glad of the compliment.

I was a lonely bird as a lecturer when I got away from New York. In many cities and States they had not heard any first-hand account of what had happened in England and what we were doing in the war. They were deeply ignorant of all this, in spite of their radio news and articles from their correspondents over here who have been generous interpreters of British valour. Probably this was due to the late Lord Lothian, our Ambassador at Washington, who when the war began said, "No propaganda, no lecturers." He was probably right about propaganda, of which the Americans are justly suspicious. I was wise in going as a private individual not backed by any Government authority and appearing before them as a literary man and journalist. Missionaries from the Ministry of Information have this taint of propaganda about them. Yet the people were greedy to hear and to know. I had big audiences, often from two to three thousand in theatres and halls, where the Town Forum, wonderfully organized, assembles its members. I told a straight tale of what England was suffering and doing and hoping to do. I described the Blitz in town and country. Without heroics I told them of the heroism of our folk, and the work of the seamen and flying men, and air wardens, and ambulance girls. They listened intently, and somehow—though I am no orator—I moved them deeply, and some of the emotional ladies surged on to the platform afterwards and kissed me. Quite a comfort to a stranger in a far land, though slightly embarrassing.

There was always the usual queueing-up of people in the audience after the talk where thousands of friendly hands grasped mine, and these people expressed their deep admiration for our civilian population who had stood up so marvellously to the air bombardment. Never once was I heckled or challenged. In the Middle West I had fully expected to come up against the isolationists. My meetings were mostly open to all who wished to come and always there was question time when many questions were asked for twenty minutes or so. I was hoping for a few eggs, but none came my way. No angry voice was raised. There was no abuse of Britain, though some of the questions were critical or suggested criticism.

"Why don't you give liberty to India?"

That one always came and any answer of mine telling them how difficult this problem was because of Indian races, religions, and castes deeply hostile to each other failed to secure conviction.

It is no use telling the American people that we have done a good job in India maintaining justice and order, preventing plagues and famines, irrigating great provinces so that the old deserts have become fertile, encouraging a great deal of local self-government, making the fullest possible offer of Dominion status. They just don't believe it. For years Indian agitators and revolutionaries have lectured all over the United States accusing the British Raj of exploiting the natives and draining India of its wealth. Nor have they yet learnt that the Empire is no longer governed from Whitehall and that the Dominions are separate self-governing nations linked only by allegiance to the same King. It was very odd that among all the questions addressed to me there was none about Japan. Not even on the Pacific coast did they seem aware of any immediate menace from the Japs, although protracted discussions were going on in Washington with the Japanese envoy. For a long time all over the United States there had been a swarm of Japanese agents buying vast quantities of scrap iron, which were being carried to Japan from many American ports. No one seemed to bother about the use which was to be made of all this metal. Yet it was a plain warning of things to come—against the bodies of American youth.

VI. WHAT THEY WERE THINKING

By these questions at my lectures—before Pearl Harbour—and by innumerable conversations in railway trains, restaurants, aeroplanes, and American homes, I was able to find out many things in the American mind. They thought the British Army was not doing well and was not living up to its old tradition. They thought we were not putting much weight behind our war effort. "Why don't you make a second front now that the Germans are so heavily engaged in Russia?" Most of the people I met—the vast majority of them—were willing and anxious to give all possible aid to Britain in munitions and supplies and wanted us to win. But—before Pearl Harbour—every American mother and most American fathers had one reservation in their minds very clearly and firmly drawn. No American expeditionary force this time. No massacre of American youth in European battlefields.

Then came Pearl Harbour. It was a most staggering blow. Not to any American mind had it seemed possible that such a thing could have happened—to be caught unawares like this, to suffer such tragic losses under a dastardly attack. I heard many bitter comments, much harsh criticism. "Surely to God," they said, "the Japanese air squadron ought to have been spotted before it reached Hawaii. Had all the officers and men been sleeping at their posts? Somebody ought to be shot for this."

I listened to excited conversations and saw how deep was the wound suffered by the American mind at this outrage and humiliation. I was ashamed of my own secret thoughts. The tragedy of Pearl Harbour was a miracle of luck to us. It had brought the United States with its immense man-power and vast material resources into this war and by our side. Overnight, by this one stroke of fate, the deep-rooted reluctance in the American mind to send men overseas or to come into the fighting line with us was overturned and abandoned. They were in this war now not only with Japan but with Germany, which had been the instigator and ally in this Japanese attack. That would mean, I knew, victory in the end, though before Pearl Harbour only faith and hope and wishful thinking could see even dimly the defeat of Hitler's legions.

The awful loneliness of Britain—which had stood against the dark menace to all liberty, ill-armed and weak except in the soul of its people —had been relieved in the Western world by the coming-in of the Americans. In the long run, whatever the price in tragedy and blood, we should win and there would be a new comradeship among the English-speaking peoples. I dared to say these things to my audiences in many States after the news of Pearl Harbour and they cheered. I was talking to different people, changed overnight. I could feel their new intensity of interest in what Britain was doing. Their questions were all directed to this. What were the women in England doing? Was the black-out effective? What was the organization of the A.R.P. services? How did we intend to defeat the U-boat menace? How soon would it be before we started a second front? What was the secret of our civilian courage? Did I think American civilians could behave so well under air bombardment?

After my talk, when I stepped down from the platform, people came up and shook hands and spoke with emotion. They were mostly middle-aged or elderly men and women.

"We are together now. England has held the fortress alone. We ought to have been in before."

"You can count on us." "Everything we are and everything we have now goes into the common pool."

"Our boys are untrained but, by God, sir, when they're ready the Germans and the Japs will know their doom."

"Our two Navies will have a lot to do, but they'll do it."

"Remember Pearl Harbour is our watchword." "We shall remember all right." "But we must beat Hitler first."

"I come from English stock. I'm proud of it."

"The courage of your people has been an inspiration to the world. Yes, sir."

Those were the middle-class folk from well-to-do homes. Some of them, perhaps many, had English or Scottish ancestors. In Boston, where I spoke after Pearl Harbour, they were sympathetic to England and had been active in work for the Aid to Britain movement and Bundles for Britain. But I had many conversations with men and women in a lower social scale. The shrewd, hard-bitten taxi-drivers of New York, the little shopkeepers in a small town of Massachusetts, and the ordinary fellow sitting on a stool at a drug store counter. Not one word of boasting reached my ears at that time. They were taking this war seriously and grimly. They didn't like it. They didn't want it. They hadn't asked for it, but now they were in it they were not going to quit for all the devils in hell.

"We shall see this through to the end," said one of them, "and we shall have to take some hard knocks before the end comes."

"We're starting from scratch. We've a hell of a long way to go before we're anything like ready. But we shall take what's coming to us and then it'll be our turn."

"Well," said another man, "this means that we'll have to live leaner and work harder. That's sure. We shall be called on for a lot of sacrifice. That's sure, too. I guess they can't ask us for too much. We're ready to give it and a lot more."

There was a general idea in each man's head, I found, that the rest of the folk didn't understand.

"They just don't understand the first thing about it. They don't understand that we'll have to give up our way of life. We'll have to give up our gas and our home comforts and maybe our food. We'll have to give up our sons. That's the hardest. That's what's going to break my wife's heart. But we've got to win this war, haven't we? We've got to make it impossible for such a thing to happen again. We've got to kill these war-makers."

The rapidity of the Japanese sweep into the Pacific startled the American people and shook them. It didn't seem according to the book of American tradition. They had been contemptuous of the Japs. They had been told that the Japanese Fleet was rotten, that Japanese aircraft was fifth-class. Now American marines on Wake Island and other islands of the Pacific could not receive reinforcements before they were wiped out by swarms of little yellow men.

The fall of Singapore was a frightful shock to the American mind as it was to the British mind. Things were going from bad to worse but there was no panic, no doubt about the end, despite all these disasters.

VII. THE SWITCH-OVER

The American people went on with the job of getting ready, switching over from peace to war, with complete unity of purpose, most grim and resolute, under the leadership of a great President who spoke to them over the microphone in words of unfaltering confidence and solemn but spirited fervour. He called upon them for sacrifice and hid nothing of the need for it.

For a time there was a gleam of light in the Philippines. The defence by General MacArthur was truly in the American tradition. The hero worship of the whole nation was given to him. "Every time he sneezed," I was told by an American critic of this excess of enthusiasm, "it was announced as a victory by the newspaper men."

There was a clamour in Congress and in the Press to appoint General MacArthur as Commander-in-Chief of all the American forces. The President smiled, and the General himself is the most modest of men, though deserving quite a lot of hero worship which still he gets from the Australians and ourselves. A splendid type, under whom all men are glad to serve.

I saw that switch-over from peace to war. It was dramatic and impressive. It was a revelation also of American character, and I was there in a time of great history in the chronicles of a great people. I saw their good humour, their good neighbourliness, their cheerful acceptance of uncomfortable changes in their way of life, and their eager demand for service in this time of national emergency. In some ways it was a repetition of what had happened in England two years before, but without the same immediate and more terrifying menace. I saw the first black-out in Massachusetts. Small towns and villages in various districts were ordered to put out all lights at a given signal at an hour not previously announced. Air wardens had been enrolled.

I was staying in a village of scattered houses. None of them had yet prepared black-out curtains. A boy on a bicycle from the house "across the street"—it was a country road—dashed up to the back door and shouted hoarsely, "Lights out." It was very thrilling to two young people who had just gone to bed upstairs. But there was no drone of hostile aeroplanes overhead as I had heard them so often in England. I stuffed a cushion over a radio set in the form of a globe which glowed with a little light and sat in profound darkness for two hours or so. One item on the radio programme was familiar. It was constantly repeated, a gay and lively little song called "Remember Pearl Harbour." It seemed to suggest that Pearl Harbour had been a merry little episode of fragrant remembrance. We were also asked to remember the juicy, delectable flavour of somebody's chewing gum.

These black-outs plunged the eastern seaboard and States into utter darkness from time to time, but there was something lacking—a single German aeroplane. Secretly the air wardens longed for an air raid to test their organization and their courage and to give reality to their eager service.

I saw the first rationing of the civilian population and the first things chosen for such restriction overturned the very foundations of American social life. For that is based upon the automobile, and when gas and rubber were strictly and severely rationed it created for a time a sense of bewilderment and frustration and immobility which was almost paralyzing. How could the housewife do her shopping in the neighbouring small town without a car? How could a mother get her children to school six miles away? How could a factory hand get to his job twenty or thirty miles away? How could people living in country houses get into Boston or Providence, or visit their friends or go to lectures and debates and committee meetings for social service?

I stayed in the house of a district rationing officer. He had led a quiet life in an old New England house beyond the scattered village. Now he was invaded by anxious enquirers. There would be a tap at the door.

A man in working clothes would be invited into the sitting-room. He looked worried.

"Now I just want to know——"

He wanted to know how to fill up the rationing form and whether he would get enough gas to take him to his job. And what about new tyres? He had been caught with old uns. They wouldn't last more than a month or so.

There was a constant procession of these enquirers. Some of them laughed, though there was worry in their eyes.

"I'm not asking for anything more than what my neighbours get. We're all in the same boat now. I don't ask anything that's unfair. No, sir. I want to win this war as much as anyone, but my old lady and I are just wondering."

American roads became quiet. There was a strange absence of traffic between small towns ten miles apart. The tempo of American life slowed down as far as social intercourse went, though it was speeded up in factories and munitions works. Rubber and gas were only for the workers on the war job.

The President was speeder-up in chief. He announced staggering figures of the war production at which he aimed.

This Year (1942)	.	60,000 planes
Next Year	.	125,000 "
This Year	.	45,000 tanks
Next Year	.	75,000 "
This Year	.	20,000 anti-aircraft guns
Next Year	.	35,000 " "

Some of his own friends and followers were incredulous. A distinguished Senator smiled when I spoke of them and said, "Impossible. We can't do as well as that." But they did as well and better in most of the units of production.

VIII. The Machinery of Destruction

I had seen something of those potentialities even before Pearl Harbour. I went over the Ford works and was staggered by the immensity of the job being done there. In one of the show halls was the proof and symbol of the mass production which had gone on until the call came for aid to Britain and Russia. It was the 29-millionth car. Now no more cars were being made. Mr. Ford's employees were beginning to make guns and tanks. The works, as all the world knows, cover hundreds of acres. They are self-contained, from the iron ore which comes up the Rouge River to the finished product of tempered steel. Great coke ovens, immense furnaces, rivers of molten metal. It was frightening and awe inspiring, like Vulcan's workshop in the world of myth. I stood on a high platform when the molten metal gushed into vast vats which were carried away on travelling cranes. One could only look at it through darkened mirrors lest one should be struck blind. Men like demons were flinging bags into the stream of white-hot liquid. They were the alloys to harden the steel. Fountains of sparks rose and fell, too near the human beings, I thought. One touch of those shining sparks would make a human torch. But the men knew to a yard how far they would fall. The metal flowed on, cooling through endless channels as they seemed, until it was steel, finely tempered for its purpose. Tanks and guns. Guns and tanks instead of Henry Ford's automobiles.

It was only one plant. In every State I visited I had seen other plants complete or in skeleton form getting ready for war production. The President had said that the United States must be the arsenal of nations defending liberty and democracy. He had thought ahead of public opinion. He and his advisers had been getting busy before actual war.

All this, I thought, will one day produce the most monstrous machine of war—aeroplanes, tanks, guns, shells, and all munitions—ever imagined by the mind of man and beyond imagination. No nation will be able to stand up against it. No nation—not even Germany with its slave labour in captured countries—can compete with this.

After Pearl Harbour, American labour, abandoning its feuds and its political passion, poured into these new plants and began production on a big scale getting bigger as the months passed. There was a shifting of populations. Cities of huts arose in a mushroom growth around the works. Luxury trades gave up their workers. Men left the fields to go into munition shops.

The switch-over from peace to war was quicker than in Britain, with the highest technical efficiency in mass production. The United States was becoming one great arsenal.

IX. Two Leaders of the Nation

I had talked, as I have said, with the man in the street, the man in the train, the man at the drug store counter, finding each one of them—

perhaps I had luck—a friendly fellow, glad to meet an Englishman, kindly humorous, above the average, I thought, in intelligent outlook on life. Never among these types of American citizens did I get anything but courtesy and goodwill to England—and a keen sympathy for what our folk had suffered and were suffering. Now I met two men who stood above the crowd in their office and responsibility. One was the President of the United States. The other was Mr. Henry A. Wallace, the Vice-President.

I was nervous that morning when I went to the White House to see Mr. Roosevelt. I thought I might find conversation difficult and say or ask him the wrong thing. One has to be wary and discreet when facing the big men. My worry was quite needless. In one second President Roosevelt puts every man at his ease. When I was left alone with him after his Press Conference—when he had been very cheery and informal with his "newspaper boys"—he waved a hand to a chair close to his own and gave me a friendly welcome as though we had met often before. He talked about the war and Britain's part in it, saying generous and reassuring things though the news that morning was bad and black, especially in the Pacific. He spoke about his own people and their difficulties in realizing the factors of time and distance which made our task so difficult against the Japanese. Much of what he said was "off the record" and he spoke with the utmost candour about all difficulties. But there was no worry in his eyes, no shadow of anxiety. His handsome face was serene and smiling. He spoke about the figures of production and put a hand on some papers on his desk.

"My critics said we could never do it. Well, we are doing it. In many cases we are beyond our schedule. Impossible, said the enemy. Well, we're doing it."

He spoke about the English Prime Minister and his eyes were alight with good humour.

"Winston Churchill and I get on fine," he said, heartily. "We understand each other."

He has, as I have written elsewhere, a radiant personality. Sitting there in his chair, very easy in the swing of his body and the movement of his hands with his infirmity hidden, something in his personality captures one and suffuses one. In very truth by this radiance of his he puts a spell on one. Whatever his critics and his enemies may say—and he has many—he has the highest qualities of leadership in the power of his personality alone. Has he not proved it by every speech he has made, by his courage in action and by his tremendous and dynamic energy as a war-time President with supreme authority as Commander-in-Chief of all the American forces? Lincoln had no harder job, nor had to face more enmity behind the scenes. There is little else in common between that dry, self-educated and rustic-spoken man and this cultured, social, smiling President. For the latter is the son of a wealthy family and has had a university education and, but for the cross of pain, has had all the opportunities for a great political career denied to Lincoln in his early years.

He has aroused passionate political hostility. I have met people in the United States, though not many, who hate him so much that they cannot even mention him by name lest they should choke. They call him That Man. A distinguished literary man referred to him in my presence as a Swindling Messiah. They cannot pardon him for his policy of the New Deal which seemed to them no better than State Socialism, his pandering—as they called it—to revolutionary Labour and his departure now and then from constitutional and political tradition. They accuse him of having tried to pack the Supreme Court and of having used his influence to appoint men of shady character to high places. The isolationists, who have gone into retreat, carry on secret and whispering propaganda against his reputation and character. But few, if any, are able to attack his foreign policy with which even his Republican opponents find themselves in agreement, and even his enemies are forced to admit that his conduct of the war has been courageous and far seeing. Behind him still stands a vast mass of public opinion, especially in the humblest sections of the American people who know him as their champion.

The other man who impressed me most among the leaders of American policy and thought is Mr. Henry A. Wallace, the Vice-President. He has not the magnetic personality of Mr. Roosevelt. He would never carry great audiences, I imagine, by dynamic oratory or popular appeal. He seemed to me a shy man with the scholar's mind, though he has done great work for agriculture and has, I am told, a shrewd and practical judgment as chairman of many committees, directing the organization of war-time affairs. When I sat on the other side of his desk one day and he talked to me about his ideas on the post-war world, I became aware, as it seemed to me, that here was a man with a sweetness in his soul and a fine spiritual quality. Here, I thought, is a man of vision far beyond narrow national interests, as far reaching as a happier and better state after the war for all nations and a common humanity. But he spoke very simply and modestly, with now and then a glint of humour in his deep-set eyes. His political opponents call him Starry-eyed Wallace. They want to ridicule these ideas of his which they detest because they challenge selfish nationalism and are hostile to that form of Big Business which barricaded itself behind tariff walls, and denied American markets to debtor nations so that they became desperate in misery and financial insecurity. Before seeing the Vice-President I had read an article by him in *The Atlantic Monthly.* It had appeared in January 1941 and was, to my mind, the most remarkable document in this war-time world. It was extraordinarily fearless in placing upon his own people, or at least upon their political and financial leaders, a heavy weight of responsibility for the downfall of world economy, the misery of many nations, the failure of the League, and the inevitability of this Second World War. He outlined his plan for a new peace and a new world in which there would be the chance of recovery in international trade, a better standard of living in poverty-stricken nations, security of prices and markets for the primary producers—reduced to bankruptcy after the last war—and a scientific scheme for stabilizing currencies, raising purchasing power and arranging credits for war-scarred countries. We spoke of these things and I was deeply moved. Here was the vision of a new and nobler world, I thought, here is the only hope of the future.

A chance remark by Mr. Wallace was partly the cause of this book being written by the authors who are here assembled.

"I don't get much support from England for these ideas," he said. "They don't seem interested."

Those words made a dent in my mind. I carried them back to England, and they reached my liberal-minded friends. Something ought to be done about it, they said. This book is trying to do something about it.

X. CAUSES OF MISUNDERSTANDING

Apart from what our two governments may do in support of international peace and economic recovery when this war comes to an end, there is a need of interpreters to explain each country to the other, to break down many prejudices and misunderstandings on both sides of the Atlantic and to create a sense of fellowship and unity of purpose between our two peoples.

I have written here honestly about the great friendliness I found in the United States towards this country. It was the same in all the States I visited. But I was touching only a small section of American life and thought at least in my audiences who came to hear me because they were friendly. But I do not wish to disguise from myself and from others the somewhat painful truth that the mass of Americans do not like the English. Why should they, after all? They have less prejudice against the Scots, but they cannot abide our English accent and our English manners.

The English accent as they call it—we call it English—of London, Oxford and the Home Counties is just ridiculous to them, seeming very affected and absurd. It is the accent which makes them jeer at the damn fool Englishman on the comic stage. We do not realize until we have been some time in the United States how the rise and fall of our voices and our way of speech irritates many American minds.

"Why don't you take the marbles out of your mouth?" shouted a fellow from the gallery when I was speaking in the Carnegie Hall, New York, many years ago. Perhaps I have taken them out since then. An American friend of mine named John Tunis, one of the most delightful of men with a highly developed sense of humour, stayed in my country house for a week-end and I invited a party to meet him. He told me afterwards that he had to retire from time to time in order to laugh behind the door. It seemed to him like a Somerset Maugham play. He couldn't believe that such people were real—the old Colonels and their dames, the country gentry who gobbled in their speech, the young girls who laughed in the English way which somehow is not the American way in the sound of mirth.

The Oxford accent, as they call our sophisticated tone of speech, annoys Americans of a certain type without making them laugh. They think we are patronizing them. They think we are putting on edge or English side as they say when playing billiards. These haw-haw people, they think, have no brains, no sense of humour and no democratic convictions. They are all snobs. It is very unfortunate for the purposes of understanding that we must still go on talking English—in our own way. The North countryman and Scot are not so handicapped.

Every American, however friendly now to us, has to break down in his mind certain historical causes of dislike. The first books he reads as a small boy about his own national heroes have England for the enemy. Their victories were against us. Their towns were burned by British soldiers. In the War of 1812—of which we read very little in our history books—American frigates fought against ours and, according to American history books, always won. We were hostile to their liberties. We interfered with their trade. They hated our guts, as they say. This historical prejudice—the Ancient Grudge—reaches the American mind in its most impressionable age. It needs a mental wrench to get over it. Some don't get over it, though Kenneth Roberts has done his best in *Oliver Wiswell* and other books to give fair play in historical romance.

Why should the American people in the mass have a natural affection for us? Many of them are descended from peoples with whom we fought or with whom we competed, or who hated our arrogance in the days when we were very proud and haughty. There are a lot of Irish in the United States. They, too, have had a grudge against us, not without cause. They have long memories, the Irish. They do not easily forget or forgive. I found myself in trouble with the Irish-Americans after the last war. They picked on the wrong man, because I resigned the best job I had ever had in Fleet Street as a protest against the Black and Tans, just before I went out to the States. But they didn't know that. They said, "Here is an Englishman who wants to address American audiences. We'll see about that." They saw about it in the Carnegie Hall, New York, where I opened my lecturing tour. Ten thousand people were in the hall when I stood on a big platform, feeling as small as a little white mouse. All went well for twenty minutes. Then something happened. In the stalls I saw, to my surprise, a stout lady in evening dress strike a bald-headed gentleman in a tuxedo jacket. It seemed to be the signal for battle. Green flags were unfurled in the central gallery, and in the topmost gallery. Great numbers of people started fighting each other. There was a great clamour of voices.

"Can anybody tell me what is happening?" I asked, from my lonely place on the big platform. Nobody could tell me. Their voices did not carry because of the uproar. It lasted three-quarters of an hour before the police restored order and ended the meeting. The friends of Ireland had been fighting those who upheld free speech and courtesy to a foreign visitor. Most of my lectures were broken up, and it was fine for me, because I seldom had to deliver a speech, and just stood there waiting until the fun began. In Chicago an Inspector of Police came into my dressing-room, putting on a pair of white gloves.

"Sir Gibbs," he said, "I'm going to tell the audience that if there's the least sign of trouble, I have a body of my men behind the scenes stripped to their jerkins."

He was disappointed when I told him I thought that was a bad introduction to an English lecturer.

Trouble began within ten minutes. The battle lasted quite a long time. I did not have to speak a word. In Chicago at that time I was accompanied, against my will, everywhere by two plain-clothes men. They were Irish, like many American cops. They found themselves in an awkward situation as they explained.

"We ain't worrying about your life, Sir Gibbs, but only about our reputation."

That seemed all right to me.

At the end of this exciting lecture tour I was given a very fine dinner in New York by those who wished to make amends for the unfriendliness of the Irish, of whom I was a friend. Many hundreds of distinguished people were there. In many speeches they said generous things about me, quite undeserved, but while they spoke little notes were handed me from the outside where a crowd of Irish had gathered. The notes were terse but significant.

"You are a dirty English rat."

"You ought to be deported."

When I went again to the United States, peace had been made with Ireland, a generous peace, and all was well. Many Irish men and women came and shook hands warmly, regretting a little misunderstanding on my previous visit. And this time, after all those years, in the midst of another world war, I had many Irish among my audiences who came up afterwards and spoke of their admiration of the way English people had sustained the terrible ordeal of the Blitz. Some of them criticized the attitude of Ireland. All the same, the Irish in the United States have a certain prejudice in their minds against England. It is one of our handicaps in achieving a unity between our two peoples for world peace and good fellowship. It is not insuperable. For hundreds of years we fought the Scots who have no grudge against us. For hundreds of years we fought the French before the *Entente Cordiale*. Then there are the German-Americans. Most of them who have been long established in the United States are among the best American citizens, utterly loyal and very good folk. But it is natural and right that in their minds there is an historical sentiment for the old Fatherland, before Hitler or Nazidom, and not for England. One would think so, though I met these people of German descent who were working generously on behalf of Bundles for Britain. Czechs, Poles, Russians, Swedes, Portuguese, Slovaks, Roumanians, Italians, now American citizens half or wholly assimilated, are without any pull of the heart-strings towards Britain except for what they read of English poetry and English books. We need interpreters out there, ambassadors of goodwill, men and women who belong to our best types and can speak to them without affectation or condescension. We have no right to condescend to the Americans, or even to seem to condescend. Their "set up" of civilization is in many ways, though not in all ways, on a higher standard than our own. They hold a mighty big place in the world. In the mass, as I have written, they are better educated than our folk in an elementary way. In New England and many States they have homes as beautiful as ours and much more comfortable. They are citizens of a great country, vast in its spaces, beautiful beyond words where there is natural beauty of mountains and forests, and lakes and rivers, as I saw when I flew great distances looking down from the sky. The most magical beauty I have ever seen in the world is where I looked down in the night upon American cities of the great plains below—Denver, Sacramento, San Francisco—like fairy cities built of shining jewels, or like clusters of diamonds on the black velvet of the earth. What could be more charming than the little towns of New England, with white wooden houses, many of them dating from the eighteenth, and even seventeenth, centuries, with avenues of trees between them?

But the American folk matter most to us, not their mountains or their lakes. Can we make friends with them? Can the English-speaking peoples get together to hold the peace of the world and shape its destiny somewhat? To my mind that is the most important thing in the world to-day—after winning the war. It is the best hope we have of getting law and order and justice and equity among nations for the prevention of another war, and the end of human slaughter and the beginning of a better era. It is of most vital importance that all liberal-minded men and women in these isles should reach out to the liberal-minded men and women in the United States. We must try to build a bridge for spiritual and friendly traffic across the great grey sea. We must greet every American over here as an ambassador of his own country, to whom we must give warm hospitality and all courtesy. It will take us long to repay the wealth of hospitality given to our visitors in the United States. We should open the doors of our homes.

We should unfreeze the ice of our insular reserve if any still exists. Do not let us botch this chance of union for world peace by blunders and stupidities of statesmanship or prejudice. There will be many hostile forces ranged on either side against Starry-eyed Wallace and men with his vision of world peace, whether they be Democrats or Republicans—and in the Republican Party—let us not forget—there are many fine minds with an international outlook and a sympathy for the common needs of humanity. These ideas are not the exclusive property of President Roosevelt and his friends. But in the United States, as here, there are reactionary minds hateful of all liberal ideals because they will prevent trade interests and big profits, and the old piratical way of life. Greed and selfishness and narrow nationalism and the rigidity of small unchanging minds will have to be fought there and here. It is not going to be a walk-over to a better world following this war.

Pessimists say that there is already a falling away from idealism based on common sense, and that Anglo-American relations are not as good now as six months ago. I don't believe that. I have no evidence to prove it. In any case, I know enough of the American people to believe that they will respond warmly and generously to warm and generous expressions of friendship from this side. Every American, however "tough," is a sentimentalist at heart.

Let us give him the chance of sentiment about ourselves by letting him know the heroic achievements of our young men and the glory of our women in time of war. We have much to tell them that they do not know and would like to know. Let the word American to us mean something more than a figure on the screen in a picture palace. They have a genius for comradeship. If we can build that bridge across the Atlantic by a warmth on this side which will reach them 2,000 miles away—the vibrations of goodwill can reach farther than that—we shall establish an alliance which will last beyond the war, and alter, maybe, the shape of things to come.

III ANGLO-AMERICAN RELATIONS

A SURVEY

By Viscount Samuel

―――――――――――――――◆――――――――――――――

I. GHOSTS OF HISTORY

THAT ANGLO-AMERICAN CO-OPERATION after the war is essential to the welfare of mankind is clearly understood in Britain and the British Commonwealth. No one doubts it. There is no dissentient voice. Everyone here would wish to see the ideas and the strength and resources of these two, the mightiest organizations that the world has ever seen, joined together in a sustained effort to solve the hard problems which, in vast complexity and formidable shapes, will confront the nations.

But is it the same in America? Great leaders, with immense followings, speak with that purport; stress the duty of America's participation, of America's co-leadership in world affairs; proclaim a willingness, an eagerness even, to share to the full in the moulding of the future destiny of man. And yet . . .

Can we be sure that the electorate, Congress, President, will be steadfast during the inevitable years of stress and controversy, and doggedly see the matter through? It is useless to conceal the fact that among us, remembering the events of 1919, there is a deep anxiety.

The British people see the strength of American isolationism. They see a reluctance to join hands, a distrust. They see a lack of confidence in our intentions; an emphasis on mistakes committed; where there is recognition of results achieved, often a grudging recognition. They see these things, and are puzzled; and sometimes hurt. This is because the mass of the British people are altogether unaware of the background of

American thought. Only a minute fraction have any knowledge at all of American history; those who have seen America with their own eyes are, of course, far fewer still. The British people do not realize that the history that every American boy and girl learns at school is mainly a history of their country's struggles and conflicts; that the antagonist in those struggles, those conflicts, has almost always been England.

Our school-books begin, after a brief Roman and Anglo-Saxon preface, with the Norman Conquest and the Middle Ages; but to the Americans that is all dimly remote—embryonic, pre-natal. For them the history that matters begins with the Pilgrim Fathers and those who followed them, setting out to face every peril and hardship for conscience' sake; seeking liberty of thought and liberty of worship across the ocean; casting off the yoke of an oppressive, tyrannous government—the government of England. Generations pass; the next struggle is in essence the same; it is again in the cause of liberty. This time the Americans have to line up in battle, to fight for years, at the sacrifice of thousands of lives, the organized forces of a King and aristocracy—the King and aristocracy of England. No long interval passes and war breaks out again. A force invades American territory, occupies the city of Washington, burns down the newly built Capitol: those troops are British troops, it is another war with England. The next crisis in the annals of the nation is the tragic conflict between North and South; the governing classes in Britain openly sympathize with the wrong side; friction grows and becomes dangerous; the countries are within an ace of war for the third time; it is only just averted by a Gladstone government, which, in the teeth of the most formidable political opposition, accepts arbitration. The Tribunal judges Britain to have been in the wrong, and under the award she pays a compensation of millions. Meanwhile, America watches the course of events in the country nearest to her shores, in Ireland—the lamentable results of an indefensible land system, established in the interest of a landowning class, foreign to the people, holding their estates through military conquest. There is a terrible congestion; a great famine; in fifty years the population of Ireland is reduced by a half; hundreds of thousands of people flee to America, there to create in the electorate a bitter, resentful, anti-British block, enduring for generations.

It is a painful story to tell. But it has to be told. For the British people will never understand the American mind unless they grasp, quite clearly, that the predominant feature in the history of the United States has been that series of clashes and conflicts with that one antagonist. Till now our people have been blandly unaware of most of this. After all, we say, the Stuarts were centuries ago, and the people at home suffered as well as the Pilgrim Fathers. We have recognized long since that the Americans were in the right in their War of Independence; they won; and we have always been willing to let bygones be bygones. As to the War of 1812 and the burning of the Capitol—every detail of which is known to every American boy and girl—here not one person in ten thousand is even aware that such events ever took place. The tension during the American Civil War and the Alabama Treaty are equally unknown. As to the Irish question, that, we say, was no doubt a very unfortunate business; but it has all been put right now, and it is a pity that people should have long memories and nurse ancient grievances. We follow the rule—"the farther we are from our bad deeds, the smaller they appear; the farther we are from our good deeds, the larger they appear."

But when, to-day, Americans see features that they dislike in the social or political systems of Britain and the British Empire as they now are, sub-consciously they may relate them to the Britain they had learnt about at school. They see surviving the old royal and aristocratic forms and formulas. They see a great section of the British working-classes still housed in slums and sunk in poverty. They see an Ireland still unreconciled and hostile. They see an India, ruled by a British Viceroy and British Governors, with, apparently, the mass of the people struggling for political liberty, and held down by armed force. They hear of neglected colonies, and can observe the West Indies, at their own doors, backward and discontented. And they watch British policy in Europe, still engaged, as it seems, in the same old sequence of complicated diplomatic manœuvres, aiming at maintaining, by shifting alliances, some precarious system of "Balance of Power." Many among them draw the conclusion that this, after all, is the same England that their forbears knew and suffered from. When they are asked to co-operate, they are deeply suspicious that they are being inveigled into policies that are not good policies, seeking aims that pretend to be good aims but are not. They feel that their country may still be best serving the cause of man if it holds aloof; evolves, as it has done in the past, a new and finer way of life of its own; promoting world progress rather by example and influence, by the economic power of a great population with vast accumulated resources, than by mixing in the unsavoury politics of Europe and Asia, and spending lives and wealth, decade after decade, in war after war.

II. THE NEW SPIRIT OF EMPIRE

We, on this side of the Atlantic, know that this view of our present-day conditions, this diagnosis of our ideas and policies, while true in certain particulars, is in the main and in essence false. There have been, during those centuries, two Englands—a Tory England and a Liberal England; America has had to deal sometimes with one predominant, sometimes the other. Now the old Toryism is quite submerged: Liberal democracy rules and is likely to rule. The issue was decided in two pitched battles; which, although fought according to constitutional rules, were as strongly contested as many a civil war: they were the battles over the Reform Bill of 1832 and the Parliament Bill of 1912. Old party names survive, although with changed meanings; some reactionary forces still furtively remain, and might, it is true, if conditions became propitious, again emerge into mischievous activity. But our politics are now firmly based on an electorate of thirty millions, and a House of Commons chosen by it in full freedom; the essential ideas of Liberalism permeate that electorate, that House through and through.

If we here are often ill-informed about the past of America, Americans are often as ill-informed about the present of Britain and the British Commonwealth. The monarchy survives—not because of mere inertia or a snobbish subservience; but because it is a link, which we cherish, with all our past, and because it renders—without friction nowadays—most useful service as the lynch-pin of our constitution at home, and as a personal unifying factor in our diffused and variegated structure overseas. The Crown remains; but, as Mr. H. G. Wells has said, it is emerging from the trials of history "a little more like a hat and a little less like a crown." As to the House of Lords, there is not a single one of its members who would defend its present composition; and if movements to change it are in abeyance, it is partly because there is no general agreement as to a substitute; and partly because, since the passing of the Parliament Act, its spirit has become more progressive and its contributions to the national discussions more helpful and constructive.

Americans understand that the old British Empire has been transformed by the gradual evolution of the white colonies into fully independent Dominions, that independence finally given the stamp of constitutional sanction by the Statute of Westminster of 1931. But, from all accounts, they do not at all understand the facts of the Indian situation. Everyone who has returned from recent visits to the United States brings the same account of a surprising lack of sound information about India. American opinion seems to have been misled into believing that the situation there is nothing more than a head-on collision between an Indian nation fighting for its freedom and a stubborn British Government refusing to grant it. It seems to suppose that Congress is not only the best organized and the most active of the Indian parties, but that it is fully representative of the Indian people. Some, it seems, even believe that "Congress" is a constitutional body, like the Congress of the United States or the other American republics. If the issue had been as simple as that, it would have been settled long ago. Let us hope that the American people will come to realize that the British Government has repeatedly offered to India a self-government as complete as any that exists in Canada or Australia, or in Great Britain itself, with precisely the same constitutional status; and that if this has not been carried into effect it is almost entirely due to the fact that a hundred million of Moslem Indians refuse to accept the majority rule of three hundred million Hindus; while the Hindus have been unable to propose any form of constitution which would not be likely to lead to immediate civil war —a renewal of the wars which, for centuries, and until the establishment of British rule, had been the chief feature of the history of India.

Nor, it seems, does American opinion yet understand that if the Irish quarrel still persists that also is not because of any continued divergence between the British Government and a solid Irish nation, but solely for the reason that the problem—precisely similar, except in scale, to the Indian situation—is not bi-lateral but triangular; that there are not two parties to the case, but three; that here again a large and powerful section of the population, consolidated in the north-eastern part of the island, differing from the rest in race and religion, still refuses to be amalgamated with the majority and cannot be overridden except by armed force. If the cause of liberty demands self-determination for India and for Ireland, is the cause of liberty to have no regard to self-determination for Indian Moslems and for Ulster Protestants?

As to the colonies, here again there has been a great advance in recent years. Not that it would be true to say that progress has only been a thing of yesterday. The history of the British colonies taken as a whole has been a remarkable record of brilliant achievement in all the elements of human well-being, accomplished through the unstinted devotion of thousands of pioneers, of officials, of soldiers and sailors. If the economic and cultural conditions of those territories, as they now are, be compared with what they were fifty years ago, still more with what they had been at the time when British influence was first established, the contrast will furnish material for an illustrious chapter in the history of civilization. None the less it is right to concentrate attention on the faults that remain. In a broad survey we must give proper weight to achievements; but in day-by-day politics we must seek out the failures and find and apply the remedies. That is now being done with greater zeal and activity than ever before. The Colonial Development and Welfare Act, passed by Parliament with general approval in 1940, marked a new stage. It provided large funds for all purposes of welfare. So far from a metropolitan State exploiting its colonies and drawing tribute, here is one of the rare cases in which it is paying large subventions from its own resources for their benefit. And all the time, in the more primitive communities, the indigenous forms of self-government, where they have survived, are being carefully maintained, though purged of their former abuses and encouraged to strike out on new lines of progress. Elsewhere, as in the West Indies, parliamentary institutions, often of long-standing, are being gradually moulded to the pattern of modern democracy.

There was a time, in the middle of the nineteenth century, when many of the best minds in Great Britain looked forward to an early day when the British people might regard their Imperial task as done; when India and the greater colonies would become wholly independent States, and the lesser colonies be well on the road to a separation not less complete. Then the British Empire would become a not ignoble memory, and the British people find their only mission in perfecting the way of life of their own island, and in conducting a mutually beneficial and indiscriminating commerce with all the countries of the world. Very few voices are heard to-day speaking that language. The reason is not a mere vainglorious pride in the vastness of possessions, a crude resolve that "what we have we hold"; nor yet a belief that to maintain the political connection is vital to our own economic prosperity. Those principles would not appeal to the many enlightened students of international affairs, sincerely devoted to the cause of political progress, who hold, with full conviction, that to maintain the unity of the British Empire is a service to mankind. There is at stake something deeper and better than a mere national egotism.

The philosophic mind, viewing the present parlous condition of human affairs, sees as one of the chief causes the multiplicity of sovereignties. There are more than sixty separate States in the world; and that is too many. The need of this age is clearly an integration, a co-ordination of States. The way of progress lies there. To adopt an opposite course, to break up such unions as already exist, would be reactionary and wrong.

No one would now deny that if the American Civil War had resulted in a permanent division between North and South, in the establishment of two wholly separate sovereignties, with an international frontier between them, each with its own army, its own tariff, its separate foreign policy—that would have been no service to the world. Still worse would it be if some political cataclysm, happily unimaginable, were to split up the present forty-eight States of the American Union into as many independent republics. So again with the Soviet Union; it would be no progressive step if that federation, of nine self-governing units, were to dissolve into nine separate nations; the consequence could only be to add to the chaos and the turmoil of world affairs. The same principle, we believe, applies to the British Empire. If, through weariness or weakness, the Parliament and Government at Westminster were to connive at the break-up of the vast system which now gives some measure of unity to fifty or sixty countries covering a fourth part of the globe; securing them at least from internecine conflict among themselves; combining them into one mighty force to resist aggression and to defend peace; if the great Dominions were cast off to become wholly disconnected sovereign entities; India to add one more—or more probably soon to divide again into two or three; the colonies, or groups of them, to constitute at least another half-dozen; and if that example were followed, for similar reasons, in the French, the Dutch, the Belgian and the other colonial Empires—then the existing sixty sovereignties would become a hundred and more; scores of new international frontiers would be created; the causes of possible quarrel would be multiplied manifold; and the prospect, already so uncertain, of an enduring peace being established upon the earth would be made still more precarious.

The continuance of such great syntheses of States is therefore justified. But it must be on two conditions: First, in each case, the unity of the whole must be accompanied by the political liberty of the parts, wherever "national" characteristics prevail; carried as far as their degree of maturity allows. Second, the influence of each combination must be used, not for its own selfish interests, political or economic, but for the general welfare. We believe that our Commonwealth, in its modern shape, does substantially fulfil those two conditions. That being so, we hold that it is our duty to resist disintegration, as wrong in principle, and as injurious, not only to the well-being of its members, but to the permanent interests of mankind. If the twentieth century were to dissolve the British Commonwealth, the twenty-first would have to re-create it.

III. The Record of Social Reform

As to the aims of British policy in Europe, it is, I believe, a misreading of history to present them as seeking, by devious and changing ways, to maintain a Balance of Power, in order that Britain herself, as a make-weight, might profitably control the issues. The real aim, pursued through every kaleidoscopic change in the grouping of the continental States, has been to prevent any one of them from establishing a domination over the rest. Spain, France, Germany—each in turn has been a menace to the freedoms of Europe, and therefore to the freedom of Britain: each in turn has thereby brought her into a league of resistance. Add to that the consistent exercise of her influence or her power to promote the national freedom of smaller countries suffering under foreign oppression—Holland, Greece, Belgium, Italy, Bulgaria—and we have a history, centuries long, which we can present to our American friends, not with apologetic shame, but with well-founded pride.

As to our social conditions, they have been greatly changed and vastly improved even during the lifetime of the older among us. I have made four visits to the United States, spread over a period of just fifty years. The advance there has been amazing; and not only in material things—the development of cities, of industries, of communications—but also in what is more difficult, and more important, in all the affairs of intellect and culture. Yet I venture to affirm that the changes during the same period in Great Britain, and particularly in the conditions of the masses of the population, have been as striking. They are changes that are continuing at this moment with ever-increasing speed. We are convinced that—through the Beveridge Scheme of Social Security, the leadership of the new Ministry of Planning in the improvement of environment, the extensions of the system of Education and of the Public Health services which are now in active preparation—unless some financial catastrophe were to prevent, we are convinced that we shall succeed at no distant time in carrying the social progress of the past sixty or seventy years to a line so much farther forward that our ancient society will have freed itself altogether from those blots and deficiencies which, we must confess, have lowered its credit in the eyes of the newer countries of the world.

In any case, what matter those old quarrels embedded in history, those minor causes of present difference, or any trivial discordances of ways and manners, compared with the gravity of the world situation in these times, and the over-riding necessity for all enlightened men, all the truly civilized nations, to join together for the rescue of mankind? The British and American peoples are moved, after all, by the same fundamental motives—respect for the dignity of man, care for the family, love of liberty, hatred of war—all springing from the humanitarian spirit, taught by the Christian ethic. These point to a common object. If there is a common object, there must be a desire for a united effort to attain it. The greater the difficulties of the task, the greater the need for unity in the effort. Once there is a desire for united action there must next be the will; and once the will is there, revealed and proclaimed, the ways to make it effective will surely be found.

IV. AMERICAN LEADERS ON POST-WAR POLICY

Let us consider, then, more definitely what are the purposes for which Britain and the United States would wish to co-operate, and what are the various practical measures through which they would hope to achieve them. I think I would render more useful service if, instead of trying to draw up a summary of my own, or bringing together statements made by British leaders of opinion, I were first to survey the series of remarkable speeches that have been made by American statesmen during the years 1941 to 1943, and to give the gist of the ideas on the principal issues which they embody. I will not include the declarations of the President himself, for they are well known, and they have necessarily been of a less specific character than those of some of his colleagues or his political opponents. But we have had a number of striking pronouncements from Mr. Henry Wallace, the Vice-President of the United States; Mr. Cordell Hull, the Secretary of State; Mr. Sumner Welles, the Under-Secretary; Mr. Milo Perkins, the Director of the Board of Economic Warfare; as well as from Mr. Hoover, the Republican ex-President, and Mr. Wendell Willkie, the Republican candidate at the last Presidential Election; and many of these are as definite as the conditions allow at the present stage. The value of any speech depends upon three things—what you say; how you say it; and who you are that says it. These speeches deal with urgent matters of the highest importance; they are cogent and clear, and they are made by representative men in highly responsible positions.

I have divided the extracts among a number of heads. I will take first those that relate to the difficult economic issues, and afterwards the political.

(a) *The Economic Aim*

Mr. Wallace: Some have spoken of the "American century." I say that the century on which we are entering—the century which will come out of this war—can be and must be the century of the common man. . . . No nation will have the God-given right to exploit other nations. Older nations will have the privilege to help younger nations get started on the path to industrialization, but there must be neither military nor economic imperialism. The methods of the nineteenth century will not work in the people's century which is now about to begin.[1]

Mr. Sumner Welles: The creation of an economic order in the post-war world which will give free play to individual enterprise and at the same time render security to men and women and provide for the progressive improvement of living standards is almost as essential to the preservation of free institutions as is the actual winning of this war. . . . The basic conception is that your Government is determined to move towards the creation of conditions under which restrictive and unconscientious tariff preferentials and discriminations are things of the past; under which no nation should seek to benefit itself at the expense of another; and under which destructive trade warfare shall be replaced by co-operation for the welfare of all nations. The Atlantic declaration means that every nation has a right to expect that its legitimate trade will not be diverted and throttled by towering tariffs, preferences, discriminations, or narrow bilateral practices. Most fortunately we have already done much to put our own commercial policy in order. So long as we adhere and persistently implement the principles and policies which made possible the enactment of the Trade Agreements Act, the United States will not furnish, as it did after the last war, an excuse for trade-destroying and trade-diverting practices.[2]

Mr. Milo Perkins: In every civilization of the past, bar none, if men took the most which it was possible to produce and divided it among all who were alive to share it the answer was always a miserable standard of living. Within your lifetime and mine, however, men have entered an era dominated by the machine and the test-tube. If we take all that can be produced at the end of this war, and divide it among the people who will then be alive to share it, we shall be within reach of a very good standard of living for the first time in all history. That will be the most important material thing that has happened to the human race since the discovery of fire and the invention of the wheel.[3]

Mr. Cordell Hull: In order to accomplish this and establish among the nations circles of mutual benefit, excessive trade barriers of many different kinds must be reduced and practices which impose injuries on others and divert trade from its natural economic course must be avoided. Equally plain is the need for making national currencies once more freely exchangeable for each other at stable rates of exchange, for a system of financial relations so devised that materials can be produced and ways may be found for moving them where there are markets created by human need, for machinery through which capital may—for the development of the world's resources and for the stabilization of economic activity—move on equitable terms from financially stronger to financially weaker countries.

There may be a need for some special trade arrangement and for international agreements to handle difficult surplus problems and meet situations in special areas. We in this country must realize that the far-reaching economic objectives of the Atlantic Charter will be impossible if we follow policies of narrow economic nationalism, such as our extreme and disastrous tariff policy after the last war.[4]

(b) *Barriers to Trade*

Mr. Sumner Welles: After the last war, at a time when other countries were looking to us for help in their stupendous task of economic and social reconstruction, the United States, suddenly become the world's greatest creditor nation and incomparably strong economically, struck heavy blows at their war-weakened, debt-burdened economic structures, that were heavy morally as well as economically. The harmful effects of this policy on the trade, industry, and conditions of living of people of many other foreign countries were immediate. Our high tariff policy reached out to virtually every corner of the earth, and brought poverty and despair to innumerable communities. Our tariff policy was striking at the very roots of our export trade. . . . The resultant misery, bewilderment and resentment, together with other equally pernicious contributing causes, paved the way for the rise of those very dictatorships which have plunged almost the entire world into war. It is essential that the United States should make clear at once their intention to stimulate world trade. If we do not have that intention, then other nations would have to plan and build for autarchy.[5]

Mr. Wallace: A movement is already under way to abandon the same tariff policy represented by our reciprocal trade agreement programme, and go back to the Smoot-Hawley days of building a high tariff wall around the United States. Economic warfare of the Smoot-Hawley type is the initial step towards military warfare. It leads first to totalitarian control of trade, then to shooting.

To win the peace, we must follow through to establish the right kind of international trade relations; we cannot hope to maintain peace by force unless the peace we are maintaining is a just peace.

India, China and Latin America have a tremendous stake in the people's century. As their masses learn to read and write, and as they become productive mechanics, their standard of living will double and treble.[6]

Mr. Willkie: Our tariff policy throughout most of this century, culminating in the Hawley-Smoot tariff, was probably the greatest single factor in creating intense nationalism in the world. By this policy, and by the dumping of the London Economic Conference in 1933, we made international co-operation impossible. These excessive tariff laws destroyed the past and prevented the future.[7]

Mr. Perkins: The job of the future would be to build up mass consumption great enough to use this mass production. It would require a bold and daring use of long-term credits by every enlightened government in the world. Governments must enter fields where private finance could not enter without assuming risks too great to take with other people's money, but by that very act the area of private investment would be broader and safer than it had been in the last two decades.[8]

I turn now to the political side, with which the military is closely associated. It is unnecessary to give quotations in support of the principles in the Atlantic Charter that the war must be carried through to complete victory, against all three of the Axis Powers; that it must be followed by their disarmament, and by safeguards against rearmament. On those points there is no doubt or disagreement in any quarter.

The following extracts deal with other matters, immediate or ultimate, that arise.

(c) *Peace Settlement to be Prepared beforehand and Effected by Stages*

Mr. Sumner Welles: The framing of post-war plans could not wait till victory had been achieved, and he announced that plans were already under way for such measures as agreements for stabilizing the prices of basic commodities. He added that we must give serious attention to nutrition and that humanitarian considerations and self-interest combined to make this subject one of outstanding importance. The final terms of the peace should wait until the immediate tasks of the transition period after the defeat of the Axis Powers has been completed by the United Nations, and until the final judgments can be coolly and rationally rendered.

The organization through which the United Nations are to carry on their co-operation should surely be formed so far as practicable before the fires of war which are welding them together have cooled.[9]

Mr. Hoover: There should be two stages: an instant "conditional peace," and then the world should take time to cool off and work out one by one and separately the solutions of lasting peace.[10]

(d) *International Organization*

Mr. Wallace: Obviously, the United Nations must first have a machinery which can disarm and keep disarmed those parts of the world which would break the peace. Also, there must be machinery for preventing economic warfare and enhancing economic peace between nations. Probably there will have to be an international court to make decisions in cases of dispute. And an international court presupposes some kind of world council so that whatever world system evolves will have enough flexibility to meet changing circumstances as they arise. As a practical matter we may find that the regional principle is of considerable value in international affairs. For example, European countries, while concerned with the problems of Pan America, should not have to be preoccupied with them, and likewise Pan America, while concerned, should not be preoccupied with the problems of Europe. Purely regional problems ought to be left in regional hands. This would leave to any federated world organization problems involving broad principles and those practical matters which affect countries of different regions or which affect the whole world.[11]

Mr. Welles: At the end of the last war a great President of the United States gave his life in the struggle to further the realization of the splendid vision which he had held up to the eyes of suffering humanity—the vision of an ordered world governed by law. The League of Nations, as he conceived it, failed in part because of the blind selfishness of men here in the United States as well as in other parts of the world; it failed because of its utilization by certain Powers primarily to advance their own political and commercial ambitions; but it failed chiefly because of the fact that it was forced to operate, by those who dominated its councils, as a means of maintaining the *status quo*. It was never enabled to operate, as its chief spokesman had intended, as an elastic and impartial instrument in bringing about peaceful and equitable adjustments between nations, as time and circumstance proved necessary.

Some adequate instrument must unquestionably be found to achieve such adjustments, when the nations of the earth again undertake the task of restoring law and order to a disastrously shaken world.[12]

Mr. Cordell Hull: It is plain that some international agency must be created which can—by force if necessary—keep the peace among the nations in the future. There must be international co-operative action to set up the mechanisms which can thus ensure peace. This must include the eventual adjustment of national armaments in such a manner that the rule of law cannot successfully be challenged and that the burden of armaments may be reduced to a minimum. In the creation of such mechanisms there would be practical and purposeful application of sovereign powers through measures of international co-operation for the purposes of safeguarding peace. Participation by all nations in such a measure would be for each its contribution toward its own future security and safety from outside attack.

The settlement of disputes by peaceful means, indeed all processes of international co-operation, presuppose respect for law obligations. It is plain that one of the institutions which must be established and given vitality is an international court of justice. It is equally clear that in the process of re-establishing order the United Nations must exercise surveillance over aggressor nations until such a time as the latter demonstrate their willingness and ability to live at peace with other nations.[13]

(e) *Co-operation with Russia and China*

Mr. Wallace: We shall decide some time in 1943 or 1944 whether to plant the seeds for World War No. 3. That war will be certain if we allow Prussia to rearm either materially or psychologically. That war will be probable in case we double-cross Russia. . . . Unless the Western democracies and Russia come to a satisfactory understanding before the war ends, I very much fear that World War No. 3 will be inevitable. Without a close and trusting understanding between Russia and the United States, there is grave probability of Russia and Germany sooner or later making common cause. Of course, the ground for World War No. 3 can be laid by actions of the other Powers, even though we in the United States follow the most constructive course. For example, such a war would be inevitable if Russia should again embrace the Trotskyist idea of fomenting world-wide revolution, or if British interests should again be sympathetic to anti-Russia activity in Germany and other countries.[14]

Mr. Willkie: There is a theory that the way to build a healthy peace is around the ridge-pole of British-American relations. Call that the Anglo-American backbone theory. This theory says that we have a powerful common culture, and that we should lead the peace, and that Russia and China must thenceforth play an unimportant part in the scheme of world power. This is a traditional theory, and much argument can be made in favour of it.

I profoundly disagree with this theory. It takes no account of the immense development of the Russian people, of the literacy and health that has been given to a new Russia. It takes no account of their just claim that they will have contributed at least as much as anybody else to winning the war. It takes no account of a new China, led by a man with a determined purpose. . . . We must meet Russia and China and the other nations at the peace table and at the reconstruction of the world afterwards as absolute equals.[15]

(f) *American Participation*

Mr. Wallace: Both Russia and the United States retreated into isolationism to preserve their peace. Both failed. Both have learned their lesson. . . . In order that the United Nations may effectively serve the world it is vital that the United States and Russia be in accord as to the fundamentals of an enduring peace based on the aspirations of the common man. It is my belief that the American and Russian peoples can and will throw their influence on the side of building a new democracy which will be the hope of all the world.[1]

Mr. Hoover: When victory comes after this war, we must jointly with our Allies again try to lead the world to the promised land across this terrible maelstrom of conflicting forces. If we are to have lasting peace, it will be by co-operation with them in finding it and making it secure.[17]

Mr. Willkie: To say there will be a reaction against internationalism when such a victory is won seems to me fatally unrealistic. We shall no more be able to isolate ourselves from the ensuing peace than we can dodge the responsibility now of fighting everywhere in the world. . . .

It is obviously fallacious to argue that because the Democratic Party was in power when these things happened the Democratic Party was a party of intervention and by the same token the Republican Party was a party of isolation. The British public should realize that some of those who raised their voices loudest for isolation right up to Pearl Harbour were leading Democrats. They should realize that the arsenal of democracy was created by American industry and that 80 per cent of the men who operate American industry are Republicans. They should realize that many of the great American newspapers are Republican newspapers, which were the strongest in advocacy of the cause of assisting Great Britain and other countries fighting aggression; that most of the essential legislation necessary to implement this programme was passed with the help of Republican leaders; that with virtually complete unanimity the American Press stands to-day for full and complete participation by the United States in world affairs and for the relentless prosecution of the war to a victorious conclusion.

With almost as complete a unanimity the Press stands for full and complete United States co-operation in the formulation and implementation of the peace to come. And none can doubt that this applies with equally forceful emphasis to the leaders of the Republican Party and to the rank and file of the Republican Party to-day. . . . I will be asked why I am so confident that the seeming intricacies of American party politics will not bring about a repetition of history. This will not happen because America is fighting this war—not merely the Democratic Party. Because the overwhelming majority of Americans to-day are completely aware that isolationism is not merely perilous but downright impossible.[18]

v. A Council of Nations

These declarations, taken together, form a consistent body of political doctrine of great value in the present phase of world affairs. The speeches have been widely reported in Great Britain, and have been welcomed by political leaders and in the Press with the warmest approval. Mr. Eden, as Foreign Secretary, and other members of the Government, have spoken repeatedly to the same general effect. So far as they go, it may be taken that these are agreed principles.

Of necessity a great deal has had to be postponed until conditions are riper. Nothing definite has yet been said with regard to the future of Germany. That is clearly right; for this is a matter which concerns intimately all the Allied Nations; and those whose territories are on the periphery of Germany more directly than Britain and the United States. Until the voices of Russia, France, Poland, Czechoslovakia and the smaller continental States can be heard, only harm would be done if spokesmen of the British and American Governments were to put forward clear-cut schemes.

What has been said also on future world organization has hitherto been very tentative. This, too, is clearly right, and for the same reason. But within the free nations a vast public discussion has been proceeding; various alternatives have been keenly canvassed; opinion seems now to be slowly crystallizing. Active movements in the United States and in Great Britain declare that international anarchy is a root cause of all our troubles—with which all would agree; and offers Federalism as the only alternative—a much more doubtful proposition. For if Federalism means, as it should mean, the creation of federations, and if that term is used, as it always has been used, to denote constitutions such as those of the United States, or Switzerland, or Canada, or Australia, then the opinion of the great majority at the present time undoubtedly does not support it. For it would involve that, within each federated area, whatever it might be, a unitary Assembly of some kind should be established, chosen by a single electorate comprising all the peoples, together with a unitary Government. This Assembly and Government would control the foreign policy and defence of the whole area, with the necessary finances. But at the same time the existing Parliaments and Governments in the capitals of whatever States might be included would continue to function—in Washington, London, Paris, Brussels, The Hague, or wheresoever they might be—without, however, anything to say on international relations: they would no longer have any voice in deciding the course of policy, not even the supreme question of war or peace. In the present state of the world this appears, to most men of political experience, an impossible proposal. The conflict between Federal Rights and State Rights has often troubled the history of the United States— although substantially a homogeneous country—leading to one of the most bitter and sanguinary of all civil wars. That conflict would inevitably recur, magnified many times, and made incomparably more difficult of solution, when the component States were ancient nations with different traditions, languages and cultures, and when the Federation was a new creation set to cope, suddenly and simultaneously, with the most formidable and stubborn problems that beset mankind.

But this is not the only alternative to international anarchy. It is coming to be recognized among the smaller nations that the old principle of complete independence and a scrupulous neutrality will no longer hold. That has been proved beyond question, by the most disastrous experience, to be no safeguard against the aggression of great predatory Powers irresistibly armed. Many of the leaders of the lesser nations are seeking a new policy, and they are turning, not to Federation but to Confederation; not to an amalgamation of States, with a unitary Assembly and Government, but to a permanent union of existing Assemblies and Governments. In such a union each would be represented in a joint legislature and executive by delegations chosen by themselves. Already the exiled Governments of Poland and Czechoslovakia, and of Jugoslavia and Greece, have agreed upon the principles of constitutions of that kind. They hope that the two Confederations may be linked together, and that, when the conditions allow, other countries may adhere. Similar tendencies are appearing in other parts of Europe.

These regional organizations, however, would clearly not be sufficient to meet the case. Here comes in the suggestion in Mr. Churchill's outstanding broadcast of March 21st, 1943:

"One can imagine that under a world institution embodying or representing the United Nations, and some day all nations, there should come into being a Council of Europe and a Council of Asia. . . . I hope we shall not lightly cast aside all the immense work which was accomplished by the creation of the League of Nations. Certainly we must take as our foundation the lofty conception of freedom, law and morality which was the spirit of the League. We must try—I am speaking of course only for ourselves—to make the Council of Europe, or whatever it may be called, into a really effective League, with all the strongest forces concerned woven into its texture, with a High Court to adjust disputes, and with forces, armed forces, national or international or both, held ready to enforce these decisions, and prevent renewed aggression and the preparation of future wars. . . . It would therefore seem, to me at any rate, worthy of patient study that, side by side with the Great Powers, there should be a number of groupings of States or Confederations which would express themselves through their own chosen representatives, the whole making a Council of great States and groups of States."

We may see adumbrated here a pattern for the post-war world. It is a pattern which might well fit in admirably with American ideas; for the Council of Europe might absolve the United States from day-by-day participation in the management of the affairs of our troubled Continent, while membership of the "world institution" might give her a sufficient voice in the governing decisions.

Many in Great Britain, accustomed to a constitution that is unwritten and finding great value in it, are inclined to think that any new arrangement should be kept as simple and as fluid as possible. We regret that, after the last war, American and continental practice, not unnaturally, led to the League of Nations being bound within the clauses of a formal, rigid constitution; we see there, perhaps, one of the causes of its failure. If the other parties agree, let the new "world institution" at the outset be furnished with the bare essentials; let the "principle of stages" apply here as in the other provinces of the peace-making; let it be planted as a sapling and left to grow of its own vitality.

vi. The Colonial Empire

Little, again, has been said in the American speeches about the future of the colonial empires; and this, too, must be accounted wise. For the initiative here should rather come from Great Britain, since she is more deeply concerned than anyone else. At the same time we must not suppose that American tactful reticence implies indifference. If we are to be partners, the kind of household each partner keeps is not unimportant to the other. Besides, if the American Fleet and Army and Air Force help to expel the Japanese from Malaya, Singapore and Burma, the American nation will feel some moral responsibility for the future fate of the peoples of those territories. In Britain, the right principles to be followed in relation to colonies have been much discussed during these years. That they should be assisted to reach the status of self-government has long been accepted as the only proper policy. It has to be recognized, however, that many of these communities, with populations small in comparison with great modern States and often at a primitive standard of culture, do not possess the political experience and ability, or the financial resources, necessary to provide for their own good government, development and defence. It is to their interest to remain for a period, and perhaps for a period of generations, under the ægis of a great Power. There is, further, the general consideration, already mentioned, that it is not to the advantage of the world to multiply independent sovereignties. The conclusion is that early and complete separation is not the policy to be encouraged.

Nor is there any wide support for the proposal that all colonial empires should be pooled and put under a combined international control. The chief objection is that such a system might prove of less benefit to the peoples concerned than that which they now have. Hitherto joint international administrations have been notoriously inefficient and inactive. They are carried on by officials drawn from different countries, with various backgrounds and traditions, trained in different systems of law, speaking different languages and obeying different loyalties; it has always been found that they have been the theatre of jealousies and intrigues and friction; the teamwork, which is of vital importance to good administration, is usually absent.

The present Colonial Secretary, Colonel Oliver Stanley, looks forward to something different. He favours some form of regional co-operation between colonial Governments—in West Africa, or East Africa, or elsewhere—irrespective of their nationality. And no doubt regular, formal consultations would be useful in pooling valuable experience and might help to promote good neighbourliness. There is a growing tendency, however, to regard this as insufficient. Some of those who are deeply interested in this matter are now advocating two other measures. The first is the establishment of a Standing Select Committee of the two Houses of Parliament on British Colonial Affairs. The duty of such a Committee would be, not to share in administration, but to investigate and to recommend. It would carry out its function largely by sending, year by year, sub-committees of its own members to visit the various groups of colonies and to report. Its activities would be likely to arouse and to maintain the interest of Parliament, Press and public in the welfare of the colonies; it would be a link between the British nation and the peoples for whose well-being the course of history has made it responsible.

The second proposal is of still wider scope. It is to be hoped that after the war it will be found possible to establish some world authority, better constituted, more widely supported, and with greater hope of achieving success than was the League of Nations. If those hopes are realized, there is much to be said for the administration of all colonies, belonging to all nations, being voluntarily placed under the supervision of that authority. The proposal in effect would revive and make general the Mandatory System. The Mandates Commission of the League, impartial, conscientious, painstaking, rendered admirable service; the present writer, having been subject to its superintendence as High Commissioner in Palestine, would offer his tribute. Although the last word must lie, not with a Commission, but with the Mandatory Power, since upon it lies the responsibility for maintaining order and for securing the necessary financial and military resources, the participation of an international body may have a powerful moral influence. And it may help to assure the other States that the ruling Power is in fact endeavouring to carry out those general purposes, expressed in the Atlantic Charter, which all are pledged to promote. I do not suggest that either of these proposals—a Parliamentary Committee or international supervision—has yet enlisted in Great Britain any widespread measure of support; but I mention them because there are indications that they may do so, and the fact that they are being ventilated may be of interest, in the United States and elsewhere, to students of affairs.

VII. RELATIONS WITH RUSSIA

With respect to Russia, American and British opinion do not appear to be yet in step, and there is danger that some divergence might arise. In Great Britain, during the Russian revolution and for some years after, the feeling of alienation, even of antipathy, was strong. It seemed at times that there might be a violent reaction, such as that which followed the French Revolution, the reaction of which Edmund Burke was the spokesman, and twenty years of war with France the outcome. Among the Russians the antagonism towards Great Britain was not less. Now all this has changed. The beginning of the change in British opinion followed the victory of Stalin over Trotsky, and the abandonment of the Bolshevik policy of fomenting communist revolutions all over the world. It was carried much farther when Hitler's attack put an end to the deplorable pact into which Stalin had entered as a measure of self-protection, and opened an era of heroic resistance to the formidable aggressive State which was already our enemy. The powers of endurance, and the military and industrial efficiency that were revealed, gave rise to a new feeling of surprised admiration and respect. It was realized here that past antagonisms and continuing differences of political opinion did not matter in comparison with the fact that we were engaged, side by side, in a desperate struggle against a common enemy detested by both.

The British people are not in the least alarmed at the prospect of being Bolshevized after the war by a triumphant Russia. If there are good things in the communist system which it would be to the advantage of our people to adopt, they will no doubt adopt them, probably by the gradual methods characteristic of our history; and adopt them of their own free will and initiative. If, in a moment of exaltation, our Russian ally were to revert to the methods of the Comintern, our electorate would know how to deal with them. But of that there is so little likelihood that the British Government, with the almost unanimous support of the nation, has gladly entered into an alliance with Russia, for the lengthy term of twenty years.

In the United States, however, it would seem that the earlier stage of suspicion and distrust still continues. There is as yet little sign of any similar drawing together.[1] Yet the same causes may bring about the same result in time. And when the concluding phase of the war is reached, and the United States, the British Commonwealth and China concentrate their forces upon the defeat of Japan, it may well be that Russia will have a part to play there also. Then would be opened a still closer comradeship between the four predominant Powers in confronting the problems of the post-war age.

viii. The Collapse of Collective Security

Meanwhile much joint consultation is already proceeding between the United States and Great Britain on the tremendous new issues that have arisen in the economic field. The classical economics no longer apply in the present-day world. The gold standard and the automatic

[1] Written in April 1943.

adjustment of the international exchanges have broken down. The question arises whether any planned economy on a world-wide scale can be substituted and be maintained, unless it were to be backed by force on the principle, definitely rejected, of Hitler's New Order. Meanwhile, clearly the first task is to devise some scheme of long-term credits and multilateral clearing which will enable currencies to be stabilized and commerce to move smoothly and securely. Here the first initiative has been taken by the Economic Adviser of the American State Department, Mr. Feis, who has put forward an ingenious scheme. Since then the British Treasury, in a White Paper published in April 1943, has presented a more comprehensive and more ambitious plan, the result of long reflection by a group of the ablest financial minds in the country. Simultaneously the American Treasury has presented a scheme for achieving the same ends by somewhat different methods. Public discussion of these plans in both countries has been widespread and keen, preparing the way until, at the armistice, the moment arrives for action.

"It is useless," President Roosevelt has said, "to win a war unless it stays won." Greater Germany, if it remained united, might have in a few years' time a population of a hundred million. The German people, as we know, are intelligent, industrious, brave. Their qualities, diverted to evil ends, have plunged the world into two terrific and disastrous wars; they may do so again. Great Britain, however staunch, is not strong enough, in population and resources, to withstand them unaided. The Dominions are remote and thinly peopled. The future policies of both Russia and France are necessarily uncertain. The smaller Powers, however united, could be swept under once more. All depends, therefore, on Anglo-American unity.

The American people, after the rise of Hitler and his all-round aggressions, hesitated long. The Japanese attack removed all doubts; Pearl Harbour consolidated the nation. The help of American ships, troops, aircraft, munitions, money, has been poured out unstintingly to all the Allies and has clinched the decision. But when the war is over, and the Japanese attack disposed of, may not the American people relapse into isolation? Is it not possible that the vicissitudes of domestic politics may sweep away the far-seeing men whose voices have been heard speaking with so much wisdom and force?

The American Constitution is strongly biased on the side of isolation; it was deliberately so designed. Isolation was obviously the right policy in the eighteenth century; it became doubtful in the nineteenth; it is impossible in the twentieth. Yet it is the hand of the eighteenth century that grips the situation.

The Government of the United States cannot, of its own authority, enter into any kind of treaty with any foreign Power. The Senate must concur. And not only that, but it must concur by a majority of at least two-thirds. If, after this war, the Allied Governments were to agree to some form of permanent union in order to prevent a repetition; if this gave rise to controversy in the United States; and if, when the matter came before the Senate, of the 96 members, 63 were in favour and 33 against, it would be the 33 who would carry the day.

Pope's maxim:

"For Forms of Government let fools contest:
Whate'er is best administer'd is best,"

is sometimes quoted as the last word in political wisdom. A little thought shows it to be wholly untrue. Fascism and Nazism are clear examples. There are many observers who think that some of the restrictive clauses of the Constitution of the United States might be instanced also—and particularly this one.

The chief cause of the present tragic world situation has obviously been the collapse of Collective Security, the failure of the League of Nations to stem aggression from the outset. The Manchurian incident was the beginning. Many attribute the League's surrender to Japanese defiance to mere lack of resolution on the part of the Member States, and particularly to the weakness of Great Britain. With knowledge of the facts as a member of the British Cabinet in the immediately preceding years, I venture to assert that that is a wrong analysis. The position was this: Of the seven Great Powers, two, the United States and Russia, were not members of the League; two others, France and Italy, showed little interest, and, in any case, could be of small assistance if the quarrel resulted in armed conflict; one, China, in a state of political confusion, was militarily very weak; one, Japan, was the guilty party. There remained only Great Britain. If war came—and our information was that Japan would be more likely to fight than to yield—we could not, in the uncertain conditions already prevailing in Europe, risk transferring our naval strength to the Far East, where, in any case, our exposed naval bases would probably be lost at the outset. Nor could we for a moment forget the possible perils to which Australia and New Zealand might be exposed. Everything, therefore, depended upon support being forth-coming from the United States. Mr. Stimson, then Secretary of State, with the best of intentions, could give no assurances; he was obviously not in a position to do so; the Constitution left the deciding voice to the Senate, and in it to a third of the Senators. In these circumstances there was no backing for the League's writ in the Far East. It might proclaim sanctions against Japan, but if Japan resisted with armed force there might be nothing to support them. No collectivity existed and there was therefore no security. That was the reason, and the sole reason, why events took the course that they did. The real test came later, when Italy attacked Abyssinia; it was the fatal Hoare-Laval agree-ment that brought down the League. There again definite American participation, pushed to the limit if necessary, would have turned the scale.

It is as well to face the fact that the annals of this century are strewn with the failures of conferences and negotiations. We may recall the Buckingham Palace Conference on the Irish question: summoned by King George V in July 1914, between representatives of the then Liberal Government, the Irish nationalists and the Ulstermen, it came within an inch of success; but it failed on a minor question of boundaries, with disastrous consequences. We may recall the World Economic Con-ference of 1932, representing all countries, sitting in London under the presidency of the Prime Minister, with the purpose of finding an outlet from the economic depression then universal, and completely futile. We may remember the Disarmament Conference at Geneva, struggling on for years, but equally without result. Recently there has been the Cripps mission to India, with the discussions between the Government, Con-gress and the Moslems that began with fair prospects and ended in nothing. And there had been the Versailles Conference itself, which did indeed effect many great things but failed in the one that mattered most.

The precedents for the negotiations that will follow this war are, it must be admitted, not encouraging. Complete success in the military campaigns is a condition of a good peace but will not of itself ensure it. Those who are most powerful with the sword are not always the most successful with the trowel. Only if there is an intimate comradeship between the American and British peoples and leaders can the great obstacles, and the innumerable minor complications and perplexities that will face us, be overcome. That is why, taking a broad survey, a bird's-eye view of the whole field of public affairs, domestic and international, political and economic, we may come to realize that Anglo-American co-operation is the most important of all the issues. Without it there can be no security, no stability. With it, everything else may follow after.

But will it be established? And once established, will it be sustained? That is the great question-mark that overhangs the future.

REFERENCES

[1]*The Times*, April 23, 1942.

[2]*The Times*, Nov. 1, 1941.

[3]*The Times*, May 26, 1942.

[4]*The Times*, July 24, 1942—*Total War and the People's Peace* (published by Oxford University Press), p. 39. *New York Times*, May 17, 1942.

[5]*The Times*, Nov. 1, 1941. *New York Times*, Oct. 8, 1941. *The Times*, Feb. 27, 1943.

[6]*The Times*, Mar. 10, 1943. *The Times*, April 23, 1942.

[7]*The Times*, Dec. 19, 1942.

[8]*The Times*, May 26, 1942.

[9]*The Times*, Nov. 1, 1941. *New York Times*, June 18, 1942.

[10]*New York Times*, Dec. 17, 1942.

[11]*The Times*, Dec. 29, 1942. *New York Times*, Dec. 29, 1942.

[12]*The Times*, July 24, 1941.

[13]*The Times*, July 24, 1942. *New York Times*, May 17, 1942.

[14]*The Times*, Mar. 9, 1943.

[15]*The Times*, Dec. 19, 1942.

[16]*New York Times*, Nov. 9, 1942.

[17]*New York Times*, Dec. 17, 1942.

[18]*New York Times*, Feb. 15, 1942. *News Chronicle* (London), Feb. 1, 1943.

IV AMERICAN POST-WAR POLICY
By Harold Callender

---

1. The Hope of Post-War Unity

WITH the collapse of German power, which may come suddenly and sooner than many expect, as it came in 1918, the opportunity will once again be offered to establish some collective insurance against further warfare. That opportunity was missed the last time a coalition of nations defeated German aggression a quarter-century ago, because the moment Germany was vanquished the coalition disintegrated. The collaboration so laboriously achieved during the war was quickly abandoned, extreme nationalism took command of the Allied countries, the United States virtually withdrew from world affairs and, as Lord Tyrrell put it, the British thought the French had become Germans while the Germans had become Britons. The perhaps inevitable results are those the world has experienced since then, culminating in the conflict that began on September 1, 1939.

It may not require excessive optimism to hope that those twenty years of uneasy, unstable, temporary peace have not been forgotten, and that this time the Allied Powers will be less eager to revert to disunity and better prepared for common action. Efforts have already begun to reach agreements for the future while war-time co-operation is still going on; and the suggestion of Mr. Sumner Welles, the American Under-Secretary of State, for a prolonged armistice period was designed to permit time for wiser decisions than those made so hastily under the influence of nationalistic emotions in 1919. Thus it is hoped to establish, first, some bonds of policy strong enough to survive the stress of the immediate post-armistice moods of war-tired nations and, second, a "cooling-off period" during which more mature reflection may counteract such separatist tendencies as those that appeared so quickly and so disastrously when the problems of peace arose after the last great victory over German aggression.

While the enemy countries in Europe are being occupied, while relief organizations are feeding starving peoples, while provisional administrations are being set up over a Continent which may well be threatened by civil wars, the war will continue in the Pacific. The bulk of the British and American fleets and air forces will be moved to the other side of the earth to subdue the third Axis partner, who will not yet have felt the full force of Allied power. Thus, as Mr. Churchill indicated in his speech of November 29, 1942, Great Britain and the United States will be fighting together as Allies in the East at the same time that they will be assuming the burdens of reconstruction in the West. Their common belligerency in the vast strategy of the Pacific may prevent or at least diminish in the West the relaxation of effort, the disunity, the quarrels, which divided the Allies when the war was over in 1918; though the resourcefulness of the two peoples is such as to permit a good deal of disagreement in the Atlantic world even while they maintain their combatant collaboration in the Pacific world.

Nothing in their history justifies the assumption that, even though fighting two wars at once and facing peace settlements that practically encircle the earth, the British and the Americans will co-operate automatically or spontaneously or completely. Nothing authorizes us to anticipate that, even when confronting economic and political tasks which are perhaps more vital to their own future than any they have confronted together or separately before, they will not be divided by their traditional differences of temperament, habit and outlook, their usual propensities for rivalry, their customary mutual suspicions. In spite of the optimistic theory that great crises produce great men to meet them and that nations learn from experience, it would be unwarranted and inadvisable to believe that Anglo-American unity will follow this war as the night the day without sustained effort to ensure it.

We may hope that the inevitable friction will be reduced by formulation well in advance of specific policies to be applied jointly to meet the outstanding tasks that we know we shall face. We may hope that the isolationist impulses which so often have influenced the public opinion and foreign policies of both countries will yield before a better understanding of the co-operative rôles that seem to be imposed upon them by events and by the needs of their own security. We may hope that the demobilization of millions of men, the transition from war-time to peace-time production and consumption, the food shortages that may conceivably result for our own countries from the relief sent hurriedly to less fortunate peoples will in neither country so absorb the energies and emotions of people and politicians as to create a wave of nationalism—like that induced by the depression in 1932 in Great Britain and in 1933 in the United States—which will turn attention away from foreign affairs. Yet it seems wise to take account of the danger that these hopes may not be fully realized. If there is a single great mistake that the two nations have made in recent times, it is that of under-estimating dangers and so failing to prepare for them.

II. The Sense of Difference

Anglo-American unity—in very few but very vital spheres—does not require that Britains and Americans should suddenly achieve a congeniality they have never felt and are not likely to feel. It does not require, as some seem to imagine, similar social and economic policies. It does not involve the assumption that a like cultural heritage and what is often, not without exaggeration, called a common language need exclude on either side the lively sense of difference and "foreign-ness" which existed even when, a century and more ago, America was far more "Anglo-Saxon" than it is to-day. It does not mean that, within whatever scope is left for it in a possibly more socialized world, our traders and bankers need be ruthlessly or completely deprived of the rivalry to which they seem so emotionally attached. Unity should not be predicated, as it has been in so much discussion, upon the often exaggerated likeness of the two peoples but upon the likeness of certain vital but limited interests. Such similarities of language and laws and traditions as exist matter less than the common need of peace and economic stability, obtainable only by their combined efforts.

What Anglo-American unity means, I assume, is that the British Commonwealth and the United States should agree that it is in their joint interests and in those of other peoples that no further world war be permitted to develop; that any war which involves either Power is likely, if not certain, to become a world war; that consequently both Powers are compelled by experience and by any reasonable estimate of the future to take cognizance of the danger of war anywhere and to take measures, in conjunction with such other Powers as are willing, to provide adequate insurance against that catastrophe, even at the cost and risk of those military commitments which both Britain and America have studiously avoided in the past;[1] that to diminish the danger of war they are ready, again in collaboration with all like-minded nations, to remove or at least reduce potential economic causes of war by ensuring a fairly free flow of trade and general access to vital raw materials.

A common policy might involve some such measures even if other Powers declined to participate, for the joint influence of the British Empire and the United States would go a long way toward forming a "system of general security," as the Atlantic Charter calls it, even if other great Powers—of which, for a considerable time, there may be only one (Russia) after this war—should hold aloof. In that case our common policy might look less like a scheme of collective security than a simple alliance. But we must be prepared for this possibility. We should consider that such an alliance, had it existed, might well have prevented the present war; and that, if it came into being in the future, it could be so utilized in the interest of freedom and peace and economic welfare as eventually to commend itself to the entire civilized world, as British naval power did, in the opinion of such German writers as the historian Dibelius.[2]

This German tribute to that wise and liberal exercise of armed might, an exercise of which Germany has yet to prove herself capable, is striking evidence of the extent to which Britain managed to identify her imperial power with the greatest good of the greatest number. Further evidence of this is the belated admission in the United States that during the nineteenth century our Monroe Doctrine and our isolation were made possible by the fact that Britain ruled the seas. It doubtless was such facts as these that led the late Senator Borah, renowned in his time as an outstanding nationalist and isolationist, to say to the writer of these lines two years before the beginning of the European war that the British Empire was a force for stability in the world and that the disappearance of that force would cause chaos from which the United States would suffer. Hence it is not mere "Anglo-Saxon hypocrisy" to cite the use of British power in recent times as an example of the essen-

---

[1]The United States declined such commitments outside her own hemisphere, save in Hawaii and the Philippines; Britain long declined them beyond the Rhine.

[2]See his book *England*, one of the best ever written on the subject in any language.

tially stabilizing and beneficent, though not primarily altruistic, rôle which Anglo-American power might play in the disturbed years that lie ahead, either as part of a wider security system or, if necessary, as a security system in itself. The opportunity of playing such a rôle, for the ends indicated above, will surely come in one of these two forms; and Anglo-American unity in recognizing and seizing the opportunity seems clearly the *sine qua non* of the brave new world of which official pronouncements hint, or indeed of any conceivable world in which our civilization can live and advance.

That this opportunity existed but was rejected two decades ago, with the consequences we are now suffering, was recalled in February 1943, by the suggestion of the American Secretary of the Navy, Mr. Frank Knox, that in future the United States should retain a string of naval and air stations in the Pacific. He apparently alluded to the stations which the United States had been obliged to occupy since attacked by Japan, stations in New Zealand, New Caledonia and the Fiji Islands. Perhaps he would include New Guinea, Java and Singapore. He certainly would include for air purposes the mandated islands which the British and the Americans so generously contributed to Japanese militarism at the Peace Conference in 1919, after which we made sure of Japanese naval preponderance in Far Eastern waters by adopting two years later at Washington a capital ship ratio which precluded our meeting Japan on equal terms in that large part of the world where extensive British and American interests were at stake.

III. REQUIREMENTS FOR DEFENCE

Before this conflict is over United States naval and air power will have *pieds à terre* in quite a lot of novel places like Dakar, which President Roosevelt described as having special strategic significance for the Western Hemisphere, Casablanca, Greenland, Newfoundland, Iceland, the Galápagos Islands west of the Panama Canal, the West Indies on the Atlantic side of the Canal, Bermuda, Iran, India, China, Australia, and possibly parts of Asia farther north. There might be then, as there is now, a disposition in Washington to believe that retention of rights to use these or a similar series of outposts—either in the name of an international authority or by means of long leases, as in the case of the bases acquired in the chain extending from Newfoundland to Trinidad— would be desirable in the interest of American security, which led to occupation of places as far away as Iceland before the United States was at war.

Thus the requirements of defensive strategy, unless we decide that strategy does not matter any more, may lead the United States to stretch out into new regions and by so doing to assume new commitments. This tendency can only be intensified by the advance of aviation, which has only recently brought to our notice the hitherto hardly known port of Dakar and magnified the importance of the remote and half-forgotten Aleutian Islands and the tiny coral atolls lying thousands of miles south of them. In this sense this war will have been an education for Americans, who can never again feel quite so complacent behind their now not so broad oceans; and this education should make the logic of Anglo-American unity clearer than it has ever been before.

These experiences of a nation not accustomed to think of itself as being in any military danger, or as being obliged to collaborate with other powers in the interest of its own security, probably will exert a far greater influence upon American opinion than any of the elaborate plans for a nice, tidy, safe and prosperous world which Americans are told might be created if they were willing to pledge their military intervention in all sorts of remote places with which it has been their traditional belief that America had no direct concern.

Mr. Welles has deprecated the nationalistic implications of statements like that made by a member of the House naval sub-committee to the effect that acquisition of the islands mandated to Japan would make the Pacific "an American lake." Mr. Welles pointed out that the security of that ocean was a subject involving other United Nations as well as the United States. This is, of course, true, and no doubt the ideal arrangement would be a general recognition of common interest in security everywhere. But there is, on the one hand, no certainty of such general recognition, and on the other hand there is a traditional and almost instinctive tendency to define security in terms of geographical spheres of more direct interest to some Powers than to others. The principal divergence in the attitudes of Britain and the United States in the past (reflected in the contention over the size and cruising range of warships in the days when we were limiting navies) arose from the fact that Britain's widely scattered territories and shipping routes created for her more spheres of interest and more coaling stations than those of the United States. But even for Britain vital spheres of interest varied in importance and had their limits, since they long included Egypt, for example, but not Europe east of the Rhine. Even if the United States finally should accept a share of responsibility for peace in all parts of the world, she would remain more concerned for the safety of the Western Hemisphere and parts of the Pacific and Atlantic than for, let us say, the Indian Ocean. Regional interests are inevitable whether or not they are written into treaties, as was so often suggested in the nineteen-thirties, notably by Sir Austen Chamberlain, who regarded them as a kind of practical substitute for the unattainable "universality" of the League of Nations Covenant. We find them reflected in this war, which some perhaps naturally regard as mainly a Pacific war while others believe the Allied forces should be concentrated first against Hitler.

Recognition by Americans of their broadening spheres of defensive interest, or what may be called the narrowing of their ocean barriers, even if that recognition takes nationalistic forms, seems likely to lead to that acceptance of broader responsibilities which is necessary if the United States is to play a greater rôle in international affairs than she played after the last war. That acceptance doubtless bears possibilities of Anglo-American disagreement and rivalry as well as of co-operation; nevertheless it seems the pre-requisite to co-operation.

Let us note three recent and significant examples of how official views may differ between Washington and London.

First, after the invasion of North Africa there were for months, in effect, two rival French leaders seeking the support of the French in France and overseas—General de Gaulle, closely allied to Britain since the days when Britain fought alone, and General Giraud, who might not inaccurately be called the official American candidate. This division resulted from the divergence of British and American policies towards France after the armistice, when Britain broke with the Vichy régime while the United States recognized it in the hope of inducing Vichy to keep the French Fleet out of German control. But it resulted from older and deeper causes as well and betrayed on the American side a certain suspicion of British motives, even at a time when Britons and Americans were fighting together. For the marked coolness towards De Gaulle in Washington represented mainly distrust of the British Government, who were thought to have created the De Gaulle leadership for their own ends.

Second, the leading article in *The Times* of March 10, 1943, pointing out that the era of Balance of Power policy was past and that only in collaboration with Russia could Britain keep the peace in Europe, caused irritation in Washington because it seemed to some to suggest a kind of exclusive regional system inconsistent with a general system of security and a disregard of the smaller neighbours of Russia whose frontiers would apparently be determined by Russia. It was also interpreted as proposing that Britain should be a mediator between Russia and the United States where, in view of officials in Washington, none was needed.

Third and most important, Mr. Churchill's broadcast address of March 21, 1943, provoked sharp dissent in Washington. Though his approach was broader than that of *The Times* article, he suggested a Council of Europe in which it seemed difficult for the United States to participate. This seemed to imply a Council of the Americas, which might be welcomed by the isolationists as a new form of limited liability as opposed to a scheme of general security. Moreover, Mr. Churchill's endorsement, on March 17 in the House of Commons, of the Colonial Secretary's rejection of suggestions for international administration of Britain's colonies was linked—odd as it may appear to Britons—with the Prime Minister's speech of March 21, both being regarded in some important American quarters as objectionably nationalistic. It was thought that Mr. Churchill failed to take into account the strategic interest of the United Nations in some of those colonies, such as Gibraltar and Singapore, or the importance of the colonies for international civil aviation.

It is a notable fact, never to be forgotten, that no American may speak of foreign policy with the authority with which the Prime Minister speaks for Britain, since the American Constitution in effect subjects foreign policy to ratification by the Senate. In this sense the Prime Minister enjoys an advantage over the President of the United States. He may—as he did in the speech mentioned—outline British aims and interests in a far more specific manner than any American may outline American aims and interests, and the impression in the United States is that he has defined the future relationship of Britain with Russia in a way to indicate that it is a fixed factor which Americans must take into account in making up their minds about their own policy. The truth is that Britain's policy, from the logic of events, has taken far more definite shape than America's policy can take at this stage. For Britain has a virtual alliance with Russia, while the United States cannot now or possibly in the future enter such an engagement with any Power. The result is that some Americans feel that Britain confronts them with a kind of *fait accompli* in the form of a *ménage à deux* even while she speaks of a *ménage à trois*. For this the American Constitution *must* bear some responsibility.

Thus Russia, because of her service in wearing down the German Army and because of her prospective position of unique power on the Continent of Europe, has emerged as one of the three great Powers of the immediate future and consequently as a major factor in the future relations of Britain and the United States. Britain, having been herself in danger, is more appreciative of Russia's service than Americans generally are.

IV. RESULTS OF MUDDLED THOUGHT

Both British and Americans are now fighting with all their strength for the freedom of the civilized world. But who can say when Britain would have challenged Hitler if, after depriving Czechoslovakia of her defences, he had not occupied Prague or attacked Poland but slowly worn down the states to the east by economic pressure and military threats? Who can say when the United States would have entered the war if Hitler had spared American ships and Japan had refrained from attacking American territory? This writer well recalls those in London in 1938 who inquired how the fate of Czechoslovakia concerned Britain, as he recalls those in the United States in 1941 who argued that the fate of Europe was not of vital import to America.

Both countries in those years muddled along in the hope that approaching danger would, at some point or other, cease to approach, and many were the ingenious arguments to the effect that the danger either did not exist or was far less than the more gloomy prophets believed. The gentleman in London in 1938 who refused to believe the Nazis actually arrested people without warrants belongs in the same category with the Americans who contended that Hitler could not cross the Atlantic, both being examples of one heritage that the two peoples have in common—a propensity for optimistic self-deception. This propensity is an obstacle to a common Anglo-American policy to safeguard peace, for only a realistic appreciation of the dangers ahead can persuade the two countries to adopt such a policy.

This muddling optimism, like freedom from militarism, was a habit acquired when Britain, behind her moat of salt water and her wall of ships, could feel assured of her safety and her leisure to come to de-

:isions; when America, separated from Europe by an ocean that was
under British surveillance and fearing no Pacific Power, could imagine
she lived in another and happier world. Both then developed a sense
of serene isolation which was reflected in their foreign policies, and the
growth of democracy in both countries owed much to their comparative
physical safety.

But with the rise of air power Britain has in a sense ceased to be an
island; and even the United States, reaching out defensively for bases
far over the water, finds other continents drawing uncomfortably close.
Defence authorities assume that even in this war the continental territory of the United States may be attacked by the air forces of nations as
far away as Germany and Japan. In a future conflict potential enemies
will have moved much nearer, so to speak, and even the greater oceans
will have lost much of their value as defensive barriers, as the English
Channel has already done. Strategists preparing the defence of the
United States after this war will consider Europe as being less than half
a day's flight from America and will lay their plans accordingly. Protection of defensive outposts everywhere will be based upon the same
drastically revised calculations of time and space.

In these circumstances the traditional margin for muddle has about
vanished. The sense of lazy power and the ability to put off action or
decision until the last moment, which Britain and America have so long
enjoyed because of their privileged geographical positions, are luxuries
that can hardly exist again if highly armed potential foes remain anywhere in the world. Security is no longer conferred by nature or guaranteed by sea power.

Nor do the old security and the old margin for muddle exist any
longer in the sphere of economic life. For Britain, that security once
seemed to rest upon her supremacy in manufacturing, shipping and the
export of capital which created reserves of wealth that contributed to
her safety, her power and her prestige. For America, security seemed
to consist in a predominantly continental economy endowed with fabu-
lous internal resources, a growing population and an expanding internal
market which greatly reduced the country's dependence upon overseas
trade. Hence her traditionl nationalistic policies in the field of economics
as well as in the field of politics.

The change in Britain's position had begun long before the Great
War of 1914–18 and became tragically clear after that war, whose physical
destruction, as Sir Arthur Salter pointed out, was less costly and less

lasting than the dislocation of international exchange. Long after the devastated areas of France and Belgium had been rebuilt, the depressed areas in Britain reflected the decline of the once great exporting trades like coal, textiles and shipping, which formed the outstanding economic problem of Britain for the succeeding two decades. Meanwhile, in the United States the greater and more sudden shock of the slump in the early nineteen-thirties shook this normally optimistic nation's faith in its mastery of its destiny and in the very possibility of economic security. The collapse of the gold standard in 1931 and the various nationalistic restraints of trade that followed—the British tariff, the Ottawa agreements, the American devaluation of the dollar, exchange and import restrictions everywhere—were signs of an economic insecurity which had direct repercussions in the sphere of political and military security.

For the collapse of currencies and the economic nationalism which was thus intensified provided the opportunity the Nazis required to institute in Germany the militaristic economy which cured unemployment by subordinating the whole life of the nation to preparation for war. The economic breakdown contributed materially, notably in countries then becoming totalitarian but not only there, to the suspicion that democracy was growing decadent and proving powerless to cope with the elementary economic problems of the nations where it prevailed. This suspicion was one of Hitler's greatest assets—in Germany and beyond it. It was for this reason that President Roosevelt described his purpose as that of demonstrating that democracy could work.

v. The Twin Pillars

It is interesting to note that Mr. Roosevelt, whose place in history probably will rest principally upon his leadership in international co-operation, began his presidency with an economic programme that was extremely nationalistic. In 1933, when the World Economic Conference in London waited for his agreement to stabilize currencies, he sent a message flatly declining to fix the value of the dollar pending a further rise in American domestic prices. It was true that a healthy American economy was essential to a healthy world economy; it was also true that uncertainty about the dollar prevented the principal measures for which the Economic Conference had been summoned.

President Roosevelt and his advisers to-day consider economic collaboration and political collaboration to be the twin pillars, so to speak, of the more secure and more civilized world that they hope may result from the present opportunity for reconstruction. In the declaration known as the Atlantic Charter Mr. Roosevelt and Mr. Churchill, and subsequently all the United Nations, expressed a desire for "the fullest collaboration between all nations in the economic field with the object of securing for all improved labour standards, economic advancement and social security." In Article VII of the Lend-Lease agreements, signed thus far by thirty nations, including all the great Allied Powers, it is provided that the final settlements between the United States and the other nations concerned shall "be directed to the expansion, by appropriate international and domestic measures, of production, employment and the exchange and consumption of goods which are the material foundations of the liberty and welfare of all peoples; to the elimination of all forms of discriminatory treatment in international commerce and to the reduction of tariffs and other trade barriers . . ." Here is a disavowal for the future of those nationalistic economic measures which governments, including Mr. Roosevelt's, deemed necessary in the emergency of the late nineteen-twenties and the nineteen-thirties; an admission that only by policies of an opposite kind can the "welfare of peoples" be achieved.

Thus we are still trying to solve the economic problems we failed to solve in the years before the war, just as we are still hoping to solve the political problems which we had an opportunity to solve but failed to solve when Germany was beaten the last time. We are still hoping, in both the economic and the political spheres, to prove that democracy can work. We reject the Nazi "New Order" and the Japanese new imperialism. But we have not yet agreed upon a new order of our own either in economic relations or in the field of collective security. This task still lies ahead.

In the political sphere, as in the economic, we have certain broad indications of intentions; as yet no more. The Atlantic Charter, the only single expression of the purposes of the United Nations, will hardly be possible to apply completely or quickly and may well give rise to disillusionment, as all such pronouncements are likely to do which set forth in abstract terms policies that can be judged only by their results. In its emphasis upon sovereignty, self-government, self-determination, restoration of conquered states, equality of economic opportunity and disarmament, the Charter recalls the Fourteen Points of President Wilson. The Charter's eight points are far less specific than Mr. Wilson's fourteen, but the doctrines and purposes it expresses run so nearly parallel to Mr. Wilson's that the Charter may almost be called a revival in briefer and more general form of that earlier manifesto. The Charter's third point, self-determination and restoration of sovereignty, repeats the doctrines of Mr. Wilson's sixth to twelfth points. The Charter's fourth point, economic equality and unhampered trade, is almost identical with Mr. Wilson's third. The Charter's sixth and eighth points, providing for lasting peace and reduced armaments, are much like Mr. Wilson's fourth and fourteenth. Mr. Wilson's "freedom of the seas" reappears in the Charter's seventh point. The Charter's "permanent system of general security" seems much the same as Mr. Wilson's "association of nations."

The close parallel between two great historic documents promulgated twenty-three years apart, carries implications of a double kind. It suggests the continued vitality of certain democratic and humane aspirations towards a more reasonable world, but it also recalls the failure of the two great English-speaking powers whose leaders promulgated the Atlantic Charter to unite their efforts to put into practice the almost identical principles defined in the similar but earlier document. The parallel also permits the inference that the Wilsonian doctrine of nationality, so esteemed by the nineteenth-century liberalism in which Mr. Wilson's mind was steeped, would again be applied on much the same lines. Mr. Edward Hallet Carr[3] has pointed out the defects of that doctrine, which formed the guiding principle by which European frontiers were drawn a quarter-century ago. Those frontiers lasted less than twenty years. The careful justice they dealt to nationalities proved transitory because nationality, as practised, excluded economic co-operation. Does the present Anglo-American programme, the Atlantic Charter, contemplate restoration of the frontiers of, say, 1939, which had cut Europe up into competing units mutually weakening one another and thus preparing the way for Hitler's conquest of the Continent? If so, how is the economic collaboration, promised in the same programme, to be ensured? How is the line to be drawn between the principle of nationality and the extreme nationalism which, growing out of that principle, proved self-destructive?

President Roosevelt's "four freedoms"—freedom of speech and of worship, freedom from want and freedom from fear—go much farther than the Charter and are at least equally lacking in precise definition.

[3]See his brilliant study of the whole question of future peace-making entitled *Conditions of the Peace.*

Designed for application "everywhere in the world" and not only in experienced democratic States, they express a desire to lift men of all colours and conditions to new levels of life, political consciousness, education and prosperity. Their achievement would involve a degree of political stability never yet attained on such a scale and an economic stability which has hitherto seemed attainable only in advanced nations and there only for limited periods.

The President's speeches, like those of Vice-President Wallace and others, are American indications of goals, vague and remote and revolutionary as they are, towards which some believe the world should move at an accelerated pace after this war, assuming the achievement of a reasonably secure peace and reasonably free interchange of goods. They represent a desire to make available to other peoples the opportunities for development which we are inclined to associate exclusively with the free institutions characteristic of the British and American constitutions and traditions. But it would be premature, to say the least, to believe that either the Atlantic Charter or the far more ambitious picture of a possible future drawn by these leaders is yet accepted by the bulk of the American people as defining objectives which should determine their political policy.

vi. What Americans Think

In a report entitled "What Americans Think about Post-War Reconstruction," issued by the Foreign Policy Association on October 1, 1942, editors in four major regions of the United States summarized what they believed to be the dominant attitudes towards the war and its problems on the part of the public in those regions. Mr. Virginius Dabney of Richmond reported that in the South, always far less isolationist than the West, there was marked sympathy towards freer trade on the lines advocated so long by the Secretary of State, Mr. Cordell Hull, and that the annual conferences on "the South and International Affairs" revealed increasing recognition of the obligations of the United States in creating an enduring peace; but he added that public opinion had not crystallized regarding foreign policy. Mr. Walter K. Schwinn of Hartford found that New England regarded the war as "a grim necessity, not a challenging opportunity" and seemed uncertain of its objectives beyond that of crushing the enemy. Mr. William H. Hessler of Cincinnati thought the people of the Middle West had repudiated isolation as a principle of foreign policy without as yet replacing it by "positive faith in any post-war programme of international collaboration." He believed few in that region regarded the war as a people's war or as a war for positive ends. Yet he thought that Westerners in general were determined, "with a fanatical and bitter earnestness," to prevent another war, and that this determination "is strong enough to carry them all the way into the citadel of international collaboration, whatever its costs and however drastic its requirements, if they are convinced that international collaboration provides a means of averting war in the future." Mr. Herbert Lewis of St. Paul reported in his section a tendency to agree that the United States must "assume responsibilities of policing and relief" after the war, but suggested that little consideration had been given to "long-run world reconstruction" and that tariff-seeking industrialists and workers might strengthen nationalistic impulses. Much would depend, he believed, upon the domestic economic situation immediately after the war.

While there are many signs of a trend away from the traditional isolation, it seems altogether probable that the end of this war will bring a reaction similar in kind, though possibly not in extent, to that which took place from 1918 onward. It will represent a natural impulse to relax from the strain of war and to postpone facing responsibilities, an impulse like that of the weary soldier who longs to return to home and civilian life. This mood may be less lasting than a quarter-century ago. It may be tempered by the experience in the intervening years of the risks of withdrawal from foreign affairs. It may be less intensely exploited by politicians. It may be less provoked by the behaviour of our Allies. But some of the officials in Washington who are most eager to prevent such a reaction are convinced that it will come and may prove dangerous for international co-operation.

In the spring of 1919 an American who is now a member of the Senate was in command of a regiment waiting at St. Nazaire for transport homeward. He read in *The New York Herald* of Paris that President Wilson had refused to agree to Italian annexation of Fiume and inferred that American troops might be sent there to prevent it. He says his regiment, who had gone through the final campaign in Northern France, were bitterly indignant at the suggestion that they might now be sent to the Adriatic, to a city of which some of them had never heard. Their mood was perhaps not unlike that of many Britons towards the policy of Mr. Lloyd George's Government in supporting Greece in its post-war

war against the Turks. No people emerging from one war likes to undertake a new one, or even prolonged military occupation of foreign lands. This attitude seems certain to recur, and in the case of Americans to be reinforced by a traditional feeling that the frontiers of Eastern Europe are not the business of the United States. For this reason it seems necessary to many Americans to lose no time in making it clear that they are our business.

The impulse towards resumption of isolation may derive strength from the alarm aroused in some minds by the somewhat revolutionary and Utopian suggestions of conferring liberty and high living standards upon the entire human race; suggestions that are implicit in the President's "four freedoms" and explicit in some of the addresses of Vice-President Wallace, who contends that "The peace must mean a better standard of living for the common man, not merely in the United States and England but also in India, Russia, China and Latin America—not merely in the United Nations but in Germany, Italy and Japan."[4] There are some who take emphatic exception to Mr. Wallace's assumption that such are the purposes of the war and who fear (though Mr. Wallace has denied it) that his proposals imply the extensive use of American wealth for international welfare projects.

The fear of social upheaval which had much to do with foreign policies in Europe in the nineteen-thirties, causing some in the democratic countries to minimize the danger of Nazi Germany in relation to what they thought the greater danger of Communist Russia, exists likewise in the United States. It probably has been intensified by the bitter social division that has dominated politics since Mr. Roosevelt became President in 1933 in the midst of depression and adopted drastic measures extending the powers of the Federal Government and vastly increasing its expenditures to stimulate recovery. Mr. James Kemper, then President of the Chamber of Commerce of the United States, addressing the Chicago Association of Commerce on January 8, 1941, opposed the entrance of the United States into the war because he thought the effect might be to change its social and economic system permanently.[5] Shortly before, on December 2, 1940, Mr. Mark Sullivan argued that in deciding whether to aid Britain to win the war, Americans would "be likely to take into account any surmised possibility that England

[4]Address before the Free World Association at New York, May 8, 1942.
[5]*New York Times* of January 9, 1941.

is to be a socialist country." However the opinions of these two gentlemen may have been altered by subsequent events or reflection, what they said at that time accurately expressed fears that existed and still exist in the minds of some Americans and may prove more than negligible factors in the response of the country to such commitments overseas as the President may propose.

VII. DOMESTIC POLITICS

It should not be forgotten that the war crisis was superimposed, so to speak, upon a domestic crisis; that unity in foreign policy was hampered by unusual disunity in internal politics; that the depression of the nineteen-thirties has its repercussions even to-day in a stubborn opposition to the President which draws less than due distinction between his acts and his associates in domestic politics and his aims in the foreign field. The fear of a Socialist Britain and its influence upon America owes much of the fear of a Socialist United States which was born of the so-called "New Deal" of President Roosevelt. Departure from past economic policies is inevitably associated with possible departure from past foreign policies. The expansion of world trade by reduction of tariffs, as promised in the Lend-Lease agreements, inspires in the minds of those who want high tariffs the same fears for American liberties that are inspired in others by the prospect of political or military commitments abroad. Those who may broadly be called conservatives, who include many of the leaders of industry and business, are disturbed lest the "shape of things to come" may be determined by the more revolutionary of Mr. Roosevelt's advisers or by British Labour leaders or by the momentum acquired by the doctrine of planned economy, rather than by themselves. They know that foreign policy is intimately linked with economic relations,[6] and their apprehension

[6] A striking example in the American Continent is the case of the expropriation by the Mexican Government of American and British oil properties in Mexico in 1938. In 1942, under the influence of the war emergency, and its desire to conciliate Mexico and the other Latin neighbours, the American Government accepted on behalf of the American oil companies a kind of token indemnity of $24,000,000 in settlement of all their claims. In so doing it recognized, without officially admitting it did so, Mexico's pretention to nationalize without compensation the subsoil rights which Mexican authorities had granted to Americans. Even this moderate payment was indirectly financed by the United States Government through loans to Mexico and through its treaty-guaranteed purchases of Mexican silver of which the United States had no need whatever. Britain has made no settlement of the similar but greater oil claims of her subjects. Unless Mexico expects a

of tendencies abroad which resemble or seem to resemble tendencies they have observed and resisted in the United States colours their views of American foreign policy, especially under the present leadership. They are inclined to overlook the differences between Socialism in Russia and Socialism in Britain, and to forget that what they consider socialistic measures in Britain have largely been adopted by Conservative governments. This is a consequence of the far more rigid economic views prevailing among businessmen in the United States.[7]

But the reluctance in Congress to sanction such revolutionary changes in foreign policy as have been suggested by the President and Secretary Hull, who has spoken frankly in favour of an international force to keep the peace, derives chiefly from the fear that they would deprive the United States, to her disadvantage, of the cherished freedom of action she has so long retained.

To indicate how those fears linger undiminished in some minds it suffices to note that, although the Republican National Committee in April 1942, under the influence of Mr. Wendell Willkie, declared that "after this war the responsibility of the nation will not be circumscribed within the territorial limits of the United States" but that it must assist in "the bringing about of understanding, comity and co-operation among the nations of the world," Republican members of the House of Representatives the following September qualified the pledge of co-operation by adding the warning that Americans must not endanger their own liberties in any international undertaking. The isolationist current of opinion or emotion still runs strongly in the party chiefly associated with the defeat twenty-three years ago of President Wilson's efforts for American participation in collective safeguards of peace, and those

permanent supply from the United States Treasury of the capital that is indispensable to her development and to the high living standard of which the Atlantic Charter speaks, she will be obliged to revise her attitude toward the private capital that gave her an oil industry.

This singular manifestation of the American Good Neighbour Policy may prove in the long run less advantageous to Mexico than it seems. It has meanwhile intensified the distrust on the part of Americans towards the more idealistic policies of the American Government in foreign affairs generally.

[7] This fear of what is loosely called Socialism—which in the United States is likely to mean any restriction whatever upon private enterprise as practised before the slump of 1929, excepting, of course, the high tariff, a restraint of trade by the State that has long been accepted—colours American feeling not only towards Britain, who is guilty of having developed social services, but also towards Russia, who has erred far more gravely by so successfully abolishing private enterprise that she was able to resist the Germans far beyond the expectations of 90 per cent of the Western world.

who hope to establish during the war co-operative arrangements that will extend into peace-time must take full account of the difficulty of ensuring Congressional support for such policies.[8]

These views in Congress reflect doubts, though they may be diminishing doubts, in the country. Foreign policy, for good or ill, is subject to public opinion, which is necessarily inadequately informed of the world abroad and possibly a trifle distrustful of those who seek to inform it. Congress may be slow in responding to changes in opinion and loath to try to lead it, but public opinion is the master that Congress recognizes. That master must be convinced that there are good reasons for a change, and until he is convinced there can be no real American co-operation with Britain which involves substantial commitments and risks. Americans in general almost instinctively recoil from such commitments. They find it hard to agree that the status of the Dardanelles or Bessarabia is a matter of national interest to them. In Congress not long ago was heard again the familiar observation that Europe had had wars for thousands of years and would continue to have them, and that "We cannot bring peace to Europe, no matter how much we sacrifice in men and money." In those words of Senator Capper was reflected the anti-European bias that reaches back to the beginnings of American history. To some of the colonists who came to America, Europe seemed hopeless, and so it seems to many of their descendants to-day.

In the interval between the two world wars a mood of disillusionment and cynicism gave rise to the belief, elaborated by numerous writers, that America's entrance into the European War of 1917 had been the work of British propaganda and a futile departure from her proper rôle. The rise of dictatorship in Europe was cited to prove that that war had been in vain. The investigation by a Senate committee of the munitions trade, revealing its international ramifications and its financial interest in war, further contributed to cynicism towards Europe

[8]When Mr. Churchill, in a broadcast speech on March 21, 1943, outlined British foreign policy by mentioning a Council of Europe and a Council of Asia, he spoke with a degree of authority that no American leader possesses, since the President requires the consent of the Senate to carry out any commitments. This constitutional limitation puts Mr. Roosevelt at a disadvantage as compared with Mr. Churchill, and compels the President to speak in more general and tentative terms. Britain has made up her mind on some points at least, and those points can be definitively formulated; America has not yet made up her mind; and if she had, the expression of that mind would have to come through two separate branches of the Government, the executive and the legislative, which are constitutionally independent of one another. This is the handicap under which the United States labours in respect of foreign policy, though domestic policies are likewise hampered.

and led to the Neutrality Act which was designed to ensure that the United States, when the next war came, would abandon her neutrality rights and withdraw her ships from the seas in order to avoid being drawn in again. That act was in effect when the war began in 1939.

Having given due attention to the dark side of the picture from the point of view of Anglo-American co-operation, let us note the very general impression among Americans and Britons who have travelled lately in the United States that since the invasion of North Africa, which placed the United States for the first time in this war in the position of an active combatant on land in the European zone, there has been fuller appreciation both of the gravity of the war and of the peace. It is certainly too early to assume, as some Britons apparently have done, that the setback for Mr. Roosevelt's party in the elections of November 1942 necessarily meant a setback for international co-operation, even if there should be in 1944 a change of the party in power. Within the Republican Party, in spite of its unencouraging record, are ardent advocates of co-operation—notably Governor Stassen of the Mid-western State of Minnesota, Mr. Wendell Willkie, Senator Ball and others. Republicans as well as Democrats have proposed that the Senate sustain the President during the war by pronouncing in favour of collective security for the future. In the Middle West as well as in the East there is marked sentiment for a co-operative policy. This war has not followed the course of the last one; nor will the response of the United States to the problem of peace necessarily be the same as twenty-five years ago. The attempt in these pages has been to give full weight to the adverse or doubtful forces, not to suggest that the battle is yet lost or need be lost.

Suspicions of British policy, which are still widespread in the United States, derive chiefly from a belief that the efforts in recent years to induce America to play a larger rôle in world affairs have been inspired partly by a desire on the part of the British to share with the United States some of their responsibilities. The emergence of the United States from isolation has been regarded as a British aim and in British interests. This view, expressed in an extreme form in a book published before the war entitled, *England Expects Every American to Do His Duty,* permeated widely through the American population; and it remains in spite of all the duties England has done in fighting alone against Germany in the air and on the seas and in the Near East in what was later to be rocognized as America's own war. For these achievements and for the leadership of Mr. Churchill there has been real admiration in the United States, and collaboration has been close and effective since the United States entered the war. Yet criticism of British policy, notably towards India, has continued, while in both the House of Commons and in Congress predictions have been made of keen rivalry, after the war, between the two countries in trade, shipping and air transport. It probably will be in these spheres that the interests of groups and companies in Britain and America will clash most sharply, creating new political problems, unless the foundation for co-operation is laid in advance of the armistice.

Meanwhile other economic influences have been at work in a region where American policy has not hesitated to assume large commitments. In Latin America the United States has been engaged for several years in doing two things: in financing expanded production of raw materials vital to the war effort, and in transforming the economies of the countries to the south by long-term loans for agricultural and industrial developments that will extend beyond the war period and in some cases will assist types of production that will compete with industries in the United States. Here is a new kind of overseas capitalism in which public funds take the place of private funds and the collaboration is between governments. It is so far a regional policy, but it might not remain regional. It is an example of the extension of American responsibilities under stress of the war.

VIII. ANGLO-AMERICAN CO-OPERATION

Anglo-American co-operation has probably been far more quickly and more effectively developed in this war than in the last. Agreement on the production and division of arms, the distribution of foodstuffs and raw materials, the operation of the ships of the two countries virtually as a single fleet, the sharing of military enterprises on sea and land and in the air have demonstrated once more the ability of Britons and Americans to work together for practical ends when they will.

A striking example is that of the joint expedition to North Africa, involving hundreds of warships and merchant ships, which departed from ports on both sides of the Atlantic for a carefully co-ordinated action on the shores of Africa. It was an enterprise requiring elaborate planning on both the military and economic sides. An Anglo-American supply committee was hard at work providing goods for North African civilians long before political differences arose there to complicate the relations of Washington and London.

The immediate approach to the problem of Anglo-American co-operation probably could best be made in these practical and limited spheres in which, through the compulsion of war needs, a large measure of common action has already been achieved. It is true that we need a clearer statement of our war aims, both for the enlightenment and encouragement of the captive peoples whose aid we shall want when we land upon the Continent and for the reassurance of our own peoples, who dislike abstractions and generalities. We should give as precise a picture as we can of the kind of Europe we shall help create, of the future of the Oriental and African colonies, of the economic guarantees that must counter-balance the disintegrating effect of restoration of many separate sovereignties, of the future status of Germany and Japan, of our relations with Russia. Meanwhile we might agree not only upon joint action in relief and reconstruction of the liberated nations (now being planned in great detail), but upon measures to prevent what might well develop into a kind of economic war between Britons and Americans in foreign markets, in shipping, in the air transport which seems certain to expand to vast proportions and which is so closely related to the strategic need of flying grounds and seaplane bases at many points round the entire globe.

Neither Britons nor Americans put much faith in general declarations, such as the Atlantic Charter, which take on meaning only as they are translated into definite programmes and acts. An agreement between the two governments to share the shipping routes of the world, or an agreement between Pan-American Airways and British Overseas Airways, would be more valuable as evidence of a real desire for Anglo-American co-operation than a hundred Atlantic Charters. It would, for one thing, put an end to discussions in the House of Commons and in Congress which have revealed on either side a good deal of suspicion that Britons and Americans are even now contemplating a kind of commercial battle for control of the air the moment the war is over. It is as if certain commercial groups could hardly wait to resume the traditional competition, or rather the traditional struggle for monopolies which was so long symbolized for Americans by the British control of much of the rubber supply, and for Britons by the national subsidies for American ships competing with British lines.

Such rivalries, which have often embittered the relations not only between business groups but between the two governments and peoples, are not necessary and are inconsistent with the economic collaboration promised in the official documents cited above. This time there will be no war debts such as those which provoked so much discussion and misunderstanding and ill feeling when Britain finally suspended payments to the American Government. But there will be Lend-Lease settlements—what the Lend-Lease Act calls "the final determination of the benefits to be provided to the United States by the Government of the United Kingdom in return for aid furnished under Act of Congress"—and they may serve as well as the older form of war debts as a subject of prolonged contention unless meanwhile genuine co-operation in both the economic and the political fields is achieved.

Americans are capable of great generosity; but their acceptance of new responsibilities overseas is less likely to be won by appeals to their humanity or idealism, or by any appeals from necessarily interested foreigners, than by considerations of self-interest in the light of the experience of the last generation. America's interest in peace for herself, which means in peace everywhere, coincides with the general interest. Britons, who suffered far more in this war and between the wars than Americans have done, have probably reflected longer and more intently upon remedies for war and for social inequalities and misery which they associate with war as evils which no enlightened community should tolerate. They have sensed more keenly than Americans have done the need of such social measures as those proposed in the Beveridge Report, and their political habits permit revolutionary change with far less friction than even moderate innovations generate in the United States. Consequently the intellectual and emotional response to the present crisis in human affairs has not come either at the same time or in the same way or with the same intensity in the two countries. It is not only that America has had no Dunkirk, no Coventry; it has had no Rochdale, no Labour Party, no Budget of 1909. It is not only that Americans are hardly yet fully convinced that they are fighting for their life as a nation; they are still farther from being convinced that their national life must be re-made on less haphazard and less unregulated lines. They have had their Pearl Harbour and they have had their economic slump (far worse than Britain's). The first destroyed the illusion that America need not go to war until she did so of her own will, while the second destroyed or severely damaged the illusion that social services of the British type were somehow beneath the national dignity and contrary to the national economic religion. But from this degree of enlightenment it is still a considerable step to the realization that even a continent is not self-sufficient as a defensive or economic entity, or that what has been called private enterprise cannot calmly resume its sway when the firing ceases.

The war may alter somewhat these differences between Britons and Americans but is hardly likely to eliminate them altogether since they are the cumulative result of two or three centuries passed in different environments. It would be helpful to Anglo-American unity if statesmen and lecturers and leader writers remembered details of this kind which, like much else, are so often forgotten on both sides.

Neither country can pride itself very much on its foreign policy in the years when this war was so visibly approaching, though both can take satisfaction from the way in which they have met the test im posed upon them by their own mistakes. A bit more foresight and a bit more unity between them could have made that test and its sacrifices unnecessary. Here, it would seem, is common interest enough to build upon.

V THE BRIDGE OF IDEAS

British and American Novelists

By Frank Swinnerton

———◆———

1. The English Mode

IT WOULD NOT BE TRUE to say that the English invented the novel; but it might be argued that they gave early lessons in writing it to all other nations in the modern world. Thus, for example, the French ingeniously adapted Richardson until they learned to be more sophisticated psychologists and much grimmer realists upon their own account. Russians as different as Gogol and Dostoevsky took what they needed from Dickens, and in turning his comic vision upon Russia magnified the men and women and fiction of their country beyond anything possible in quieter England. As for the Americans, they rightly considered English literature to be their own; for a century and more copied and adorned the European product; and, in spite of such men of genius as Herman Melville, have only in the past quarter of a century separated themselves completely from the English mode.

That English mode, according to the English habit, defies precise definition. It has given rise to English novels; not, strictly speaking, to an English novel. Even in the eighteenth century, a greater than Richardson irresponsibly began by mocking the author of *Pamela* before settling down to lead, in his original work, one considerable order of the craft. I shall not venture, as some lovers of big words have done, to name the greatest novels in our tongue; but *Tom Jones* is monumentally one of the most truly English novels ever written. Besides epitomizing life in the eighteenth century, it establishes the masculine line in our national fiction. The feminine line, which found Richardson, as he is, a truly pene-

trating student of the heart, began with Fanny Burney, and reached per-
fection in Jane Austen. Since Jane Austen it has continued, with vicissitudes, by way of Susan Ferrier, Emily Eden, Rhoda Broughton, and
Angela Thirkell, to the present day. But it has never surpassed Jane
Austen. And, much as Fielding might have lifted his eyebrows at *Mans-
field Park,* he and Jane Austen had one certain resemblance and left
one perfect legacy to their successors: both were comic writers, who
relished and were tender with human kindness, folly, and even hypocrisy. Their legacy was that of indulgent, tolerant ridicule, with love
for the good and some derision for the extrusively noble.

Since we speak of the English, the stories told by Fielding and Jane
Austen of simple characters moving agreeably in congenial environments did not become idolized models for those who lived at the same
time or later. The English novel was already moving in several other
directions. One could not bring *Tristram Shandy* within an existing
order, any more than one could, in a later age, find English models for
the novels of Peacock. The so-called Gothic tales about castles, monks,
spectres, and dungeons, which were not wholly without influence upon
the Brontës and some more recent dealers in the macabre, took another
road. And before Walter Scott ran away with the novel and made it a
dramatic, antiquity-filled romance, the moral philosopher, William God-
win, whose several tales followed no single pattern, had written the
first wholly successful critical social study in English fiction, *Caleb
Williams.* So by the early years of the nineteenth century the English
novel had set off along half-a-dozen paths, which accorded only—except
for those Gothic tales—in telling, with however broad, trim, or eccentric
a technique, probable stories about a small number of well-observed
and often well-loved characters of no previous importance in society.

This all happened, you will observe, in the pre-industrialized world
of the eighteenth century. It happened, especially, in an island which
was not more cut off by the sea than by freedom from European
turmoils. Wars were fought, not in England, but elsewhere. Revolutions
occurred at a distance. When foreign warriors and foreign revolutionaries reached England, they sought sanctuary: once here, they became
very tame, and for the most part were pleasantly amazed at the spectacle
of a free people going with easy confidence about its daily life. England
was a quiet country: the novels which recorded its life (they were
written neither about aristocrats nor about labourers) took their note
from this, and make us feel that dwellers in an island have themselves

many of the observable features of islands. Islanders live apart from the rest of mankind. They are largely preoccupied with their own domestic concerns. If they travel, it is by road, and to another part of the same island, inhabited by those who are also islanders. Some may think the doings of islanders parochial; but it is interesting to remember that, although they have been greatly about our world in the last three hundred and fifty years, the English are still islanders. Those who consider it a defect in our novels that they deal with isolated groups (in other words, with character alone) will also object to the Englishman's preference for an empty railway compartment, a closed front door, life behind hedges, and the sombre joys of personal privacy.

II. ETHICS THE BASIS

Now although exiles grew discreet as soon as they reached England, the political ideas whose defeat or proscription had caused them to flee from the Continent travelled separately to this country. We did not have a revolution in eighteenth-century England, because whatever our social inequalities may then have been they were not intolerable to the majority. Only small parties of what would now be called intellectuals were affected by them. The English, if they are a political people at all (which some have doubted), have hitherto been reasonable in their political actions. They are not very good haters. They are not even very good critics. But they readily pick up a moral rebuke, and, while denouncing the author of that rebuke as a firebrand, unobtrusively attend to the matter complained of. Hence English political novels have been, not propaganda for any party or cause, but ethical discussions or rebukes. They have never advocated the destruction of tyrants; what they have done is to direct moral indignation to some particular social injustice, and they have almost always assumed that this social injustice is due to thoughtless, selfish ignorance, rather than to the wickedness of any class in the community.

When, therefore, the eighteenth-century novelists had passed, and *Caleb Williams* had had its success and its day, and all the excellent feminine novels which advised patience, prudence, self-control, and moderation in all things had passed into limbo, Dickens, beginning as irresponsibly as Fielding had done, and taking four trivial gentlemen for a jaunt upon the coach routes of the country, lifted *The Pickwick Papers* into point and vigour by most brilliantly ridiculing political partizanship, exposing the sinister processes of shady solicitors and advocates, and bringing the horrors of the Fleet Prison for debtors into the homes of those who read solely for amusement. Dickens was in the grand masculine tradition; he wrote as much for his own diversion as for the diversion of a public; but he had been born very poor and he had experienced in life much that the feminine novelists could barely have heard of. The fact that he was a great inventor of comic characters secured him immortality: he is without doubt the greatest inventor of comic characters, apart from Shakespeare, in English literature. But he was at the same time a moral scourge of social injustice, who wrote with such power that he more than once, as no more persistently didactic man could have done, shocked the sensitive conscience of Victorian England into remedial activity.

We were then past the days when the individual worker had been drawn ever more stringently into the servitude of wholesale production. What is called the industrial revolution had occurred. Our manufacturers were becoming the wealthy class, and the landowners whose capacity for evil had been shown in *Caleb Williams* retained only a portion of their economic and political influence. It was at the new and terrible tyranny of the factory age that a succession of novels, the sequels to *Caleb Williams,* aimed their criticism. These novels were not many; and most of them—by Mrs. Gaskell, Charles Kingsley, George Eliot, Disraeli, Mark Rutherford, and George Gissing—have undeservedly slipped from the close attention of British and American readers. All were ethical novels. The authors of them, having drawn attention to this or that social evil, did not proceed, very professionally, to some other aspect of industrialism (as Zola was to do, and as, in the United States, Upton Sinclair has done), but turned without sense of incongruity to picturesque history, autobiography, or pleasant tales of love and happiness in which also the lessons of the Ten Commandments might be reinforced. It was upon the conduct of the individual, and not the conduct of the community, that English eyes were turned.

If Dickens surpassed the critics it was not because he gave more attention to the community, but because his creative gifts, unlike those of the critics, were transcendent. He laughed, and the reading world laughed; he pictured, and the reading world saw; he told with breadth a sometimes melodramatically invented, always an animated and richly diversified, story; and he became, for readers all over the world, the prototype of the English novelist. His influence upon novel-writing in

France, in Russia, in the United States, and at home persisted titanically until the day before yesterday.

III. LATER VICTORIANS

Dickens, nevertheless, was far from being the last of the Victorians. First George Meredith and then Thomas Hardy did something to the novel for which perhaps readers had been half-prepared by the ambitious tales of George Eliot and the passionate tales of the Brontës. They imparted to it something of the extremely concentrated comic and tragic force of Elizabethan drama. Whereas earlier writers had dwelt affectionately upon manners (as they did, too), and Dickens and Thackeray had brought many characters to the fulfilment or bafflement of fortune, both Meredith and Hardy dwelt, in colour, as it were, as Shakespeare had done, upon the conflict of heroic individuals with fate. They made the novel a lengthy prose-poetic drama, in which—each in his own way—they demonstrated that, in Meredith's words,

> *"Passions spin the plot.*
> *We are betrayed by what is false within."*

They were dramatic novelists. Whatever Meredith's intensely self-conscious style may have concealed of commonplace invention, there can be no doubt that his concern with men and women as tragic comedians needs to be recognized for what it is, a new and very important contribution (I cannot now discuss whether it was a decadent contribution) to our sense of what the novel may be. For the first time since Jane Austen the English novel was given a limitation of form, and for the first time at all it was made purposefully heroic, as the Elizabethan plays were purposefully heroic. It provided the cynosure of personal, spiritual drama, lacking in the dispersed and sometimes pedestrian drama of incident supplied by earlier Victorians. Hardy, coming later, and nowadays too censoriously blamed for an arbitrary philosophy and a creaking artificiality of plot, was a greater creator and equally a spiritual dramatist. I sometimes think that Meredith took his cue from the early virtuoso Shakespeare of, let us say, *Love's Labour's Lost,* while Hardy, just as much of an Elizabethan out of time, was as racy as Udall's *Ralph Roister Doister* and as tragic as John Webster.

It is usual at this point to indicate briefly that the age of the novel in England was at an end. That is true to the extent that the Victorian era was drawing to a close, and that a new era was beginning. British prosperity, the busy manufacturing and mercantile success of our nation, had passed its full tide, and the influence of scientific theory and bold inquiry into the causes of human actions was shaking the faith of restless thinkers in Great Men, the benevolent Greatness of Great Britain, and that conception of perfectibility which used to be called Progress. But the novel was not yet dead in England. It only ceased to be Victorian. Novelists, at last absorbing the new thoughts which Darwin and Huxley, Tyndall and Lyell had brought to the world's notice (which all, it must be remembered, diminished the heoric stature of the individual, and made him but a momentary instance of blindly surviving species), had to adapt their endangered craft to a new measure of life and importance. What did they do? They looked closely at home; but at the same time they looked abroad for advice. They looked as far as France.

IV. THE AMERICANS

They did not, as yet, look to the United States; for American novelists, in the matter of manner and technique, were still strongly influenced by the familiar productions of the country from which they drew their language. They were also largely concentrated in that part of the United States, New England, which had most affinity with the homeland. Delicate as was the genius of Hawthorne, and American as was the scene he pictured, *The Scarlet Letter* and *The House of the Seven Gables* were readily absorbed into English literature, and there can have been no demur when, at a later date, Henry James wrote a book about him for the English Men of Letters series. Powerful as was the genius, the extraordinary genius, of Herman Melville, the origins of that apocalyptic style of his were to be found in the work of Carlyle and De Quincey, and his first popularity was established in England. Moreover, the influence of Dickens among men of lesser genius continued to be as strong as it was in England. One might have been excused, late in the nineteenth century, when Meredith and Hardy were becoming the last literary Grand Old Men, for thinking that the American novel was but a younger brother of the English novel.

One might have been excused; but one would not have been wise. For while such a writer as Bret Harte—a very good writer who to-day is too little esteemed—owed much in vividness and sentiment to Dickens, he was already pointing the way to what we have since seen. The

United States in his day were no longer intellectually dominated by Boston. Bret Harte wrote of the West. And he thus established a fact which has grown ever more important in the history of modern literature, which is that, whereas the English novelist was always an islander, dwelling in a country whose order, however exemplary, was of a piece with his love of domesticity and privacy, the American novelist, as soon as he began to look about him, thought and wrote in terms of a continent.

New England was not, of course, to yield supremacy at a touch. For a long time English readers (who rejoiced in Mark Twain's *Tom Sawyer* and *Huckleberry Finn* to such an extent that they thought of the author as transcending time and nationality) saw the normal American novel in terms of Henry James, William Dean Howells, and Mary E. Wilkins. All three writers were admired in Europe, as they were admired in the United States. They were considered the fine flower of prose fiction in the English language at a time when England was wolfing the problem novels of Hall Caine and Marie Corelli, and thrilling to the costume romances of Anthony Hope and Stanley Weyman. But they were still not un-English, un-European; the unworthy gibe made by an American when Henry James had established himself, at ease among his familiars in Europe, was that, while Henry James had come to Europe to imitate Turgenev, W. D. Howells had stayed at home to imitate Henry James.

v. The Jacobean Novel and Its Successors

What, when he was domiciled here, did Henry James find? In his own art, so sensitive and so fine-spun, he was drawn ever inward through shyness. He could have little broad contact with the islanders— only some association with the most refined among them. He was himself an island; and he lived secluded, pulling down the blinds, and sitting in darkness, conjuring before him the nerves and pale contacts of imaginary people. By doing this he perfected a really beautiful technique, which did not fail to arouse the admiration of connoisseurs and to inspire the more sensitive among them, if they were of the craft, to imitation. What he discussed was frequently remote from reality, the serious negotiation of a concourse of ghosts; but not to recognize the exquisiteness of the discussion is to betray invincible obtuseness. What did James find when he arrived in England and became, as willingly as a novice with unquestioned vocation for monastic life, an islander?

He found something which he must have assisted considerably to confirm. He found that in the inner circles of taste the reputation of Dickens had declined. He found that Dickens was considered, as he is to-day considered by the superfine, vulgar. And the superfine of all ages are like those men who listened to Tony Lumpkin's song in *She Stoops to Conquer,* of whom one says, "Oh, damn anything that's *low.* I cannot bear it," while another, who is by profession a bear leader, indicating his drink, exclaims energetically: "May this be my poison if my bear ever dances but to the very genteelest of tunes." But, besides being thought vulgar, Dickens had been discovered, by reference to novelists more recently bred in France, not to know the novelist's job. When one had studied the craft of novel-writing in all its European finesse, he was seen to be rather slapdash, clumsy, and in fact not an artist at all.

That, for Henry James, was a damning charge. He had given himself so anxiously to the task of indicating everything, while never in so many words mentioning it (so that, in *The Ambassadors,* he never did bring himself to name, and perhaps could not bring himself to imagine, the small patented article from which a rich American family made its extravagant income), that to be told he was not an artist would probably have killed him. And one of his friends, or at least one of his biographers, Ford Madox Ford, who was as ardent an admirer of Turgenev as Henry James had been, said plainly that no Englishman, especially no Dickens, had ever—in the adult, sophisticated sense of the term—written a novel. He said our national fictions were "nuvvles." We have been on the defensive about them ever since.

This, I must say, strikes me as most becoming national modesty. But I am not wholly in disagreement with it. Nor were a number of those writers who have influenced the novel most decidedly in post-Victorian England. Developments followed. The moment George Moore decided to write novels in the French manner, he changed the course of the English novel. And when, transplanting French realism to Ireland and the English provinces, he set Arnold Bennett upon a path midway between French technical precision and eighteenth-century English kindness and moral tolerance, he did something more than he realized. For although Bennett was as English as Samuel Johnson, he did learn and brilliantly follow the French close manner of writing. (If anybody wishes to realize how good in this manner Bennett was, he should read *Whom God Hath Joined* and the remorseless picture of old age in *Lord*

Raingo). And although *The Old Wives' Tale* is as English as an oak it has a pattern which would have seemed strange to Dickens and indeed to all older English writers. In 1908 it was thought very French, and was everywhere described as "meticulous."

About the same time, H. G. Wells, at first a comic writer as easy and inventive as Dickens, departed from comedy and scientific romance in order to preach the new cause of Sociology, or the planned perfectibility of mankind. He did this with the aplomb of genius; but he left his master, Dickens, far behind, and cast back to that earliest moral and political English novel, *Caleb Williams*. And a Polish seaman, who in his scruples over words and thoughts was not inferior to Henry James, decided to write in English, because that was the language of his adoption. He may have studied Rudyard Kipling; he may have derived from Kipling the first hint for that succession of contributory narratives in the first person singular which practically applied James's "blest law of successive aspects"; but his study of Kipling had not formed his style or his choice of theme. It had only helped to make him realize that the English had room for a psychologist who had been a sailor and traveller in strange latitudes, where he had seen and dreamed curious, melancholy things, and where he had noticed that sometimes, contrary to the beliefs of literary men, human beings do behave melodramatically in good faith.

By 1910, that is, by the end of the short reign of Edward VII, the English novel ceased altogether to be the garrulous inventive hodgepodge of nature and comedy and tragedy which it had been for two hundred years. Fielding, Dickens, Hardy, and Meredith had lived in vain. Our authors, instead of looking out upon the world and describing it as creators and enjoyers of life, began to look querulously upon the mess mankind had made, to use fiction as a vehicle for political propaganda, to follow the intricate artistic models of the Continent. Conrad had not more than one or two imitators; the followers of Arnold Bennett and H. G. Wells were legion. They wrote fluently, sometimes brilliantly, about their own young lives, while the very ingredients of those lives were being mixed. They distorted the characters of their friends, working from the living model, and blended them into the fictional autobiographies which had become the rage. Only one of them, Compton Mackenzie, had a comic sense which, largely in his minor books, linked him with the masculine tradition in English fiction. Only one, tortured by genius, a strange upbringing, and perhaps sexual frustration, gave to the novel a new, fierce intensity. D. H. Lawrence had a great effect upon novelists younger than himself. Upon his contemporaries, as well as upon some of these juniors, another influence was also very powerful. They discovered a new theory which accorded very well with the inward-looking spirit of the time. They found Freud, and in him they found an explanation of the sickness which all intuitively knew to be destroying society.

vi. America to the Rescue

It was fortunate indeed that at this point American novelists were ready to continue the adventure of novel-writing upon their own account. As the century turned, and the nineteen-tens and -twenties were swallowed by war and the disillusions of peace, a new generation of American writers was growing up and detaching itself wholly from the earlier generations. But even before this young generation appeared the American novel had begun its abundant presentation, so sharp and so extremely critical, of the life of a powerful and expanding community. It was to be especially vigorous, and especially full of criticism.

One reason for the vigour was the overwhelming vitality of the young nation, which grew and spread itself across immense territory at a speed inconceivable to the closely packed and stringently confined European nations. The world had known nothing like this rapid progress. The similar spreading growth of revolutionary Russia can alone compare with it. America was driving from East to West, hindered only by natural obstacles, which were met to be overcome, in a wave of energy. It was absorbing into its population at unheard-of speed enormous numbers of men and women from Europe. It was headily rich, active, and prosperous; it was producing food and trade in a bulk impossible to most of the older communities; it was improvising a great machinery of manufacture and distribution with which to supply its population. And, although (because so many of them still had their roots in the old world) the newer Americans maintained their love of and interest in Europe and the books of Europe, and the older ones clung to British ways and English writing, there came a moment when the Americans paused in their pioneering to exclaim, with delightful astonishment, "Why, we are a great nation! In possessing ourselves of a continent, we have become, in size and achievement, the greatest nation in the world!"

This was true. But the rapidity of American expansion, otherwise so
inspiring to the spirit of man, had had several extraordinarily evil consequences. They entirely surpassed the evil consequences of the industrial revolution in England, because the worst features of that revolution,
almost immediately observed in so small a country, had aroused sensitive consciences to unsuppressible protest. The influence of public opinion in England is irresistible. We have been long civilized, and are un-
restrained by fear; only by respect for order. The aristocratic tradition in
this country, of which criticism (in assuming its resemblance to the
aristocratic tradition in France or Russia before their revolutions) has
often missed the virtue, has been on the whole a tradition of disinter-
ested political service to the community. But in the United States there
could be no aristocratic tradition:

"Have you outstript the rest? are you the President?
It is a trifle . . .
Unscrew the locks from the doors!
Unscrew the doors themselves from their jambs!
I speak the pass-word primeval, I give the sign of democracy,
By God! I will accept nothing which all cannot have their counterpart of on
    the same terms."

In the United States, growth had travelled at a speed far in excess of
control by a national public opinion. Wherever men had been gathered
together in local communities distances were so great, and the coercive
power of the most resolute and ambitious members of the communities
was so uncontrollable by any central force, that exploitation upon a
gigantic scale inevitably occurred. And so, when American writers were
inspired to tell stories about their country, they had, upon the one hand,
its terrific expansion to record, the vehement struggles with Nature of
its brave men and women to extol, the idylls of young lovers in isolation,
such as Bret Harte pictured in *Cressy,* to sentimentalize; but also, and in
effect upon a later literature so importantly, the extreme anomalies and
inequalities of a swift-moving industrialism to condemn. The rough
justice of small towns, the graft of cities, the crushing of workers by the
machine of mass-production were irresistibly a call to criticism. Consequently, although there were many American writers who sported with
the manners of New York—I myself have grateful memories of early
works by Richard Harding Davis in this style—and expressed with
beauty, as Edith Wharton did in *Ethan Frome,* the relations of human

beings in remoter settings, the significant novelists were those who saw, behind the prosperities of the new continent, bleaker facts upon which they proceeded to build sober and terrible works of fiction. Stephen Crane was the most brilliant of these authors; Theodore Dreiser and Upton Sinclair, both longer-lived than Crane and for this reason more impressive in the range and bulk of their work, were the obvious leaders in a crusade for truth.

That, speaking of course with careless disregard of dates and other memorable names, was the position when the great European War of 1914–18 was fought. In England, as far as the novel was concerned, Henry James was an æsthetic dictator. When he chose Compton Mackenzie, Hugh Walpole, and Gilbert Cannan as the hopes of the day, with D. H. Lawrence, in his words, "toiling in the dusty rear," he established these reputations. But James, although we did not know it, was at the end of his life and at the end of his power. Already, a new and even more French æsthetic was being formulated; already we were entering upon a period which must be described as distinctively *literary*. The strength, but it must be admitted not the literary distinction, of Dreiser and Sinclair, could well be contrasted with the intellectual and intuitional gymnastic of subsequently much extolled British writers, Dorothy Richardson, James Joyce, Virginia Woolf, Lytton Strachey. It was upon such writers, with the brilliant addition of Aldous Huxley, that American observers based their estimates of English post-war fiction. I think it is worth while to observe that, whatever their other strengths, which are many and incontestable, American novelists have not anywhere challenged any of the gymnasts in their unique quality of literary and intellectual finesse.

VII. MODERN AMERICANS

But what an extraordinary outpouring there has been of a fiction which has kept closely in touch with the senses and surface of American life! There can be hardly a facet of that life which has not been brilliantly presented for the world's regard. In Sinclair Lewis we have seen, deliberately undertaken, and in terms of international comprehension, the mimicry of typical Americans in trade, in the pulpit, in medicine, in matrimony, and in conflict with their juniors. In Fannie Hurst gravely circumstantial social pictures of women which range from silent immigrants to the talkative sophisticates of New York; in Edna Ferber sharp vignettes of a dozen orders of life, observed with an eye which, while never falsifying, picks the individual from the type and gives it personal importance. In the dazzlingly arrived post-war generation we have had the new romantic impressionism of Ernest Hemingway, ruthless pictures of life in the South from William Faulkner and Erskine Caldwell (Faulkner sometimes pretentious and too often turgid, but at his best piercingly vivid; Caldwell bitter, salutary stuff for queasy stomachs), ruthless pictures of decadents in New York and Hollywood from John O'Hara and men and women farther afield from James M. Cain, gusts of tumultuous youth from Thomas Wolfe, overwhelming studies of the cruel effects of poverty and evil upon suffering humanity from John Steinbeck. The close, malicious scrutiny of wicked, or temporizing, or feeble-willed city dwellers supplied by Jerome Weidman, Dawn Powell, and Josephine Lawrence are instances which I take almost at random from names and *tours de force* which crowd to memory; for in such brief space as remains to me I could not attempt to do justice to the undeviating drive and punch of a whole generation of observers. All have this in common, that they are intensely critical, alert, sophisticated (so that personal corruption seems almost to be taken for granted, while social conditions are exposed for indignation or scorn), and intensely professional. Between them, they are presenting a sharp black and white picture of the life of the United States which—in its exactitude—would give outsiders a wrong impression if it were not rectified by the less brilliant but not less valuable interiors of Ruth Suckow, the classic studies of Willa Cather, the milder satires of James P. Marquand, and, curiously enough, by the writers whom we in England can compare to our own sentimentalists, aiming no higher than the library lists.

The impression created by all these books is of a life of twenty-four hours to the spirited day, of rapid movement, heavy drinking, love reduced to its simplest elements, and society at war. And of course, since everything in the United States is upon a continental scale, of vast spaces and enormous journeys (even the night lorry drivers have had their thrilling novel), of extraordinary gregariousness and good fellowship, and of adventure which sometimes spreads beyond the law and into life-taking, flight, and terror. All this is to say no more than that the American novel, released from the moral bondage which has always restricted the range of English novels, is expressive of the large scale experimentalism of American life. American novelists, many of whom are graduates from newspapers all over the United States, come to their work of novel-writing as unimpressible by protestation as policemen; and, filled with inexhaustible knowledge of human behaviour under stress as they have seen it from boyhood, may seem cynical. They are in fact, to the great admiration of British colleagues, hopelessly expert in the professional utilization of their own scrupulous honesty.

VIII. MODERN BRITISH NOVELISTS

What have the British to set against this remorseless exposition of the life of a continent in which, in the cities, everything moves with such speed and such freedom from restraint? I do not think they have anything at all. The tempo and texture of life in England is altogether different. The English novelist who wishes to be "tough" tends to re-move his characters to some much wilder country than England, and at once removes himself thereby from any possibility of comparison. The English novelist who would write as "meticulously" of life in Birming-ham as, for example, James T. Farrell writes of life in Chicago would have few readers; the English novelist who explored village life à la Caldwell or Faulkner would have to invent almost everything. The truth is that England is a largely uneventful spot, joined to two other uneventful spots; and only from one of these spots, Wales, chiefly in the work of Caradoc Evans, does there come anything approaching in spirit the American histories of remote districts. Caradoc Evans, a poetic and diabolically skilful writer, is our one legitimate scourge, and he is not English.

No, if American readers wish to understand the novels written to-day by English authors, they must not look for counterparts to their own brilliant fictions. They must not look to find works exhibiting a high de-gree of observant curiosity and irreverent judgment. They must turn the American binoculars the wrong way round, so that they embrace, not a continent in which there are incalculable ways of living, most of them conducted at high pressure, but a crowded island in which—though with much kindness and goodwill, and often surprising affection—it is the wish of almost every family to live very respectably in a small detached or semi-detached house with a workable garden full of flowers as well as a few vegetables, without any interruption from neighbours or fellow-citizens. I do not wish to give the impression that there are no discon-tented or adventurous people in England; I hope there is no need, in 1943, to protest against any assumption that the nation is lost in apathy;

but when one returns to the country from abroad the first impression one has is of a rampart of cliff or downland, and the second is of almost irreproachable orderliness. Out of such orderliness, and such complaisance as one finds in the ugliest provincial cities ever put together by man, it would be impossible to draw thrilling social criticisms. Our novels must be taken for what they are, sometimes as musings upon the general spectacle of life, more often as studies of individual character. As studies of character, I believe some of them to be excellent.

Let me take, with extreme tentativeness, a few names from the far too many rushing upon me at this moment. And I must now, so striking is the number of Welsh and Irish names in my list, depart from all reference to "English" novelists. At this point we become indeed "British." Let me begin with the women. I. Compton Burnett is a wit who portrays in fiction everything I have suggested of the restrictions of English life. Her *dramatis personæ* are members of completely isolated families; they do nothing but talk without end, and with great rudeness, often with superlative bravura. Embedded in the exchange of bitter observations are vestiges of melodramatic plot; indicated in it are seven or eight frightful illuminations of eccentric character. Equally static, less brilliant, but not less subtle (at her best in the short story), is Elizabeth Bowen. Kate O'Brien's fictional biography of an English nun, *The Land of Spices,* shows her to have altogether exceptional talent. Jean Rhys is appallingly precise in the portraits of shiftless young actresses or tippling spinsters. Jean Ross is courageous in harsh pictures of school, stage, and wayward character. Norah Hoult, in the unpopular vein of realism, has drawn the life of drifting people in Dublin and London with the greatest possible candour and truth. And in more generally acceptable styles we must not undervalue, because they are acceptable, wise, kind Dorothy Whipple and mischievous Angela Thirkell.

Among men, I mention as ornaments of the regional or rural novelist's craft Crichton Porteous and John McNeillie, the author of *Wigtown Ploughman.* High in class above most of our other novelists is Joyce Cary, equally at home in describing family affairs in Ireland, the life and artful thoughts of an African negro, and the doings of cockney kids evacuated during war-time to the English country. We have L. A. G. Strong's powerful Highland studies, such as *Brothers,* and his nostalgic pictures of a boy's happy days near Dublin. And John Brophy's remarkable narrative gift is turned ever more vigorously upon normal character in great variety of circumstance and emergency. John Llewellyn Rhys, unhappily dead, left mordant studies in the life of airmen. A very gifted young Welshman, Rhys Davies, who observes Welsh village life with love and malice, can be contrasted with his more flamboyant fellow-countryman, Richard Llewellyn, who, however, is not (in the matter of literary composition) remaining in Wales. And lastly I must by no means omit R. C. Hutchinson, who seems to me to be an author in the grand classic tradition, who transcends the life of the islander by a boldness and range of scene and character and episode which may yet rank his with the greatest names of all.

What of the future? It may well be that all I have said about the English novel will be falsified when the authors of tomorrow return from the fighting fronts. They will be both men and women. They may well want a different England from the England of the past. Then perhaps we shall see the English novel taking yet other paths. That the American novel can take other paths seems to me to be less likely; but I should not be surprised if the American novel lost speed, lost toughness, lost its critical note, and changed. It is now the most striking novel in the world. It cannot go on being the most striking novel in the world. And so I think it may turn, with new strength, to classic conceptions and classic heights of comedy and tragedy.

VI THE WAY TO WORLD RECOVERY

By F. W. Hirst

———————◆———————

I. EARLY STUDIES

I BECAME INTERESTED in American statesmen and economists from Franklin, Jefferson, Alexander Hamilton and Carey onwards to Francis Walker and Taussig when I was studying political economy with the late Professor Edgeworth nearly half a century ago. But my actual personal knowledge of the United States and Canada dates from the autumn of 1908. Having recently been appointed editor of the *Economist,* I thought it would be useful to the paper to investigate on the spot the causes and effects of the great banking and stock exchange crisis of the previous winter. I was fortunate in carrying letters of introduction from John Morley to President Theodore Roosevelt and his distinguished Secretary of War, Elihu Root, as well as to Andrew Carnegie, Dr. Nicholas Murray Butler and Goldwin Smith, who was then living in retirement at Toronto.

I was also fortunate in having made friends with two distinguished Harvard men—Charles Burlingham, who knew almost everyone worth knowing in New York, and Lawrence Lowell, who died recently after a great academic career. At Harvard I met Professor Taussig. In Canada I stayed a few days at Quebec, Montreal, Toronto, and (with our Governor-General Earl Grey) at Ottawa. Sir Wilfred Laurier was then Prime Minister and Fielding was his Minister of Finance. It was an interesting moment not only in financial history but in the relations between Canada, Great Britain and the United States. Sir Wilfred told me that he was a great admirer of John Bright and of the Liberal Gladstonian

School, which then controlled the destinies of our country under such leaders as Campbell Bannerman, Asquith, Morley and Bryce. Canada's connection with Great Britain and the Empire was more highly prized than ever after the banking collapse in the United States, and the Laurier Government, to mark its recognition of the enormous value of the unrestricted free market which Canadian products enjoyed in England in contrast with the highly protected market of the United States, had given us a small preference in their own moderately protective tariff.

The bankers and financiers whom I met at Montreal and Toronto were very friendly and communicative. They appreciated our banking institutions and their safety in comparison with those of New York. London was of course a great investor at that time in Canada, whose enterprises were then directed by two groups in Montreal and Toronto. Though the relations between Canada and the United States were strained by tariff difficulties, there was a school (represented by Goldwin Smith) which held that the long frontier between Canada and the United States must eventually lead to far more intimate relations between the two countries, which were already associated in many ways, not only by language but also by the use of the dollar currency and a large commerce which defied even the high American tariff. Moreover, Canada was already to a large extent a favourite playground for American travellers and sportsmen.

When public opinion in the United States, Canada and Great Britain is released from the agony of war, and the temperature of all classes has cooled down, it is pretty certain that our passionate and ingrained love of personal freedom will revive in full strength. How will it manifest itself in the economic sphere?

II. FIFTY YEARS OF ECONOMIC HISTORY

During the last fifty years, of which I can speak with some personal knowledge of trade and finance, faith in the virtue of private enterprise has been strong in both countries; but there has been one very important difference. From 1846 to 1914 the mighty expansion of British commerce, manufactures and shipping, which brought ever-increasing wealth and welfare to the whole population, was accompanied by, and dependent on, our policy not only of free markets at home, but of the open door to imports from all countries. This guaranteed a low cost of production, and so enabled us to compete successfully with our manufacturing rivals in all parts of the world. The corresponding expansion of wealth in the United States was built not on freedom of trade with the world, but on complete freedom of trade between the States of the Union, which—through the interchange of their domestic products and manufactures and the inventive enterprise of their business men—made the United States by far the richest free trade area in the world. After the war between North and South the Republican and Democratic parties contended on the subject of tariffs; and the Republicans, who always wanted high protection, generally had the best of it against the Democrats, who favoured tariffs for revenue only. I attended hearings of the Tariff Committee during Taft's presidency, and heard the vain protests of Professor Taussig and other enlightened economists like Charles Francis Adams against the ready assent of political groups to the greedy demands of manufacturers for more and more tariff protection. I recall, too, several talks with Underwood, the author of the tariff which bore his name during Woodrow Wilson's first presidency. He effected large reductions of duties, but complained that manufacturers in Alabama and other interests in the South raised such opposition, as subscribers to Democratic funds, that he was unable to carry the reductions nearly as far as he had intended. I remember also Mr. Carnegie testifying that the steel trade no longer needed a tariff; and it is not long since Mr. Ford took the same line about the motorcar industry. To protect consumers against exploitation by monopolies, the Democrats resorted to "trust-busting," and managed to pass anti-trust laws which broke up and punished illegal combinations, but without much general effect; for prices can only be kept down by competition.

I think it is generally admitted now that the very high, and in many cases prohibitive, American tariffs following the defeat of President Wilson after the last war had many mischievous effects. As tariffs could not protect American farmers, tobacco growers and cotton planters, they caused that severe depression in agriculture which President Roosevelt and Mr. Wallace endeavoured to cure mainly by subsidies under the New Deal, and also in a smaller degree by Mr. Cordell Hull's freer trade reciprocity treaties. Again, by depressing the import and export trade, these tariffs caused much unemployment in the ports. Then again by ruining or half ruining many manufacturers in European countries, whose export trade with the United States was cut off by the Hawley-Smoot tariff, they aggravated poverty and unemployment in Europe. Finally, by creating artificial prosperity in manufacturing centres they promoted "the New Era" of speculative optimism and soaring prices on the stock exchange during the reign of President Coolidge, and so precipitated the appalling collapse of credit and trade in the autumn of 1929. It was the biggest and costliest crisis ever witnessed in modern history during peace. It spread from the United States all over the world, and the ruinous consequences in Germany and Austria undoubtedly contributed to the rise of Hitler. The collapse in the United States gave President Roosevelt an overwhelming majority and an opportunity, which unfortunately for the world he did not take, of associating a great reduction of the American tariff with the New Deal.

In our own country the same crisis struck us sufficiently hard to cause a suspension of the gold standard, besides providing our tariff reformers with their long awaited opportunity of overthrowing our free trade system, and of introducing first a general protective tariff, and secondly at Ottawa a preferential and discriminating system for the British Empire. This led at once to much friction with foreign countries, which adopted retaliatory quotas and exchange restriction. But in 1941 by signing the Atlantic Charter, our Government has pledged itself, with the approval of the Dominion Premiers, to put an end to preferential trading after the war.

Neither our general protective tariff nor the much higher protective tariff of the United States was much lowered by the Reciprocity Treaty, negotiated with a series of others by Mr. Cordell Hull. It was a disappointment. I remember a manufacturer of woollen blankets in Yorkshire, who once had a flourishing trade with the United States, telling me that it had reduced the tariff on his blankets from 92 to 90 per cent. One would have hoped that the alliance would have freed Anglo-American trade from protective tariffs; but they still stand except for administrative remissions in connection with war materials. Mr. Cordell Hull's Reciprocity Treaty with Canada brought substantial advantages to both countries, and I understand that since the war many tariff duties between the United States and Canada have been removed.

III. ECONOMIC LIBERTY

If Anglo-American co-operation in the economic sphere, including, it is to be hoped, the self-governing Dominions of the British Empire, is to be really effective, it must be accompanied and sustained by a very great reduction of tariff barriers, and a much freer flow of overseas trade.

In that way all the inhabitants of the British Empire and the United States may enjoy not only cheapness and plenty and profitable employment, but also the friendliness and good feeling which would result from the division of labour, and the liberal interchange of diversified products—food, fruit, raw materials, metals, and all kinds of manufactures. If this is achieved, British and American ports and British and American shipping will attain in a few years a prosperity never before known—a prosperity which will be shared by friendly nations, and ultimately by those which are now hostile.

By way of illustration let me take the case of the cotton trade. Before the first Great War Lancashire was dependent for the bulk of its supplies of raw cotton on the United States; and its yarns and finished goods, besides supplying most of our home requirements, went to all parts of the world, and indeed comprised 90 per cent of the world's overseas trade in cotton manufactures. In 1911 our exports of cotton yarn totalled 223 million pounds; and our exports of cotton piece goods totalled 6,653 million square yards. In the same year our imports of raw cotton, mainly from the United States, were valued at 71 million pounds sterling. The war played havoc with this trade, and great inroads were made upon it by Japan. In 1938 our exports of cotton yarn totalled only 122 million pounds, and our exports of cotton piece goods totalled only 1,387 million square yards. Our imports of cotton from America, Brazil, Egypt, etc., were of course proportionately reduced; but I cannot give the figures.

Since the second great war broke out the whole cotton trade has been taken under the guardian care of the Board of Trade, and its immensely enlarged bureaucracy, which is now planning to retain its management of the cotton and other staple industries of the country, including imports and exports when the war comes to an end. The result of its efforts to maintain our exports is not encouraging. From 122 million pounds of yarn in 1938 our exports have fallen to 18 millions; and from 1,387 million square yards of cloth in the former year our exports were reduced last year to 484 millions. Large numbers of cotton mills have been closed. Concentration and conscription have done their work under the new controls, which have also operated with deadly effect on the Liverpool and Manchester exchanges and on the merchants who have been driven out of business by the bureaucrats.

I need not dwell on the plight of our small shopkeepers, retail traders and manufacturers, who are being squeezed out in order to make room for the big monopolies which are to be fostered and supervised by the Board of Trade. But the general picture, if it could be filled in, would sufficiently explain why the revolt of the average Englishman against the bureaucratic State is as strong as that of the average American, though less vocal; and when the war is over my own firm belief is that this feeling for economic liberty will operate strongly and effectively in Anglo-American co-operation. This means that co-operation will not be wholly or mainly between the administrations of London and Washington, but between the individual manufacturers, producers, merchants, bankers and shipowners of Great Britain and America, as it has always been in times of peace. Trade is not between governments, but between individuals. It follows not the flag but the price list. If only governments would allow nations to remain at peace, if competition and friendly rivalry and co-operation were universal, and the peoples were not crushed down under the burden of armaments, freedom of exchange would lead to a fruitful association between labour and capital everywhere, and human industry would reap the rewards that it earns and deserves. Every soil would yield that for which it is best suited, and the fruits of the earth from all climes would find their markets in due season.

That is the dream of an economic and social Utopia; but the visions of idealists are the lamps that illuminate civilization along the difficult and thorny path of progress, often obstructed, arrested and set back, as it has been in the last thirty years, by storms of barbarism.

It is true that even in peace-time what has been called economic nationalism is apt to assert itself to the detriment and exclusion of commerce, sometimes under the inspiration of patriotic philosophers seeking to restore or safeguard the independence of their countries. Thus when Napoleon overran Germany, Fichte wrote a pamphlet in favour of what he called "the closed trade State" which would be as far as possible independent of imports and exports, sacrificing all the plenty and comforts which its people might acquire by trading with their neighbours. A State based on these principles came into existence when Lenin organized the Soviet Union, put an end to the private commerce of Russia and confiscated the private property, not only of all Russians, but of all foreigners and all foreign investments. Even he, however, could not do entirely without foreign trade; so he created the Arcos, a government organization which sold timber and other surplus products in foreign markets and bought with the proceeds foreign manufactures for distribution or sale at very high prices in the Soviet Union. This is the nearest approach on a large scale to a complete system of communism and national economic independence that has ever been tried in modern history. But the attempt to eliminate private property with the profit motive and to equalize the pay of all workers has already been abandoned by Stalin; and it is not likely that an economic system which has failed will be widely adopted, least of all by the Anglo-Saxon races. The communist parties at home, in the self-governing Dominions and in the United States, though loud and noisy in their praise of Russia, are as yet not only insignificant in numbers but devoid of the talent of leadership which enabled Lenin to overthrow the corrupt and enfeebled government of the Tsar in a moment of desperation and defeat. Personal liberty, the inheritance of the Magna Charta, the right to choose your own vocation and your own trade, the right to save and the right to spend, the right to buy and sell freely within the limits of just laws are not likely to be surrendered by the British and American democracies. Democracy and liberty, guarded by representative institutions, are the heritage for which we are fighting; and whether we can or cannot induce other nations to adopt our political habits when we have restored their independence, we shall not surrender our own liberties, or condescend to base imitations of servile institutions.

IV. The Christian Bases of World Order

In the United States there is a widespread and honest desire to combine security and liberty after the war by agreements with the Allies to extend a co-operation which has been so effective in war for the purpose of consolidating peace and fortifying it against future aggression. Political thinkers are looking ahead. Democratic statesmen, remembering President Wilson's failure at Versailles and the disastrous American period of isolation which followed, realize that this time when peace comes good Americans must act together not merely as patriots but as citizens of the world and as leaders in a policy which will make international good will its ultimate objective.

It was in this spirit that Mr. Henry Wallace, Vice-President of the United States, addressing a conference on "The Christian Bases of World Order" at Delaware, Ohio, on March 8, 1943, referred to three philosophies now in competition. The first, he said, was that of the Nazis —the philosophy of might over right, which regards wars as inevitable until "the master race" dominates and pacifies the whole world. The second is the philosophy of Karl Marx, which declares that class war is inevitable until the dictatorship of the proletariat is everywhere established. The third, which Mr. Wallace proclaims as the Democratic Christian Philosophy, denies that man is made for war either between classes or nations, and asserts boldly that ultimate peace is inevitable since all men are brothers and God is their Father. Thus he would reconcile individual freedom with the general welfare, finding in democracy the hope of civilization. The downfall of Hitler, he argued, would not be enough in itself to bring about a permanent peace. "Germans by blood are neither better nor worse than Englishmen, Americans, Swedes, Poles or Russians"; but during the last ten years Nazi education has degraded millions of German boys and girls into the cult of war. "Marxism has used the Cheka (or Ogpu) just as Prussianism has used the Gestapo; but it has never preached international war as an instrument of national policy. It does not believe that one race is superior to another." Mr. Wallace's conclusion is that, to prevent a third world war, the Western democracies must reach a "close and trusting" understanding with Russia.

He admits sharp differences, economic and political, between the Russian and the British or American conceptions of democracy and liberty. But "the future well-being of the world depends upon the extent to which Marxism, as it is being progressively modified in Russia, and democracy, as we are adapting it to twentieth-century conditions, can live together in peace." To promote collaboration, and avoid a clash after the war is over, the Russian Government must abandon the idea of fermenting world revolution against what it calls the capitalist system; and the democracies which believe in individual liberty with freedom of trade and enterprise must be tolerant of Russia and other countries when they try to work out their own economic problems in their own way.

It is at least a hopeful sign—to pass from Mr. Wallace to measures of reconstruction—that a beginning has already been made towards the relief of famine-stricken countries after the armistice. A survey made by a committee of Save the Children Fund, published shortly before Mr. Wallace spoke, shows that modern Europe has never suffered such a combination of calamities. In the First Great War pestilence and famine followed in the wake of the armies and spread behind the lines.

But conscription of labour by the Nazis has added slavery in its worst form to famine. The case of France is less bad than that of Greece or Belgium or Poland or Czechoslovakia. But the mortality statistics even of France are alarming. In the first year of the war the general death rate rose by 18 per cent and the infant death rate by 48 per cent. There is no doubt that both rates are now much higher.[1] We know, for example, that in February 1942 the mortality rate of Paris was 37 per cent higher than in February 1941. That there has been an appalling increase in tuberculosis was proved by medical examination of children in one large city of unoccupied France. The Red Cross has done what it can, but its supplies are nearly exhausted, and the transport of food in neutral ships has been obstructed by fear that it might help Germany, "though it is clear from the reports" that it is possible to give help in special kinds of foodstuffs and medicines without weakening the effects of the blockade on Germany's strength. Here I am quoting a leader in the *Manchester Guardian* of February 16, 1943, which remarks truly enough: "Nothing but the liberation of Europe can rescue children from these consequences of Nazi rule, and these consequences become graver the longer that rule lasts."

Owing partly to good harvests, but still more to the Anglo-American naval blockade, great stocks of grain have accumulated in America, and a considerable reserve has been set aside for transport to Europe as soon as the war is over. After the last war the private efforts of wealthy British and American philanthropists, co-operating with the Red Cross and other organizations under the guidance of Mr. Herbert Hoover, did much to relieve starvation; but the vast accumulations of debt and the tremendous severity of war taxes will reduce the scope of private philanthropy, and the difficulties of governments to provide the necessary funds will be enormously greater than in 1919. Yet famine relief will claim priority, not only in order to reduce human suffering and avert the death of millions, but also as a police measure against the chaos and anarchy, pillage and banditry which will inevitably break loose if multitudes are left to starve.

It is of good augury that President Roosevelt's administration is alive to these dangers, and has been insisting, ever since the promulgation of the Atlantic Charter, that distribution and exchange are just as essential as production. The interchange of food and commodities and manufactures cannot be reconciled with economic nationalism. The danger is

[1] In the spring of 1943.

real and obvious. As Mr. Henry Wallace put it in a speech at Columbus, Ohio, following that which I have already cited:

"A movement is already under way to abandon the sane tariff policy represented by our reciprocal trade agreement programme, and go back to the Smoot-Hawley days of building a high tariff wall around the United States. Economic warfare of the Smoot-Hawley type is the initial step towards military warfare. It leads first to totalitarian control of trade, then to shooting. To win the peace, we must follow through to establish the right kind of international trade relations; we cannot hope to maintain peace by force unless the peace we are maintaining is a just peace."

v. The Freedom of the Seas

During the first part of the last war the principles and practice of naval blockade were extended by the British Government to what was called a long range blockade, and it was accompanied by severe rationing of neutral countries like Holland and Sweden, which bordered on Germany, lest they should sell any overseas importations to the enemy. This policy, or strategy, caused much controversy and led to several disputes with the United States. But German retaliation in the so-called U-boat blockade, with sinkings at sight, eventually brought America into the war on the side of the Allies. The barbarity of U-boat warfare, which has consigned multitudes of seamen to a watery grave, and is now equally practised by all the combatants, has brought about a state of things which, conjoined with the practice of bombing towns by day and night, has made this war more inhuman and ferocious than any in the annals of civilized history. Whether the universal horror which these atrocities by sea and air have inspired will eventually produce adequate preventive measures to secure the human race against a repetition remains to be seen.

In the last year of the First Great War President Wilson included in his peace "Points" the American doctrine known as "The Freedom of the Seas." That doctrine, which was first formulated in 1784 by Benjamin Franklin, and was actually brought into operation in a treaty between the United States and Prussia, provided that in war-time "all merchants and trading vessels employed in exchanging the products of different places, and thereby rendering the necessaries, conveniences and comforts of human life more easy to be obtained and more general, shall be allowed to pass free and unmolested." No further progress was made in this matter until 1856, when the European Powers abolished privateering at the Conference of Paris. On that occasion the Government of the United States was only willing to do the same provided that all property of private individuals, not contraband of war, on sea as already on land, should be exempted from capture.

The American policy was supported by Richard Cobden and by many of our Chambers of Commerce. It was again pressed upon the British Government with great ability by the then Lord Chancellor, Loreburn, at the time of the Second Hague Conference, but without success. But the lessons of the last war and the lessons of this war have added strength to the contention that food and ships containing food without contraband of war should be exempted from capture or detention on the high seas, so that innocent populations should no longer be subjected to famine, and the great surpluses and gluts of food which exist and are unsaleable in America could be employed to relieve the famine now decimating many countries of Europe. The difficulties and objections are obvious, but the arguments on both sides deserve to be carefully weighed and balanced before the American doctrine is rejected. Those, for example, who argue that famine will reduce Germany to subjection, or at least assist in her defeat, may be reminded that Hitler has used the famine in France and several other occupied countries ruthlessly and effectively for the purpose of forcing great numbers of enslaved people to work in war factories for Germany.

I do not profess to know what may now be the opinions either of President Roosevelt or of his leading opponents on freedom of the seas, or on the equally perplexing and important problem of freedom of the air, when the principles of peace have to be discussed and settled at the next conference of nations. But thanks to a piece of good fortune I had the pleasure of making what proved to be an enduring friendship with Mr. Herbert Hoover during the time in London when he organized Belgian relief, with such wonderful success, between 1914 and 1916. I had talks with him afterwards when he was directing the distribution of supplies to the famished countries of Eastern and Central Europe in 1919; and again ten years later, during the financial crisis which swept over the United States, I stayed with him in the White House. So perhaps I may be allowed to express my satisfaction that he is already being consulted as to the means and methods of dealing with the famine in Europe when this war is over. I have never found that my political philosophy has in any way interfered with American friendships. In this regard James (Viscount) Bryce set the example. He was on equally good terms with the leading men of both parties and with independent thinkers in the universities and the Press who happily abound in the States of the Union. American parties are so different from British parties that the political philosopher on either side of the Atlantic can always find subjects of agreement as well as of disagreement.

When President Roosevelt invited me to stay at Hyde Park, where he talked "with the freedom of history" to quote Burke's famous phrase—I soon found that I could share his admiration for Jefferson; and though I had written a biography of that great man, the President in his table talk told me of several picturesque incidents which had escaped my notice.

On a previous visit to the States as Editor of the *Economist* I was cordially welcomed by Woodrow Wilson in a year when he was Governor of New Jersey. He had taught political science for many years at Princeton, and took the opportunity of talking with me about Walter Bagehot. Of all the English writers on politics, Walter Bagehot (who edited the *Economist* in the 'sixties and early 'seventies) was the one he most admired. And, by way of contrast, I came into most friendly relations with Senator Aldrich, a dyed-in-the-wool Republican, when he became chairman of the National Monetary Commission and visited London in order to collect information on money and banking. He consulted me about the City, and I was able to arrange for him a highly profitable talk with my friend H. W. Search, then Discount Officer at the Bank, who knew perhaps more about the principles and practice of sound banking, and the detection of unsound banking, than any man in England. The labours of the Commission are enshrined in many volumes, to one of which I contributed papers on national debt and credit. Its findings were taken over by Woodrow Wilson's Democratic administration, which modified and, in my judgment, improved the system of Federal banking which Senator Aldrich and his colleagues had recommended for the much needed reform of the National and State banks. If the reformed system was inadequate to stem the torrent of Wall Street liquidation during the collapse of 1929–32, it has since proved its efficacy, and will, I hope, serve as a bulwark of credit for the United States and their allies in war and peace.

vi. Money and Exchange

At the time of writing (April 1943), the American dollar is the only important currency in the world which is harnessed to gold; for the

American Treasury will accept and pay dollars for gold in unlimited quantities at a fixed rate per ounce; and as there is also an official rate for Anglo-American financial and commercial transactions of 4 dollars to the pound sterling, the output of the South African gold mines and of other gold mines can count upon saleability in the two best currencies at a fixed profitable price.

Had it not been for the Lend-Lease agreement, there is no doubt that in the first part of the war after Britain had disposed of all its gold in order to pay for American food and munitions (the U.S.A. being then a neutral though a friendly neutral) the pound would have deteriorated in terms of the dollar. If, for example, the average sterling prices of the necessaries of life, of raw materials and war munitions had doubled in Great Britain while dollar prices in the United States remained stable, the dollar sterling rate, if left free, might easily have become two dollars to the pound instead of four dollars.

But the entry of the United States into the war, and its gigantic programme of munitions and supplies for itself and the Allies are causing such an increase of prices in the United States, that the American Government is adopting price ceilings and rationing more and more in order to combat this inflationary rise in the cost of living and production. Consequently what is called the equilibrium between the value or purchasing power of the pound and the dollar seems to be altering in favour of the pound, though both are diminishing in real value; and we may assume that as in the last war the value of gold is also diminishing, though the value of silver may be actually rising as it did for a time at the end of the last Great War

Mr. Oscar Hobson, the City Editor of the *News Chronicle,* has recently examined this highly complicated and difficult subject. On February 26th he took the case of the cost per ton of building a cargo ship of average size in Great Britain and the United States. The cost in the United States has always been higher than in the United Kingdom, at any rate since the 'fifties of last century. Since the outbreak of war in 1939 the cost of building merchant ships in this country has of course increased considerably. Our ships are certainly of better quality than the American mass-produced ship, and ours have risen in price since 1939 (according to Mr. Hobson) from about £12 or £13 to about £20 per ton at the present time. But the cost of the American mass-produced merchant ships appears to be no less than 360 dollars, or about £90 when converted at the official war-time rate of exchange, of 4 dollars to the pound. Therefore, it would seem, the current cost of building ships is at least four times as much in the United States as in Great Britain. Hence if shipbuilding costs were a true indication of the costs of production generally "the fair current conversion rate between pound and dollar might well be as high as 16 dollars to the pound!" Mr. Hobson, in this most interesting article, admits of course that it would not be at all safe to treat the limited, though highly important, sphere of shipbuilding as an indication of the true comparative price levels in the two countries. But they do give "powerful support" to the theory that it is now the dollar and not the pound which is over-valued in the official exchange rate.

Lest I should in any way convey a mistaken view of Mr. Hobson's argument I will quote his summing up:

"Some readers find the notion that it is even theoretically possible that the American dollar might be over-valued in terms of the pound unpalatable. To them I would reply that I have never argued, and do not now argue, that present relative costs will determine either the equilibrium rate or, which is a different thing, the actual working rate between pound and dollar after the war. I do say, however, that the war-time soaring of costs in America will have some as yet indeterminable influence on the post-war actual exchange rate."

If instead of taking ships we took munitions of war generally and also took account of wages and soldiers' pay, it is probable that the British Government with an expenditure of one pound here can get more than the American Government with an expenditure of four dollars in the United States. On the other hand, if there were complete freedom of exchange and both currencies could be converted without difficulty on both sides of the Atlantic, as they were (allowing for the American tariff) thirty years ago, it is obvious that some American products which we import on a very large scale, such as cotton, petrol, bacon and tobacco, would be cheaper in the United States than here by at least the cost of transport.

VII. GOLD AND PAPER MONEY

The enormous difficulty and, I think, impracticability of maintaining the exchanges between countries with a great and varied trade if the two currencies were inconvertible without relationship to gold is strengthened rather than diminished by this uncertainty about what is "the equilibrium," the only certainty being the fact that it is rapidly changing and subject to enormous vicissitudes now and in the future. Free currencies based on gold or silver, free competition and free shipping are to my mind indispensable if we are to hope and strive for that expansion of Anglo-American trade, and ultimately of world trade, by which alone our two nations can hope to live and prosper.

It is now known that the British Government became aware some time ago—in the autumn of 1942—that most of the world's currencies after the war, being composed of inconvertible paper, will be in a state of fluctuating depreciation with no relations to one another. At best an inconvertible paper money only passes current in the country in which it is issued. It cannot be exported and is of no use for foreign trade; whereas gold or silver money has the same value in all the world's markets and can be exported or imported if necessary to correct the trade balance. On February 2nd, 1943, Sir Kingsley Wood, our Chancellor of the Exchequer, outlined in the House of Commons the type of international exchange system which, he said, our Government would like to see established after the war. It is supposed to have been drawn up by J. M. Keynes (Lord Keynes), who thinks that gold or silver currencies are relics of barbarism and unworthy of the civilized age in which we live. However that may be, Sir Kingsley Wood's project may be described as an international clearing house for current balances of payments, linked with a partial exchange control, also international, over capital movements and investments. He said:

"We need an international monetary mechanism which will serve the requirements of international trade and avoid any need for unilateral action in competitive currency depreciation. We want a system in which blocked balances and bilateral clearances would be unnecessary. We want an orderly and agreed method of determining the value of international currency units to eliminate unilateral action and the danger which it involves that each nation will seek to restore its competitive position by exchange depreciation."

Unfortunately for this scheme, which owes its plausibility to the long technical words in which it is wrapped, perhaps for the mystification of plain people, it suffers from several theoretical and practical objections, any one of which would be fatal. In the first place no sensible government depreciates its currency in order to gain foreign trade, i.e., "to restore its competitive position." Inconvertible paper currency is over-issued by bankrupt governments when they are in extremities and can devise no other means either by taxation or borrowing to pay their creditors. The other side of the shield from depreciation is an inflationary rise of prices—*la vie chère,* which afflicted France and all the belligerent countries of the Continent after the First Great War, and ultimately induced most of them to harness a new currency to gold in order to attain stability for prices at home and for foreign trade. There is no fear that any sane government will adopt the ruinous course of competitive depreciation suggested by Sir Kingsley Wood in order to improve its foreign trade.

Secondly, there is no reason whatever to suppose that after the war individual countries and governments will be ready to surrender their financial and economic independence to an international bureau. Such a bureau would have to consist of representatives or delegates of each country, and it is difficult to suppose that they would agree on the relative value at any given time of their currencies, or be able to promise that their Finance Ministers would adopt the same measures (even if it were possible) for creating and maintaining an equilibrium between their respective inconvertible paper currencies. Nor is it any more likely that they would agree to control in accordance with the wishes of an international bureau their investments, if they have any money to invest, or to guarantee that they will not endeavour to attract investments from abroad. In any case it is very unlikely that any nation which believes in economic freedom would allow its government in time of peace to interfere with the right of private individuals and citizens to invest their savings as they think best.

Thirdly, it is inconceivable that the United States, having absorbed and stored in public vaults nearly the whole of the world's stocks of gold, should agree to a scheme which, if successful, would eliminate gold from the world's currencies, and, in the words of one English critic, "risk the reduction of her gold stock to so much dross." "Dross," of course, is an absurd exaggeration of the danger; for gold will always possess a high intrinsic value even if it were relegated to the arts. But demonetization would ultimately close nearly all the gold mines, and incidentally ruin the finances of the Union of South Africa.

Sir Kingsley Wood was evidently not very confident; but he had the hardihood to declare that the present British Government, which may or may not survive the next general election, is willing to submit its internal economic policy and consequently its budgets to the check of consultations.

VIII. SECRET CONFERENCES

An announcement was issued by the Treasury on March 3rd, 1943, that a conference of the Finance Ministers of the Allied countries, including representatives of the French National Committee, had been held under the chairmanship of Mr. Ralph Assheton, M.P., Financial Secretary to the Treasury, at which "currency arrangements in Europe after the war and other post-war financial questions of common interest were discussed." It was further stated that this conference was one of a series which had been proceeding and that arrangements were made for further discussions at an early date.

In the past British diplomacy has suffered more from concealment than from any other cause; and it is especially true of our relations with the United States that all discussions of the principles, not the details, of our commercial and financial aims, which require the co-operation of our Foreign Office with the Treasury and the Board of Trade, should be conducted in the open air. I was glad to read in my *Manchester Guardian* of March 5th the following observation on the Treasury's communiqué:

"Assuming that the news of the official talks was issued (to the Press) as an invitation for comment, one must first insist that the Treasury cannot stop there. The general principles on which the effort is to be based should be aired in public."

One might add that if the broad principles and policies of financial and commercial reconstruction are not "aired" and freely discussed here, there will be no escape from criticism in the United States, where party politics and scores of independent newspapers, not under the control of half-a-dozen Press lords, ensure a thorough canvassing of projects affecting the taxation and welfare of American citizens. In this case secret diplomacy would be particularly objectionable.

There is, for example, the danger of large commitments to European Allies and émigré governments which might not only greatly augment our national debt and involve big transfers of British capital imperilling our own currency, but would also fail in their purpose in the absence of American co-operation. Let me quote the *Manchester Guardian's* Financial Editor on the economic aspect of European rehabilitation. After noting that—though representatives of the United States, China and the Dominions were present at the Treasury conference—the subject was confined to Europe, he proceeded:

"The adherence of the European Allies would be a good beginning, though without American participation the scheme would mean little or nothing. . . . Meanwhile a few of the currency problems awaiting solution can be easily recognized. One is the danger of runaway inflation at the first relaxation of the rigid controls established by the Germans. Here is a chance to make a fatal mistake, and the danger is that the financial authorities will make it. The worst service we could render the liberated Continental countries would be to grant stabilization loans to the governments or central banks without first making sure that such loans will really do the job.

"Inflation control is a matter of public faith in State authority, and if people do not trust money they will not obey rationing regulations and other controls. . . . There are other purposes for which foreign loans would do more harm than good. Governments will want foreign loans to meet budget deficits, and central banks will want them to re-create currency reserves.

"Such claims must be carefully studied. . . . Relief and rehabilitation supplies might be well linked with the restoration of assured currency régimes; but such supplies must not be linked with loans. This is a warning which will apply particularly to the United States, which will be the chief capital-exporting country for some years to come. Loans must never again be made without certainty that they will create the extra transfer capacity for the debt service. If that cannot be guaranteed, it is far better to give things away free and obtain indirect payment through the improvement of markets and the restoration of the world trading structure."

Every intelligent banker, everyone conversant with the history of stock exchange investments and speculations in currency after the last war, and all who are still smarting from the collapse of credit after 1929 will appreciate the wisdom of these cautionary observations.

IX. THE BANCOR

A few days after this Treasury communiqué some further information about the British project was allowed to leak out to the Press. It provides, we are told, for the establishment of an international unit of account styled the bancor. But the bancor, we are also told, is not money. It is said to be merely a measuring rod for expressing relative exchange values by those governments which decide to participate in a new clearing authority. The new clearing house would resemble the bank for international settlements, which keeps its accounts in the Swiss gold franc. But as the bancor is not a coin, neither is the clearing house a bank. Nor is the project made less mysterious by the statement that the international unit of account, which it seeks to establish, called "the bancor," is based on gold. For we are also told that the adoption of the bancor would not mean the setting up of an international gold exchange standard. If there were to be a genuine international gold exchange standard, countries participating in this new system would be able to get bancors in exchange for gold, and gold in exchange for bancors. But the case will be like that of a mouse and a trap—the gold mouse can get into the trap but it can't get out; at least, we are informed that "while countries owning gold will be able to tender it in settlement of their international debts, creditor countries will not be able to insist on payment of debts due to them in gold."

Meanwhile, another scheme, it is reported, has been prepared in America which provides for an international gold equalization fund. Whether it is as ingeniously complicated as the British scheme remains to be seen.[2] It is at least noteworthy that, after all the talk of a certain class of monetary experts about the advantages of a managed paper currency and the wonderful success of sterling after we suspended gold payments, both the British and American plans are attached to gold. The reason is obvious. Inconvertible paper money has no intrinsic value, and is in disrepute throughout the world. Only gold and silver currencies command confidence.

x. Recovery of Trade

Undoubtedly it is tremendously important to maintain economic and monetary collaboration between Britain and the United States, between London, Washington and New York. The City of London understands Europe and Wall Street understands America. If they don't work together, there will be no chance of solving post-war international exchange and trade problems. Then there is the danger of inflation—the danger of paper currencies all, or nearly all, becoming worthless, and consequently of State creditors and private investors being cheated of

[2]Since the above was written the American Treasury's scheme has appeared. It is simpler and more intelligible than that inspired by Lord Keynes. It aims at the removal of exchange controls, and the "unitas" is more like a gold coin than the "bancor."

all, or nearly all, that they have lent to their separate governments. And for the United States there is the special danger that their huge stocks of gold will lie barren and sterilized, when they ought to be helping to set right the currencies and exchanges of the world.

There is a pretty general agreement among economists that the best currency and exchange scheme cannot do much good without a reduction of tariffs and other obstructions to international trade. America cannot sell and exchange its surpluses any longer for gold; for it has absorbed practically all the surplus gold in the world. It must therefore exchange its goods for goods or lend them on credit, with poor prospects of the loans being redeemed.

One of the favourite fallacies, fashionable in the Press among writers who have had no time to digest the lessons of history and experience or to study logic and political economy, is the theory that a poor nation cannot afford to indulge in such luxuries as freedom of trade or hard money; and now we are frequently told that tariffs and restrictions on our external and internal trade, including the suppression of free markets, and the retention of official controls over our manufactures and shipping and wholesale and retail trade after the war, in defiance of the Atlantic Charter, will be essential if Great Britain is to survive in the post-war world.

Surely the precise opposite is true. The more impoverished a nation is by war, the more necessary is it for the recovery of its trade and the removal of poverty and the creation of profitable employment that the brains and sinews of its people should be freed from the shackles of bureaucracy. In that way the millions of men and women returning from the war and from destructive employment on the manufacture of bombs, explosives, guns, and all the other munitions of war, to productive employment in manufactures, agriculture, shipping, merchanting and shopkeeping would find their way back to peaceful liberty and be able to earn the rewards of industry.

All classes in this country must expect to be worse off and to suffer privations as compared with pre-war days. That cannot be helped. We have lost nearly all our great reserves of gold and overseas investments. We have become for the first time a debtor instead of a creditor nation. We shall have to work much harder in order to import the raw materials of industry and the necessaries and comforts of life. The position may be compared with that following the Hungry Forties. After thirty years of stagnation in our foreign trade under a system of protective and preferential tariffs and heavy taxation on everything, the springs of industry were released by the policy of economic freedom incorporated in the budgets of Peel and Gladstone. Imports and exports, shipbuilding and shipping expanded so marvellously that we became more and more a creditor nation until in 1913 wealth and welfare in Great Britain were comparable to wealth and welfare in the United States, and the commerce of this small island came to exceed that of any nation on the globe.

In his first important statement on economic conditions after the war, the broadcast of March 21st, Mr. Churchill based his views of prospects and policy on the assumption which he thought "probable," that the war in Europe would come to an end in 1944 or 1945. As leader of the Conservative Party and Premier of a national Cabinet representing all three parties, he laid before the country a broad policy for post-war conditions in which conservatism, liberalism and socialism, individualism and collectivism, private enterprise and functions of the State were judiciously and cautiously compounded. In welcoming Sir William Beveridge's recommendations for the reform and unification of social insurance, he definitely refused to commit the Government on the financial side, reminding the nation of the constitutional principle and practice that ours is an annual budget, and that it is impossible during the war to foresee and forecast the problems of the first and succeeding peacetime budgets which will have to be settled after the general election. His outlook was not unlike that of President Roosevelt; for he saw that after hostilities cease the British Commonwealth of Nations and the United States will encounter "a heavy task in trying to avert widespread famine in some at least of the ruined regions." He saw that our own future is bound up with that of other countries, not only for the settlement of Europe and the prevention of future wars, but for "the whole economic process and relationship of nations in order that the ruin of our wealth may be rapidly repaired, that employment and production shall be at a high level, and that goods and services shall be interchanged between man and man, and between one nation and another, under the best conditions and on the largest scale." He reminded his hearers that the British nation had been saved by "the free trade policy of Victorian days." It had brought us the capital and the foreign investments which have been expended in the common cause.

To repair these losses agriculture, public health and education must be fostered; but in moving steadily forward we must not forget our traditions and our glorious struggles for the rights of the individual and for human freedom:

"We must beware of trying to build a society in which nobody counts for anything except a politician or an official, a society where enterprise gains no reward and thrift no privileges. I say 'trying to build,' because of all races in the world our people would be the last to consent to be governed by a bureaucracy. Freedom is their life blood."

Is this not equally true of the United States and the British self-governing Dominions? To secure equal opportunities for all is a component part of this freedom in the economic sphere.

And lastly, in relation to what I have said about finance and money, it is instructive and encouraging to observe three strong features in Mr. Churchill's policy. The first is that taxation after the war must not be so heavy as to remove personal incentive or to destroy initiative and enterprise. The second, closely related to this, is that we must promote the expansion of our commerce, our imports and our exports, which will have to pay for one another. The third is—and on this everything will depend—that we must take care to maintain the value of our money.

A leading member of the Labour Party, Mr. Arthur Greenwood, had said in the House of Commons that "pounds, shillings and pence are meaningless symbols." But if the currency is lost, all is lost. Mr. Churchill's reply is worth repeating:

"At the end of this war there will be seven or eight million people in the country with two or three hundred pounds apiece, a thing unknown in our history. These savings of the nation, arising from the thrift, skill, or devotion of individuals, are sacred. The State is built around them, and it is the duty of the State to redeem its faith in an equal degree of value."

Without good money and freely working exchanges industry and commerce cannot flourish either at home or abroad. State trading and inter-State trading under bureaucratic controls with trade barriers, quotas and restrictions of all kinds are incompatible with the restoration of peace and prosperity.

Fortunately the Atlantic Charter promises to all States, great and small, "access on equal terms to the trade and the raw materials of the world." Until the troops come home it would be premature to predict with certainty what the electors here and in the United States, or in the democratic countries of the Continent, will want most after the war, or what will be their priorities. But it is pretty certain that they will not wish their lives and thoughts to be controlled as in a Police State, and they will certainly wish their wages and savings to be paid, or repaid in good money. It is reasonable also to suppose from the language of nearly all statesmen and reputable newspapers here and in the United States that the broad principles and generous pledges of the Atlantic Charter will be honoured by harmonious co-operation between the British and American peoples.

In the introduction to this essay I have presented a few credentials to show that, like Sir Philip Gibbs, I can claim some knowledge of American psychology. My acquaintance with American politics, finance and economics dates from 1908 when I first visited the United States and Canada. Alas, many of those who opened their doors and minds to me so generously and freely in New York, New England, Virginia, the Middle West and California have passed away; but I cannot lay down my pen without expressing my special and peculiar obligations to Mr. and Mrs. Herbert Hoover, Mr. R. L. Wilbur and Professor David Barrows, who drew me to California; to Mr. Thornton Cooke and Mr. Haskell of Kansas City, who helped me to understand the Middle West; to Mr. John Stewart Bryan, who initiated me into the glories and joys, past and present, of Virginia, our Old Dominion. For what I know of Harvard and New England, I am particularly indebted to the late A. Lawrence Lowell and Mr. J. L. McConaughy. In New York my guide, philosopher and friend was, and is, Mr. Charles C. Burlingham. I owe more thanks than I can express in words to him and to Dr. Nicholas Murray Butler, President of Columbia University and Director of the Carnegie Endowment for International Peace. In the latter capacity I have collaborated with him and his distinguished colleagues for many years, and am happy to have retained his confidence as representative in England of the Endowment, whose offices are now established at Dunford House. Nor can I forget in recording these impressions friends like Oswald Garrison Villard and James Truslow Adams, both members of the Century Club where I learnt much about American journalism and literature. But in nothing have I been more fortunate than in the possession of a sister, Gertrude Hirst, who has taught in the United States for more than half a century and has been for many years a professor in Barnard College.

VII MOTHER OF PARLIAMENTS

By Sir Percy Harris

1. THE OLD TRADITION

A NOVEL FEATURE of London to-day is the number of American officers and men to be seen visiting the sights of the town; they share this with our Dominion soldiers but perhaps they are more diligent in their search for places of interest because they are more conscious of being in a foreign land. Often when I go to my work in the House of Commons I see them gazing up with curiosity at the drab but dignified Parliament Buildings.

In 1834 it was decided to burn the old wooden Exchequer Tallies used as Tax Receipts in bygone days. Unfortunately, the fire got out of control and the old timber offered little resistance and soon the building was reduced to a lot of rubble and charred wood.

The new Palace of Westminster took ten years to build. It is designed in a Tudor-Gothic style and elaborately decorated with ornament and detail including a number of effigies of kings and queens which, owing to the ravages of London smoke and fog, are difficult to distinguish. The soft stone with which it was built has proved exceptionally sensitive to weather, with the result that it blends with the ancient Westminster Hall adjacent that dates from the fourteenth century and has survived both the Fire of 1834 and the German bombs of to-day.

Parliament has met on this site ever since the sixteenth century, when Edward VI handed to it the Monastery of St. Stephen. Upon dissolution of the monasteries by Henry VIII some of the buildings went to kings' favourites, others provided foundation for grammar schools like the Charter House or hospitals for the sick like St. Bartholomew's.

In the Middle Ages the naves of the churches were used as public meeting places where disputes were settled and problems solved and the sacredness of the edifice gave authority to decisions and smoothed out differences. It was not inappropriate, therefore, that Parliament should meet in a church, in fact previously it had met in the Chapter House of the Abbey of Westminster close by.

But for three hundred years it met in this ancient chapel of St. Stephen. Many of its old customs, some of them handed on to other Parliaments of the British Commonwealth, owe their origin to the fact that they met in a church. When members enter the House of Commons opposite the Speaker's chair, they bow, not as it is sometimes supposed to the Speaker, but to the High Altar that was nominally behind his chair in the old original chapel. Here the great debates took place between Walpole and the elder Pitt, and the younger Pitt faced his old rival, Fox. Those were the unregenerate days of the unreformed Parliament, the time of the Pocket Boroughs, when Tories wrangled with Whigs, when Lord North threw away the American colonies by taxing their tea, and the King's friends allowed themselves to be the servant of that half-wit, George III. Perhaps it was not inappropriate that the passing of the Reform Bill of 1832 should be followed by the burning down of the building associated with an era of privilege and vested interest so soon to give way to the industrial age and democratic ideas.

After the Great Fire the chapel was rebuilt on exactly the same foundations, and brass nails mark the place where stood the Speaker's chair and the table on which the mace was placed, and by which eighteenth-century orators stood to make their speeches. But the new chapel, dignified and lofty, designed in the Perpendicular style, is but the ante-chamber or entrance hall to the new House of Commons that was moved to a different site, closer to the river bank and Westminster Bridge.

Alas, the Chamber of this new House of Commons, completed in 1844, has also "gone west," destroyed by a Nazi bomb, and is now a mass of ruins with little left but part of the outer walls.

But although that part of the building is destroyed, the House of Commons has never missed a single Parliamentary day. How we have managed it and where the Chamber is actively located, I am not allowed to say, although many people must know. Many American soldiers, sailors and airmen visit our Chamber and gaze down with curiosity at our House of Commons—so different both in custom and appearance to their own House of Representatives at Washington. Here we are steeped in traditions, many of which have remained unaltered since the days when a short-sighted Parliament lost the American colonies through the folly of Lord North against the protests of the elder Pitt.

Every day, the Speaker, in full bottom wig, with knee breeches and silk stockings and buckled shoes, the very costume of that eighteenth century, walks from his residence inside the precincts of Parliament and alongside the Clock Tower from which Big Ben every evening heralds the nine o'clock news. He is accompanied in solemn procession by his chaplain, his secretary, his train-bearer, and the sergeant-at-arms who carries the gilt mace—the symbol of royal authority.

The proceedings open with prayers for Parliament read by the chaplain, with the Speaker kneeling at his side. Here it might not be inappropriate to say a word about our Speaker, a very different functionary to the person with a similar title in the U.S.A. Speakers have been elected ever since the fourteenth century and in the library are engraved the names of 138 holders of that office. As recently as March 3rd of this year, our Speaker, Captain Algernon Fitzroy, after fifteen years of office, and after only a fortnight's illness, died in harness, the first to do so since 1789. In the intervening period, no Speaker had died while actually in office. The information of his death was brought to the House when it was sitting, actually when a member was speaking, and the proceedings had to terminate immediately. According to constitutional practice, the House cannot sit without a Speaker, leave for the election of whom must be obtained from the King, and although the choice is with the elected members, his name has to be submitted to His Majesty for his approval. In these days the choice of the Speaker is very much in the hands of the "rank and file" of the House. Other appointments are more or less made by the Government. But the election of Speaker is claimed to be the prerogative of the Commons themselves. In Tudor times the Speaker was more or less the nominee of the Crown. During the struggles between King and Parliament in the reign of Charles I the independence of the Speaker from the Crown was asserted. In fact when Charles tried to arrest the five members who defied his authority and escaped by barge to find refuge in the city, and the King, who had forced his way into the Chamber, demanded of Speaker Linthall where they were, he replied: "May it please your

Majesty, I have neither eyes to see nor tongue to speak in this place but as the House is pleased to direct me whose servant I am here." This is one of the incidents that led to the Civil War and the revolution that cost Charles his head.

With the restoration the struggle between King and Parliament continued, culminating in the flight of James II to France and the accession of William and Mary to the throne and the gradual development of Constitutional Monarchy as we now know it. But even in the eighteenth century members of Parliament were most jealous of their ancient privileges. Never again was the King or even his messenger allowed to enter the sacred portals of the House.

II. Safeguards of Liberty

When the King opens Parliament in person or when he signifies his consent to a bill passed by both Houses, which he does through a commission of three Peers sitting in the House of Lords, the equivalent of the American Senate, the "faithful Commons" are summoned to attend at the Bar of the House of Lords. They are summoned not by letter or written word but the message is conveyed by a Court official whose office dates back to the sixteenth century or earlier. He carries a black wand or rod and walks solemnly from the House of Peers to the House of Commons. When he arrives, instead of being welcomed the door is slammed in his face, to assert the ancient rights of the Commons to manage their own proceedings. Black Rod knocks three times at the door of the Chamber, one of the House of Commons messengers announces "Black Rod," then opens the door when the intruder is allowed to enter, bows, advances down the floor of the House and says: "Message from the King" and delivers it by word of mouth. Many members during the last quarter of a century, elected for the first time, have been inclined to scoff at these ancient ceremonies as a waste of time and as needless "pomp and circumstance." But, without exception, they come to revere them as picturesque and harmless old customs that link the present with the past and give dignity to what otherwise would be dull and drab proceedings. James Maxton, one of the Independent Labour members who has found the Labour Party too right wing for his ideas, is one of the most loyal guardians of our ancient customs; and even our one and only Communist, Gallacher, watches to see that our formalities are properly carried out.

On the death of our late Speaker, Captain Fitzroy, who had held his office for fifteen years, the House had immediately to adjourn for permission to be obtained from the King for the election of his successor, which is according to tradition, but of course would never be refused as His Majesty must act on the advice of his Ministers. Incidentally, Captain Fitzroy had been first elected when the Conservatives were in a majority, but when a new House was elected and Labour and Liberals were in a majority, Captain Fitzroy was re-elected without a contest, though a Conservative. And re-election is the invariable practice! Once in the chair, the Speaker ceases to have any political affiliation and becomes the guardian of the rights and privileges of the House and particularly the protector of minorities. Speaker Fitzroy lived up to the best of those traditions and had the respect and affection of all parties.

Permission having been obtained, after five days' adjournment, the House of Commons reassembled to elect a new Speaker. The Conservatives being in a majority, not unnaturally claimed to make the selection, but care was taken to ascertain that their nomination was generally acceptable to all parties. Their choice fell on Colonel Clifton Brown, a man who had gained much experience as chairman of committees and Deputy Speaker. Actually his nomination was proposed by an old Liberal M.P. and seconded by a Labour member. The clerk of the House, sitting at the table and not in the Speaker's chair, points his finger at the proposer and the proceedings are more or less informal, so as to emphasize that the choice is with the members themselves. According to tradition, the man selected has to make a display of reluctance to occupy this great post and the mover and seconder have to drag him to the chair. This is a survival from the time when the Speaker often found himself in conflict with the Crown and in danger of losing his head by the axe as a result of the King's displeasure.

In the afternoon the new Speaker presented himself at the Bar of the House of Lords when the King's Commissioners—four Peers, wearing red robes and cocked hats and presided over by the Lord Chancellor—read the King's approval of the choice of his faithful commoner. Then members returned to the Commons' Chamber and, after the lapse of a few minutes, the Speaker appeared in all regalia of office, full bottom wig, knee breeches—clothing which gives that dignity and authority that our ordinary costumes fail to provide.

Perhaps I have dwelt too long on these old British customs, but without understanding them Americans cannot get a true picture of the workings of our Parliamentary machinery. As I have said, each day our proceedings open with the prayers for King and Parliament read by the chaplain, with the Speaker kneeling at his side.

III. METHODS AND MANNERS

Then comes question hour, perhaps the most interesting and useful part of our daily work. At almost every sitting these days there are numbers of American service men gazing down at our proceedings, and very puzzled they are with the difference between our House of Commons and their House of Representatives. First, their chamber is semi-circular—as is the French Chamber—and each member has his own desk. Both in our House and the other place, as we call the House of Lords, the Government and its supporters sit on one side and its opponents sit facing them, separated by a considerable floor space. The Government side is on the right side of the chair, the Opposition on the left.

During war-time these differences have lost some of their meaning because, both in the last war and in this, we have a National Government drawn from all three parties, Conservative, Labour and Liberal. However, the physical arrangement of the House remains and the Chairman of the Labour Party, though not in opposition, maintains the style and function of leader of the Opposition. Two days' notice must be given of a question which must relate to the work of a particular department and be passed by the clerk at the table as relevant. The questions are numbered; the Speaker calls the member whose name is printed on the order paper, who rises from his place and merely gives the number of his question. The Minister gets up and reads out his reply, carefully prepared for him by a skilled civil servant—which is often of an evasive character. Then the fun starts. Supplementary questions can be asked, not only by the person in whose name the question is, but by other members filled with curiosity to know the truth. The Speaker has to hold the ring and see both the Minister and questioner get fair play, and see the supplementaries are relevant and keep the cross-examination within bounds. As questions are limited to an hour, the Speaker must see that no question gets more than its fair share, as there is a danger that a skilled member who is persistent in his search for truth may get out of hand.

Questions range over a large field: Foreign Affairs, Home Security, the three Service Departments, Education, Transport, Colonies and Dominions; each have their Minister, who, in turn on their appropriate day, will be put on the rack. This is so very different from anything in the U.S.A., where the Executive is divorced from Congress and independent of it and therefore the Ministers are spared the daily ordeal.

But what surprises Americans most is to see the Prime Minister put through his paces. Questions 45 and after are always allotted to the Prime Minister or his Deputy. Normally, the Prime Minister is Leader of the House of Commons and directs its proceedings. Until a few months ago, Winston Churchill did double the posts of Prime Minister and Leader of the House. But it was the House of Commons itself that pleaded with him to relinquish the second post, because he is not only Prime Minister, he is also Minister of Defence and not merely in name, but in fact. There is no doubt he is the driving force behind the war and he has his finger in every service pie. He not only presides over the War Cabinet but also over the meeting of the Service Ministers as well as the Ministry of Defence. And he finds time to go to the U.S.A., to Russia, to Casablanca, to Turkey, and to Egypt. He is no kid—not short of seventy—and he has never led a life of leisure or comfort but has taxed his energies to the limit, in his youth fighting in various campaigns in Egypt, in India, in South Africa, to give only a selection; in middle age being First Lord of the Admiralty and Minister of Munitions in the last war; in the post-war period, Secretary of State for War, Secretary of State for the Colonies, winding up as Chancellor of the Exchequer. Out of office, he amused himself writing best sellers, a history of the Great War, his own early life, as well as the life of his ancestor—the Duke of Marlborough—to say nothing of numerous newspaper articles. Even his leisure was strenuous, occupying himself by brick-laying and painting quite good pictures. And he found the time to act Cassandra and play the part of the true prophet and warn the nation of the need to prepare for the Nazi danger, a warning that went unheeded. But this is a digression. The Prime Minister reluctantly yielded to pressure and has given up the active leadership of the Commons, first to Clem. Atlee, the Labour leader and Deputy Prime Minister, then for a time to Stafford Cripps, and now to Anthony Eden. Incidentally, during the absence of Mr. Eden in Washington, he could not resist the temptation to take it on again. But on occasions when there are questions of importance affecting the conduct of the war, the Prime Minister himself does turn up and face the music. And a very good account of himself does he give. A favourite pastime for certain members, especially Shinwell, Dick Stokes, and Aneurin Bevin, is baiting the Prime Minister. He is inclined to be quick-tempered and fire up, but he usually gives as good as he gets. But it does amaze our American visitors to see our Prime Minister—whom they class with their President—doing the rough-and-tumble on the floor of the House. The fact is, in spite of all our ancient traditions and customs and all our links with the past, there is no more democratic constitution than the British. It may occasionally creak a bit and want some oiling, but the House of Commons is supreme and if it decides to take action, it can more or less do what it likes. The American President is elected for four years and nothing Congress can do can shift him, short of a revolution. But if the House of Commons turned nasty and the Prime Minister incurred its displeasure, out he would go to-morrow.

Neville Chamberlain had behind him at the outbreak of war an immense majority but things went a bit wrong: the Norway campaign failed; some forty Conservatives voted with the Opposition parties, and he felt he had not the confidence of the House and handed in his resignation. If he had asked for a Vote of Confidence, no doubt he would have got it, but he sensed the feeling of the House was for a change in war direction and he was wise enough to accede to it. It is true in his case other influences were at work. There was a desire for a National, instead of a party, Government, and Chamberlain was led to believe that Labour and Liberal would serve under Churchill and not under him.

IV. FREEDOM AND PRIVILEGE

Perhaps the outstanding example in recent times of the working of the democratic machine was the abdication of Edward VIII. It is more than probable that if the House of Commons had approved his marriage to Mrs. Simpson, he would still be King. But Mr. Baldwin, the then Prime Minister, satisfied the House of Commons that it was not in the public interest—and that settled it. A bill was introduced into the House of Commons, "The King's Abdication Bill": it went through a second reading, committee stage, report stage, third reading, all in a few minutes. Then through the same process in the House of Lords: a Royal Commission summoned the Commons to the Bar: the clerk read out the name of the bill, "The King's Abdication Bill," the clerk to Parliament indicated the King's consent in the accustomed formula in old French,

"Le Roi le veult" (the King wills it), the bill became "an Act of Parliament" and the King ceased to reign. Tragic in its speed but a great testimony of the power of Parliament.

Which brings me to the orders of the day that are called out after questions. If it is a second reading of a bill, a motion or a resolution, the Speaker remains in the Chair. If it is a finance matter or anything dealing with money, the mace is taken off the table by the sergeant-at-arms and put underneath. The mace is the symbol of Royal Authority, and ever since the revolution, the Commons has claimed the sole right to vote supplies and so the mace is removed. The Commons do not even allow the Lords to interfere with money matters, and they keep a very tight hold of the purse-strings. There was a long struggle between the two Houses on the finance issue. The House of Commons, as the elected chamber, claimed the sole right to control supplies and the dispute finally culminated in the struggle over the Lloyd George Budget of 1910, rejected by the Peers. The Asquith Government appealed to the electors and, fortified by their support, claimed the right to recommend to His Majesty enough new Peers to swamp the Upper House.

Unlike the American Senate, our Upper House is not elected. It is a hereditary institution and the majority sit there by right of birth. The King has the power to exercise the right, on the advice of his Minister, to make new creations. And so the Prime Minister, in order to avoid a dead-lock, could advise the King to create enough new Peers to secure that the will of the Commons should prevail! Under the Parliament Act, not only is the control of the Commons over finance established but it is laid down if any bill in three consecutive sessions passes the Commons in its original form, it automatically receives the consent of the King and becomes an Act of Parliament over the head of the Upper House.

In peace-time the legislative machine moves mighty slowly. In war-time it goes very quickly, and the checks disappear. The Opposition ceases to function properly and bills go through like sausages through a machine—perhaps too easily—and some of the bills might gain by a closer examination. But in peace-time there is every safeguard against hasty legislation. Most of the legislation is at the initiative of the Government and private members have very little chance of getting their ideas embodied in an Act of Parliament. But of that later. The first process is to get leave to print—that is, the first reading. Then a day is allotted to the second reading when the principles of the bill, as the proposals are then called, can be discussed in general both for and against. If it passes its second reading, it can be referred to a committee of the whole House—which is sometimes a way of shelving the bill altogether as it may be difficult to find Parliamentary time for the discussion. In fact it is a recognized dilatory method for an opponent to move that "the bill be referred to a committee of the whole House." The alternative is to refer it to a Grand Committee, composed of about thirty members only, and which sit generally when the House is not in session. These Grand Committees do not function in war-time, which many of us think is a pity as they really give more effective examination to proposed legislation than the whole House—which is too large and formal an assembly for discussion in detail. If a bill goes to a committee of the whole House, the Speaker leaves the Chair and the Chairman of Ways and Means presides, not in the Speaker's Chair, but at the table on the floor of the House where he sits alongside the clerk. When the Speaker is in the Chair, a member can speak only once; but in Committee he can speak as often as he likes. But at any time the motion can be put "the question be now put," although it is up to the discretion of the chairman to accept this closure motion at his discretion.

But there is a more effective method of meeting possible obstruction that dates from the time the old Irish members used to hold up business deliberately in order to bring Parliamentary business into discredit with the avowed forcing from Great Britain a separate Parliament. That is closure by compartments or the "Guillotine." A time-table is fixed and if by a certain time a number of clauses are not through, the axe falls, the debate comes to an end and the clauses have to be voted on together. Honour demands loud cries of gag. But it is a way of getting a contentious bill through Committee without undue expenditure of time. Obstruction is a useful weapon for the minority to use against unpopular legislation, but a majority regards the matter from another angle. In the end the electorate has to judge between the contending forces. If the act proves a good one, the Opposition will suffer accordingly: but if the act is a bad one, it will be praised for its pertinacity.

When the committee stage is through, the bill is still a long way from becoming an Act of Parliament. The chairman reports it to the House through the Speaker in its amended form, with some clauses dropped and others amended, and then comes the report stage where it cannot be changed in mere detail, but with the Speaker in the Chair and at his discretion new points can be raised and old ones of principle can be discussed again. Then comes the third reading, when a day or two can be spent discussing the bill as a whole in its altered form. But it is still not an Act of Parliament. It must go to the House of Lords, where the same process has to be gone through over again: first reading, second reading, committee stage, report stage, and third reading. Often it is found convenient to alter by arrangement to use the stock phrase "in another place." But if the changes are not acceptable to the Commons House, the motion is put that this House doth disagree with the amendment. On some occasions agreement cannot be come to on vital issue and then the bill is dropped. But if they are adjusted, there is still one final stage, i.e., the King's consent which—under our constitutional monarchy unlike the authority exercised by the President—is never withheld. But it is given with great formality in the House of Lords through a commission sitting in state specially appointed for the purpose, with the Commons summoned to attend by Black Rod and stand at the Bar headed by their Speaker and accompanied by the sergeant-at-arms carrying the mace. Then it is an Act of Parliament approved by the three estates, Commons, Lords and Crown.

v. Constitutional Differences

Procedure in the House of Lords is not unlike that in the lower House except for one or two features. First the Lord Chancellor, sitting on the Woolsack, presides. Unlike the Speaker, he is a member of the Government and takes an active part in debates. When he does he stands to the left of the Woolsack. He wears wig and costume similar to the Speaker. But his work is not limited to his Parliamentary duties. In addition to being a member of the Cabinet, he is also head of the judicial system, appoints the Judges and presides at the Highest Court of the Land, when the House of Lords sits as a final Court of Appeal. That is something very different from what they have in America.

There is one other astonishing feature to American visitors. The bishops in the Church of England have seats in the House of Lords and sit there in their lawn sleeves and take part in debates. In fact the present Archbishop of Canterbury takes a very active part in discussions on a great variety of subjects, by no means limited to ecclesiastical matters.

In one other matter our House of Commons is very different from the House of Representatives. The American Constitution provides that a member must reside in the district which he desires to represent. In Great Britain a candidate need not have any association with the division he stands for. The present Prime Minister has sat in turn for Oldham, Manchester, Dundee, and Epping—which he now represents. In none of his divisions has he had any residential qualification. The American system makes the association of the members much closer and dependent on his constituents, while our method gives more opportunity to the ambitious and independent member who, rejected in one district, can try his luck elsewhere—and often does. Of course a man with local association has undoubtedly an advantage in a contest with a stranger who is often styled a "Carpet Bagger."

But the most striking difference between the two systems is while the Executive in the U.S.A. is independent of Congress and can carry on and does, even if it has an adverse majority in both or either of the Houses, in Great Britain an adverse majority in the House of Commons can at any time force a Government to resign. In America the President is elected by the people, his Ministers are his servants and can be dismissed by him. Nominally, British Ministers are the servants of the King and they receive their appointments from the Crown. But His Majesty acts on the advice of the Prime Minister and accepts his recommendations. But the Prime Minister is dependent for his office on the goodwill of the House of Commons, and an adverse vote on a question of principle will cause his downfall. If a General Election goes against a Government the Prime Minister can either immediately hand in his resignation or wait for an adverse vote, when his resignation follows. But I am going outside the subject of this article.

Though their machinery works very differently both the British Parliament and the American Congress have this in common, they are both thoroughly democratic in substance and secure that the will of the people prevails. My purpose has been to show that though the British Parliament is steeped in the past and bound by tradition, in actual practice the constitution does provide a sound efficient plan of Government.

VIII THE HOPE OF FEDERATION

By Lord Davies

I. INTRODUCTION

As THE WAR DRAGS ON and victory begins to loom in sight, it becomes increasingly apparent that the success of any plans for post-war reconstruction in the domestic, no less than in the international, sphere will mainly depend upon the collaboration which can be achieved between the English-speaking peoples. It is not too much to say that the future of civilization and the progress of mankind for a long time to come will be decided, for good or ill, by the degree of solidarity and the sense of unity which can be developed between the citizens of the British Commonwealth and the United States. Included in the former are the self-governing Dominions—Canada, Australia, New Zealand and South Africa. Furthermore, it is clear, as Lord Lothian pointed out, that the closest and most complete form in which unity could be expressed and collaboration achieved would be through a federal union of the American and British peoples. Such a union would constitute the best guarantee for a lasting peace, because it would become the nucleus of any international authority or confederation of the United Nations entrusted with the duty of erecting and maintaining the structure of peace. It would also help to solve those difficult problems which have to do with native races and colonial territories. Hitherto amongst the English-speaking democracies the white man's burden has been shouldered almost exclusively by Great Britain. If, however, the people of the United States were willing to share the responsibilities of trusteeship, many of the obstacles obstructing the path of progress might be removed. The future of India is a case in point.

11. ROLE OF U.S.A.

It is true that at the conclusion of the war the task of winning the peace will become the responsibility of all the United Nations who have endorsed the Atlantic Charter. But if they are to keep in step and to remain united, there must be some effective leadership, and this will not be forthcoming unless the British and American peoples are able to speak with one voice at the council table of a World Authority when the programme of reconstruction is decided upon. But to agree upon a plan is not enough. There must also be the assurance that the policy emerging from the plan will be adhered to and that the plan itself will be carried out.

After the last war the United States took the lead in drafting the Covenant of the League of Nations. It failed, however, to play its part in implementing and executing the plan, and this was probably the main cause for the failure of the League.

The fact that America abandoned the infant at Geneva—which she had been mainly responsible for bringing into the world—afforded an excuse to the members of the League, and especially to Great Britain, for refusing to give it teeth and to equip it with adequate sanctions, including an International Police Force. Rightly or wrongly, it was held that so long as the United States remained in isolation it would be impossible to maintain an effective blockade against an aggressor, and that any attempt to enforce it by the forces at the disposal of the League might result in a clash with the American Navy, if the Government at Washington insisted upon carrying on normal trade relationships with the aggressor or recalcitrant nation. It was this state of uncertainty as to what the attitude of the United States Government would be towards the application of sanctions that helped to sabotage any real and effective system of collective security. Supposing, however, that the peoples of the Republic and the British Commonwealth had formed themselves into a federal union at the conclusion of World War I, it is probable that their combined energy and drive would have succeeded in developing the League into a real International Authority, and would thus have prevented, not only the outbreak, but also the preparations for World War II.

III. Democracy and Federalism

Both these nations are democracies. They have practised parliamentary government over long periods, and if the House of Commons is the cradle of representative government, Congress is the nursery of federalism.

It follows that if the American and British peoples are determined upon the fullest and most complete collaboration in the task of world reconstruction, they should apply those political principles and methods which they have successfully practised in the development of their national institutions. Such a policy involves an extension of democracy and federation in their post-war relationships. Regarded from this standpoint, it is by no means a revolutionary proposal, because it was Great Britain that invented the parliamentary system, whilst the United States and the Dominions are the modern exponents of federation. Consequently, if in the changed and shrinking condition of the world a closer union has become necessary, not only to prevent future wars but also to promote their mutual welfare, the English-speaking peoples should be prepared to merge their national sovereignties at least to the extent of securing democratic control of a common foreign policy and of making provision for their mutual defence. Moreover, if such collaboration is to be permanent, it can be achieved only through political institutions based upon democratic principles; the direct, not the indirect, participation of the peoples. In other words, democracy must leap the frontiers, a bridge must be built across the Atlantic, and thus, through the creation of a federal parliament, the durability of the new order will be assured. If Atlantic unity can win the war, Atlantic disunity can certainly lose the peace.

IV. Friendship

It may be said that this is the wrong approach, that all we need do is to promote mutual understanding and strengthen the bonds of friendship between the English-speaking peoples. No one would wish to disparage the importance of friendship or the efforts which are being made to foster the growth of mutual confidence and esteem. These feelings help to create the right atmosphere in which difficulties can be overcome. But the play of emotions, valuable though it may be, does not provide a safe or durable solution of our problem, which is how to develop a common consciousness and a sense of unity. To achieve this result it will also be necessary to create those political institutions through which public opinion, expressing the views of the majority of citizens in the federated countries, can become effective. An automobile cannot run without petrol; conversely the petrol will run to waste if there is no car. Similarly, if we rely exclusively upon friendship, based upon sentiment, it may prove a broken reed, as it has so often done in the past. The emotions are like gusts of wind; they blow hot and cold.

Even in the relationships of individuals, the friend of to-day may become the enemy of to-morrow. Unfortunately this applies in an even greater degree to the relationships of states and nations. How many treaties of friendship have been signed during the last twenty-five years, and how many of the signatories are at war with each other to-day? Mussolini set the fashion when he concluded a treaty of friendship with Abyssinia. "'Walk into my parlour,' said the spider to the fly." Then came the turn of Albania. Germany induced Czechoslovakia, Poland and Russia to sign pacts of friendship with the Third Reich. Nowadays commercial treaties and friendship pacts may be regarded as danger signals, the precursors of aggression and invasion. They can never become a substitute for the rule of law. As Rousseau once wrote: "Every community without laws and without rulers, every union formed and maintained by nothing better than chance must inevitably fall into quarrels and dissensions at the first change that comes about." That is the real trouble. In the every-day hurly-burly of the sovereign states in the political arena, where all sorts of conflicting interests and atavistic tendencies come into play, the absence of laws and legislative machinery perpetuates the state of anarchy and dissension which every sane person desires to terminate. It follows that if we rely exclusively upon friendship we are merely courting disaster and are liable to become the victims of "the first change that comes about."

v. Economic Remedies

We may also be told that the vital necessity is to reach agreement upon economic questions. We are often assured that once these have been satisfactorily settled everything else will fall into line. Never was there a more complete fallacy or a greater delusion. Mr. Agar, in *A Time for Greatness,* writes: "An example of our confusion between means and ends is the tendency to put economic problems first on our list of woes.

... A world which thinks it can understand itself and cure itself by concentrating on the economic problem is a world which has failed to put first things first, which has substituted the means for the end." There may be many causes of war, but the main cause underlying all the rest is the overweening desire for mastery and domination, the urge to become the top dog. This motive is deeply ingrained in human nature, and manifests itself in every sphere of society. There is always the tendency and temptation to impose one's will upon one's neighbour. In the national community this natural propensity is curbed in many ways. It can operate only within the limits prescribed by the customs and laws of the land. In the international community, however, there is no law, and the desire to dominate everything and everyone is given free rein. This is the paramount motive that drives nations into the international slaughter-house, not the lure of economic loot or territorial aggrandizement.

In recent years there has been the controversy between the protagonists of the haves and the have-nots. We have been told that the have-not powers—Germany, Italy and Japan—were compelled to wage World War II in order to secure the economic advantages hitherto enjoyed by the United Nations but denied to them. Apparently, however, this is not Hitler's view. In *Mein Kampf* he tells us that "men do not die for business." This is true. They die for a mystical idea, concept or aspiration; for an ideal—religious, ethical, political, racial—or it may be that they are inspired by loyalty to a leader, whose personality and magnetism has for the time being captured their imaginations. They do not die for a purely materialistic or economic objective, and it is an illusion to think otherwise. This view, however, does not imply that trade barriers, economic quarrels, industrial depression and unrest may not become contributory factors which help to produce the atmosphere and irritants of war. Undoubtedly they do, but although the economic blizzard of 1930 assisted the dictators in their plans for world conquest, it was not the primary cause of World War II.

No one would wish to minimize the importance of improving the trading and economic relationships between the national sovereign states, and mutual agreements will become a vital necessity at the conclusion of the war. The Lend-Lease arrangements initiated by the U.S.A., a capitalist country, is the first instalment of this policy. It may, however, be doubted whether economic rapprochements and ententes will ever become a reliable substitute for the rule of law, or that they will eliminate the real causes of war. It is true that when the cease fire has sounded, the abnormal conditions—starvation, distress and general impoverishment—will compel the United Nations to adopt an economic policy of mutual help and collaboration.

But once these strains and stresses are removed, vested interests, national prejudices, and other forms of sabotage will begin to assert themselves once more, and unless the economic structures—trade agreements and commercial treaties—are supported by a consciousness of political unity they will crumble into ruins as so many of their predecessors have done in the past. It follows that a common policy can only be evolved and resolutely adhered to if some kind of International Authority or Confederation is established, which means that political institutions must be created through which co-operation between the United Nations can be made effective, not only in the economic but in the political arena as well.

In the case of the English-speaking peoples it is of even greater importance that they should not be lulled into the belief that their problems can be solved merely by economic adjustments, trade pacts and commercial treaties. To rely exclusively upon these instruments, and to imagine that they will ever become a substitute for political union, is to follow a Will o' the Wisp which in a few years will leave them stranded once more in the morass of national sovereignty.

VI. POLITICAL UNION

The next question which confronts us is whether any federal union is practical and whether it is likely to contain the elements of stability. The answer mainly depends upon what are described as the imponderables, namely, those intangible links between nations which cannot be weighed or assessed, but which can only be classified and surmised. These constitute the scaffolding which holds the political structure together. As the history of the United States proves, not even a federal union can withstand the attacks of the factions and vested interests unless it is based upon the solid foundation of the imponderables, those aspirations and ways of life which appeal to the good sense of the average men and women in the communities forming the federation. In the Civil War Abraham Lincoln proclaimed the ideal of "One and Inseparable." He declared that North America could not continue half slave and half free. He mobilized the imponderables, sealed them with the blood of the nation, and re-established the Republic upon a solid foundation, where it has rested ever since.

What do these imponderables consist of? Briefly enumerated, they are as follows: First, there is the historical background, the relationships of the federating peoples in the past. Another is language, giving expression to their thoughts and ideas. Obviously, if they speak the same language, it is much easier to arrive at mutual understandings and agreements, especially when under the electoral and Parliamentary systems a common policy has to be endorsed by millions of human beings living perhaps in widely separated parts of the globe. Other imponderables are race, culture and religion; the political, legal, educational and economic institutions reflecting the philosophies and general outlook of national communities upon the problems of life. These, of course, are bound to differ. It may be only a question of degree or the cleavage may be fundamental and go deeper. For instance, one community may practise the principles of democracy, another of totalitarianism. One may believe in the freedom of the individual, another in the divinity of the state. In the economic domain one may support communal ownership, another private enterprise. One may loathe, another glorify, the ideology of war. One may be the protagonist of the rule of law, another of international anarchy. One may accept the implications of federalism, another may be intoxicated with the spirit of nationalism. These are some of the national philosophies. None are stable or permanent, all are liable to gradual or violent changes. It must also be remembered that states and nations belong to different strata of civilization. There are the backward races whose customs, institutions and ways of life are extremely primitive. Obviously, they should be classified and placed in their proper categories. So long as they remain in the rudimentary stages of cultural and political development it is difficult to compare them with the older civilizations, and their treatment will differ accordingly.

VII. PROMISING FIELD

It may be true that one can only generalize about the imponderables. No one, however, can deny their existence. But their potency or otherwise cannot be proved until the transformation from national sovereign states to partners in a federal union has actually been achieved. And if we embark upon a survey of all the sovereign states of the world it will probably be agreed that the most promising field for a durable union, if it could once be realized, would be the federation of the English-speaking peoples—"the foundation of sane solidarity," as Stephen Leacock has put it. If they are unable to set an example to other democracies in curbing the political pretensions of nationalism, if they cannot create the federal institutions which will enable them to evolve a common policy and speak with one voice in the council chamber of a World Authority, it is quite certain that no other nations or group of nations will be likely to do so.

Where else in the world, it may be asked, do the same imponderables stand forth so conspicuously as they do when we compare the characteristics and ways of life of the English-speaking peoples?

VIII. HISTORICAL BACKGROUND

In the first place they share an historical background. A little more than a century and a half ago the thirteen states of North America were included in the British Commonwealth. It may be true that this background is not a particularly happy one. On the other hand, the implications of the War of Independence have been grossly exaggerated on both sides of the Atlantic. Moreover, the treatment subsequently accorded to other colonies proves that Great Britain recognized the terrible mistake she had made in her dealings with the colonists of North America. Even at that time there were many people in Britain—Burke, Fox, William Pitt, Richard Price and others—who believed then what everyone believes now, that George III and his Government were wrong in the attitude they assumed towards the peoples of the thirteen states. But why should this ancient quarrel rankle for ever? Why should the stupidity of one British Government poison the wells of friendship and co-operation, or prevent for all time the closest collaboration between two great peoples?

Furthermore, modern discoveries and scientific inventions, eliminating distance and culminating in two world wars, must surely have some bearing upon the future relationships of all countries, especially of the English-speaking peoples. In both these crises we find the antagonists of a hundred and sixty years ago fighting shoulder to shoulder against a common enemy in defence of a common cause. Why then should they stubbornly refuse to let bygones be bygones or look askance at any proposal to constitute a political reunion based upon those principles of democracy and federation in which they both profess to believe?

IX. RACIAL TIES

Then there are the ties of race which, in the circumstances we are now considering, do not possess the same significance as they did in the days of Washington and George III. We are prone to think that because Americans speak English they are all descended from British stock. This, of course, is a complete fallacy, and the old adage that blood is thicker than water no longer applies in this case. The fact is that the blood has been drastically diluted. Although the original stock in the United States was mainly British, there has been a profound change during the intervening period. To-day the citizens of the United States trace their descent to all the nationalities of Europe. Their ancestors shook the dust of the Old World from their feet when they founded their homes in the broad and fertile lands of North America. In their new surroundings they lived in a freer and more exhilarating atmosphere than they had ever known before. Nor must it be forgotten that a considerable number had migrated in order to escape persecution and tyranny at home. Some of them, the Irish for example, were filled with hatred for Great Britain, a baneful influence which unfortunately still exists, in spite of the belated freedom that has now been accorded to the Irish people. Moreover, the increase of immigration during the second half of the nineteenth century, and the fusion of nationalities, has lessened, if not almost obliterated, the imponderables of kinship and race, though here and there scattered throughout the republic there are groups and communities who still retain cultural contacts with the homelands of their forefathers. The outstanding fact, however, is that the people of the United States have now developed into a distinctive and virile nation, and owe their political allegiance exclusively to the federal and state governments of the Republic. In proof of this it is interesting to note that in the last war the first contingent of the American Army to cross the Atlantic and man the trenches alongside their British and French Allies was composed of German-speaking units recruited in the Middle West. Racial affinities did not prevent them from fighting for a cause in which they believed, and making sacrifices for the country of their adoption. But this new nation, composed of men and women of so many races, would never have espoused the cause of the United Nations in both world wars had it not inherited from the parent stock the imponderables—the traditions, culture and institutions—which the British pioneers had transplanted in the New World when the colonies were first founded. It is true that settlers of other nationalities also made their contributions to the progress of this advanced outpost of European civilization, but it will probably be agreed that its main inspiration was derived from the principles of Magna Charta, the Bill of Rights, and other historic documents which were subsequently improved upon and embodied in the Declaration of Independence. It was at this stage that they severed their political connection with the Old World, but the imponderables remained and exercised a profound influence upon the development of the youthful Republic, where loyalty to the principles of freedom and democracy still remains its most treasured heritage. This heritage is essentially British in character. It is based upon the rights of the individual citizen. It includes freedom of thought, of worship, of speech, of association and of education, a free Press, private enterprise and equality in the sight of the law. In the march across a continent from the Atlantic to the Pacific, this heritage has ousted the "lawless heritage" of the pioneering days through the gradual extension of the rule of law.[1]

To-day one has only to read the speeches and declarations of President Roosevelt and Mr. Willkie, the leaders of the two great American parties, both of whom are of European—though not of British—descent, to appreciate how completely and realistically the noblest ideals and aspirations of the Pilgrim Fathers have been reinterpreted and applied to the new conditions of the twentieth century.

X. RELIGION

Moreover, we find that from the outset religion and education were deeply rooted in the lives of the new communities. The creeds of the Mother Country flourished on a new and freer soil and Christian churches belonging to various denominations sprang up everywhere, whilst colleges and universities were also established. As the tide of immigration rolled westwards, schools multiplied and courts of law steadily increased. Broadly speaking, all these institutions bore a striking resemblance and conformed to the same patterns which had characterized their predecessors in the old country. Similarly in business, commerce and industry, individual enterprise discovered new fields for

---

[1] "Lawlessness has been and is one of the most distinctive American traits . . . Americans . . . have one of the most sinister inheritances in this matter of law from which any civilized nation could suffer."—*Cf.* Truslow Adams, *A Searchlight on America*, Chap. V.

economic expansion, unhampered by the inhibitions and restrictions which clogged the wheels in Britain. It will be readily admitted that the new régime across the Atlantic was in many respects far in advance of the parent communities in Europe. There was a greater readiness to take risks, to embrace novel ideas and to embark upon new ventures—hallmarks of the pioneer—which contributed to the speedy development of this vast continent. In comparison the economic progress of the older English-speaking community may have been less rapid and dramatic. On the other hand, ever since the Reform Bill of 1832 the British Parliament has made great strides in the domain of social legislation and it may be claimed that in some respects, at least, it has outstripped the activities of Congress and the state legislatures in this important sphere. The net result is that the broad outlook towards these problems —religious, cultural, educational and industrial—appears to be much the same on both sides of the Atlantic. There are, of course, different points of view, but these are shared by sections of public opinion in both countries; they are horizontal, not vertical, divisions.

XI. Language

Lastly, there is the imponderable of a common language which enables millions of ordinary folk, men and women, living in scattered parts of the world and separated by thousands of miles, to understand each other's thoughts and ideas. It is obvious that to ensure the smooth working of democratic institutions a common medium of speech is invaluable. And if we survey the history of mankind it appears that the misguided men who built the Tower of Babel were the friends of nationalism and sovereignty and the enemies of democracy and peace. They were probably the ancestors of the Axis peoples and the first apostles of the Fascist, Nazi and other totalitarian creeds. The handicaps which they imposed upon the human race have helped to perpetuate mutual antipathies and misunderstandings which may develop into extreme forms of nationalism and ultimately pave the way to violence and war.

Anyone who has attended international conferences cannot fail to have been impressed with the difficulties and inconveniences created by the absence of a common language in these proceedings. How much greater then is the handicap when the daily intercourse between peoples is involved! It is true that this difficulty can be surmounted and must be overcome. Nevertheless, it is a serious obstacle in the path of international reformers. But in the case of the 200 millions who inhabit the English-speaking countries this hindrance to their collaboration does not exist. They have at their disposal a common literature which does not need to be translated and republished. They can read newspapers and periodicals in their own tongue printed, it may be, on the other side of the globe. We may live to see the day when editions of one daily newspaper will be published simultaneously in London, New York, Chicago, Montreal, Sydney, Johannesburg and other cities. Through the drip, drip, drip, day by day, week in, week out, of a popular Press whose policy is based on the principles of democracy and federalism and whose reading public embraces all the English-speaking peoples, it may be possible to do more to create a common consciousness and sense of unity than through almost any other agency. Where are the Press pioneers who will embark upon this adventure and help to build up a solid wall of public opinion in support of the new order? Moreover, in the twentieth century the theatre, cinema and, above all, the microphone have enhanced the value of a common language. To-day, in their broadcasts the President of the United States and the Prime Minister of Great Britain are able to address vast audiences and appeal to a huge electorate stretching around the entire globe. Not only can they convey their ideas, but they can impart the personal touch in their speeches, which is of immense importance in any democratic community. It would almost seem as though Providence, disclaiming its alleged share in the debacle of Babel, has bestowed this priceless boon upon the English-speaking peoples. In recent years its value has been increased by the discoveries and inventions of man. Will the peoples cast this imponderable aside and refuse to employ it as an instrument for widening the scope of democratic and federal institutions or will they use it to extend and uphold the rule of law and thus contribute to the advancement of civilization and the progress of mankind?

XII. THE DOMINIONS

Let us now consider the case of the Dominions. Naturally, their development has followed on lines similar to those of the United States. They also are free communities who began their careers as pioneer colonies. They have now blossomed forth into national sovereign states each equipped with a Department of External Affairs for the conduct of its foreign policy and controlling its own Army, Navy and Air Force. But in spite of this desire to exalt the pretensions of national sovereignty, their keen sense of loyalty to the British Commonwealth has been reinforced up till now by the same imponderables which have helped to mould the outlook and policy of the U.S.A. As the events of the war have proved, the future security of the Dominions will mainly depend upon the support of the Mother Country and the United States. If the former can overcome their nationalist tendencies, there seems to be no valid reason why they should not welcome a union of the English-speaking peoples and become partners in the enterprise.

XIII. FEDERATION OF U.S.A.

We now come to the political side of the picture which has already been alluded to. Maybe it will provide us with inspiration and lessons for our future guidance. It will be remembered that when, at the instigation of Alexander Hamilton and his federal friends, representatives from the thirteen states were summoned to the Convention at Philadelphia in 1789, it almost seemed as though the dissolution of the Union was at hand. The Confederation founded on the morrow of victory in the struggle against Great Britain appeared to be going to pieces. The governments of the thirteen states, caring little for the general interest represented by the Confederation, were immersed in jealousies, quarrels and strife, which at this distance of time it is difficult for us to realize. So bitter was the feeling that three minor wars were in progress and eleven disputes were outstanding between them. Taxes were hopelessly in arrear and the Confederate Exchequer was empty. Political disintegration and the breaking-up of the Confederacy into thirteen or possibly into a smaller number of federal or regional units appeared to be imminent and inevitable. The imponderables had not come into play because the political institutions through which they could assert themselves effectively were still lacking. Then the scene suddenly changed. In *The Federalist*, Hamilton and his friends led the attack upon the isolationists, separatists and protagonists of state sovereignty. He persuaded the Convention that the general interest, the future progress and welfare of the whole country, was linked up with the creation of a federal government, a federal parliament, a federal Supreme Court and a federal army. When the new Constitution was drafted it was submitted, not to the governments but to the vote of the electors in all the thirteen states. The average citizen rose to the occasion; he realized the issues at stake; he recognized that his interests were bound up in the general interest—

the peace, progress and welfare not of any individual state but of the whole North American Republic. In spite of bitter opposition from the vested and sectional interests, especially of some of the leaders and politicians in the state governments and parliaments, the new Constitution was endorsed by the majority of the electors, and the Federal Government at Washington set out upon its adventurous voyage.

Perhaps the federation of the thirteen states in 1789, the nucleus of a Union which now includes forty-eight political units, is the greatest democratic triumph of all time. It derived its inspiration from the example of the City States of Ancient Greece. But in those far-off days democracy could only function when it was bolstered up by slavery, which enabled every freeman to take a direct, not an indirect, share in the administration of his city and the framing of its laws. It is the supreme merit of the United States Constitution that after the lapse of centuries it succeeded in merging the federal conceptions of the Greeks with the system of representative government which the British people had developed and which may be regarded as their greatest contribution to the advancement of political science and the progress of civilization.

But it was reserved to the pioneering branches of the English-speaking people to create those federal institutions which would enable their citizens to control their inter-state relationships through the medium of a federal parliament. Thus it became possible to separate external from internal questions and to ensure that in pronouncing its verdicts the electorate would be able to distinguish between foreign and domestic issues. It also enabled each state to exercise its powers of Home Rule and at the same time to collaborate with its neighbours in a common policy towards the outside world. Deprived of its sovereignty in external affairs, the state community would still be free to develop its national characteristics, propensities and institutions without becoming a menace to the security of its neighbours in the federation. Hamilton insisted that the existence of a strong federal government, resting upon the assent and direct representation of the peoples, was the surest guarantee of durability and peaceful development. That he was right is proved by the experience of the U.S.A. during the last hundred and fifty years where the rule of law has conferred the blessings of peace upon a vast continent. Only once during this period—in the Civil War of 1861—was the authority of the Federal Government ever challenged by a resort to force.

If we contrast this result with the history of the adjoining continent of South America, we cannot fail to be impressed by the difference between them. The states of South America were originally Spanish and Portuguese colonies. When, however, they severed their connection with the parent communities in Europe they refused to federate and developed into national sovereign states. Although they were descended from the same stock, spoke a similar language, and shared the same culture, they failed to provide the political institutions through which these imponderables could assert themselves. The result has been that during the last century and a half, whilst the federated community in North America enjoyed an almost uninterrupted period of internal peace and growing prosperity, the national sovereign states of South America have been engaged in numerous wars and internecine strife which have seriously retarded their economic development. With this concrete example before us, can anyone doubt that the future progress of the world is bound up with the extension of democratic and federal institutions?

xiv. The British Commonwealth

On the other hand, the political development of Great Britain proceeded upon lines of unification, not of federation. The Parliaments of Scotland, Ireland and Wales were merged in the British Parliament, which in more recent times has been wrongly described as the Imperial Parliament. Had it been truly Imperial, the self-governing Dominions would have been represented in it. The truth is that the federal solution has never been regarded with enthusiasm in Great Britain, partly on account of the happy-go-lucky attitude of the British people. There were also the practical difficulties of applying it because of the enormous distances separating the parts of the Empire; now, however, owing to the development of transport these difficulties no longer exist. The case of the Dominions is somewhat different. In spite of considerable opposition they were able to unite their states or provinces under federal governments. But, although they understood what federation means and the advantages they have derived from this system, nevertheless up till now they have refused to consider any plan for the federation of the British Commonwealth because they dreaded the possibility of being dominated by the senior partner in a federal parliament at Westminster.

The result has been that no concerted measures were taken to provide for their mutual defence. The absence of any co-ordinating political machinery to ensure that the Empire would be adequately defended played into the hands of our enemies, who deluded themselves with the belief that the Dominions would stand aloof from the Mother Country in any future war. When the crisis came, however, the former threw themselves into the breach because they understood in 1939 what they had already realized in 1914, that if the Mother Country was defeated their safety would be gravely imperilled. It was this lack of a common policy during the last twenty-five years that culminated in a state of deplorable unpreparedness and proves how vital it is that in dealing with foreign affairs and mutual defence the members of the Commonwealth should act together and pool their resources. In practice this means that these paramount questions can be satisfactorily settled only through the medium of a federal parliament where plans can be fully discussed and decisions taken. Only thus can the interest of the democratic electorates be stimulated and an informed public opinion developed. Perhaps such a procedure was unnecessary in the nineteenth century when Great Britain was able to police the seas. During that period the British Empire was relatively powerful enough to prevent the outbreak of world-wide conflagrations. It is, however, an illusion to imagine that it can impose the *Pax Britannica* to-day, although it would appear that up till a few years ago this view was still held in Whitehall. Speaking in the House of Commons in 1925, Sir Austen Chamberlain, then Foreign Secretary, said: "After all, it is in the hands of the British Empire and if they will that there shall be no war, there will be no war." To-day we realize that on two occasions within the last thirty years the British Empire has failed to prevent the outbreak of world wars. What is the lesson? It is that a new and much more powerful combination is now needed to secure respect for the public law, and the nucleus of this organization is to be found in a political union of the 200 million citizens who live in the English-speaking countries.

If through their representatives in a federal parliament they could control a common government equipped with one Foreign Office and one defence organization—instead of six or seven as at present—they would be able to speak with one voice in the Council of a World Confederation and present a united front to any would-be aggressor in future. It is suggested that such an arrangement would not only increase their own security but would also be a permanent contribution to the cause of peace. Let us now consider what are some of the obstacles which stand in the way of a federation of the English-speaking peoples.

XV. VESTED INTERESTS

First of all there are the vested interests, namely, those relatively small but nevertheless powerful sections of every community who thrive under the system of national sovereignty and imagine that their power, influence and livelihoods will be endangered if this system is superseded by a federal union of peoples. In *The Federalist,* Hamilton has described one section of the vested interests as follows: "Among the most formidable of the obstacles which the new Constitution will have to encounter may readily be distinguished the obvious interest of a certain class of men in every state to resist all changes which may hazard a diminution of the power, emolument and consequence of the offices they hold under the state establishments; and the perverted ambition of another class of men who will either hope to aggrandize themselves by the confusions of their country, or will flatter themselves with the prospects of elevation from the subdivision of the empire into several partial confederacies than from its union under one government."

XVI. POLITICAL INTEREST

In this passage Hamilton alludes to the political vested interest. It included the Ministers and members of the thirteen State Parliaments, all of whom in greater or lesser degree would be affected by the transfer of powers and functions from the State governments and Parliaments to the Federal Authority and Congress at Washington. For instance, Hamilton's plan provided that, in future, foreign affairs and common defence would be outside the purview of the State Parliaments and would come under the exclusive control of the Federal Executive and Congress. Naturally, to the Ministers and members of the State Parliaments this was not a pleasing prospect because it belittled their importance, restricted their powers and diminished their "prospects of elevation." Nor was it likely to meet with the enthusiastic approval of another vested interest—the civil and military services of the state governments. They could not help being apprehensive that their positions and livelihoods might be threatened by these new arrangements. A third vested interest was those sections of the business and trading community, especially vendors of arms, whose immediate prospects and contracts might be prejudiced by the transfer to, and concentration of, certain powers under the Federal Authority.

These are a few examples of the vested interests, as opposed to the general interest, namely, the interest of the ordinary citizens in all the thirteen states, who had no direct or personal interests to serve by maintaining intact the legislative and administrative machinery of their particular state. In the debates at the Philadelphia Convention, Hamilton and his friends proved conclusively that the general interest could best be served through the creation of a federal constitution, and in the plebiscite or referendum which followed his views were endorsed by the majorities in the thirteen electorates, despite the opposition of the vested interests. This was democracy functioning at its best; the people saved themselves by asserting their supreme authority over the sectional political, bureaucratic and economic interests of the state communities. To-day a union of English-speaking democracies may be more difficult to achieve than it was in 1789. If, however, the common folk, who have nothing to lose but everything to gain, can be convinced that the future welfare of their children, the security of their hearths and homes, and the advancement of civilization depend upon their collaboration and solidarity in peace no less than in war, then it is possible that democracy will be able to record its greatest and most resounding victory not only on the blood-soaked battlefields of Armageddon but also in the chaotic arena of the political world.

XVII. ATAVISTIC TENDENCIES

But perhaps the greatest obstacle to a federal union of the English-speaking peoples is the innate conservatism of human nature reinforced by the apathy, prejudices and atavistic tendencies of two hundred million citizens of the British Commonwealth and the United States. These may be described as the negative, as distinct from the positive, imponderables already enumerated. The negatives and positives are constantly at war with each other. But the former can be most successfully attacked when mankind has struck its tents and is on the march, when there is a general upheaval, a clash of ideologies and a gigantic struggle such as we are witnessing in World War II. These are the psychological moments when men and women everywhere are roused from their lethargy and are compelled to face up to the major issues and moral problems of life. Confronted with the widespread misery and impoverishment imposed by war and the appalling slaughter of human beings, including their own sons and daughters, they cannot help calling into question the meaning of human existence and wondering whether it has any meaning at all. Surely the vast majority must instinctively feel that this outburst of brutality and insanity is a challenge to the preconceived ideas and ways of life to which they have been accustomed in the past. They may consider that it is an affront to the whole human species because it is a repudiation of the spiritual and intellectual values which, ever since the dawn of history, have distinguished the animal we call man from the beasts of the field. Having prostituted his discoveries and inventions to the art of killing under the thin veneer of a deteriorating civilization, he has displayed in two world wars a cunning, ferocity and barbarism unparalleled in the annals of mankind. It follows that in these new circumstances every man and woman with a spark of humanity must feel a sense of shame and humiliation which may prompt them to investigate the problem for themselves and insist that their rulers should find a satisfactory and permanent solution to prevent a recurrence of this evil thing.

XVIII. Attitude of English-Speaking Peoples

No one will suggest that the two hundred million citizens of the English-speaking countries desired to engage in wars against Germany or any other country. On the contrary, their antipathy to war carried them to the opposite extreme. They forgot that some things—slavery, for example—are even worse than war. Enveloped in the mists of appeasement, selfishness and cowardice, they even went so far as to betray their honour and the noblest traditions of their forefathers in vain attempts to avoid the catastrophe. Eventually, in sheer self-defence, they have been on two occasions forced to participate in these struggles. In the first encounter, twenty-five years ago, they inflicted an overwhelming defeat upon Germany. How then does it come about that they are now compelled to fight the same battle all over again? The reason is obvious. It is because they tolerated, and indeed supported, a lawless international system in which each nation was the judge in its own quarrel and decided what the size of its national armaments was to be. So long as this system exists war is inevitable sooner or later—it is merely a question of time.

It must now be clear to the meanest intelligence that if competition in armaments is allowed to continue and no effective procedure or machinery exists for the administration of justice and the peaceful settlement of all disputes, a crash is bound to come as soon as an aggressor appears upon the scene who imagines he is strong enough to impose his will upon his neighbours by force of arms. This has always been the case in the past and always will be in future so long as the national communities choose to tolerate the anarchic system of sovereign states. Moreover, war to-day is a totalitarian affair absorbing the entire energy, resources and man-power of the nation. Further, the distinction between soldier and civilian, combatant and noncombatant, has almost disappeared. The advent of the bomber has decreed that in future everyone—men, women and children—shall be in the front line, and as the potentialities of the air are still further developed and the range of the aeroplane is increased, the destruction of big cities and nerve centres will become the main objective of the belligerents. In future, whatever its geographical position may be, no country will be immune from attacks from the air, not even the U.S.A. It follows that the elimination of war, the international duel, is the most urgent need of mankind, not merely on account of the mortality, suffering, misery and impoverishment it brings, but because it is an insane, brutal and criminal method of legislating for human affairs.

Some nations still glorify war, others regard it as a relic of barbarism. Among the latter we find the English-speaking peoples. From the moral standpoint the vast majority of them have condemned this gory institution. It is true there have been occasions in the past when they have been the aggressors, but in the twentieth century they have renounced war as an instrument of policy.

xix. The Anarchic System

Nevertheless, despite this repugnance and renunciation they have taken no effective steps to transform their duelling weapons into policing instruments or to dissociate themselves from the system of national sovereignty that breeds war. It is now clear that so long as they cling to this worn-out system they will be victimized by dictators and warlike communities and will be compelled to fight again in defence of their freedom and existence. It appears, therefore, that the unforgivable sin of the British and American democracies was a negative, not a positive, one. They outlawed war but forgot the common obligation of hue and cry for the apprehension of the criminal and the murderer. They established a court, but neglected to appoint the sheriff and his *posse comitatus*. Wrapped in the cloaks of appeasement and isolation, they lacked the courage to take a decision at a moment when their combined intervention would have been decisive and irresistible. Although they had won World War I they continued to tolerate the system of anarchy instead of putting an end to it by establishing the rule of law. Like Hitler, they preferred to remain above the law and to exercise their national sovereignty in pursuit of what they wrongly and foolishly imagined were their national interests. Thus they helped to pave the way for the second Armageddon in which they now find themselves engulfed. It may be true that the political leaders who led them into this morass cannot be exonerated, but in democratic countries the guilt must rest upon the shoulders of the peoples who allowed themselves to be doped under the spell of the negative imponderables—ignorance, apathy and selfishness.

xx. Nationalism

It follows that we cannot escape from the toils of this horrible system of international relationships unless the peoples are prepared to save themselves from themselves by themselves for themselves. They can never dedicate themselves to the supreme task of salvaging civilization so long as they cherish the belief that their loyalties are circumscribed by the geographical expressions in which they happen to live or are limited to the national communities in which they happen to be born. If the citizens of any branch of the English-speaking peoples hug the illusion that they are vastly superior to all the rest, they are only a feeble imitation of the *Herrenvolk*. Further, if the highest allegiance of which they are capable is to governments and states instead of to principles and ideals, then, in effect, they become the unconscious exponents of an anæmic totalitarianism, which will degenerate into what Mr. Agar describes as "the passive barbarism, the negative corruption that arises within a civilization that is going soft."[2]

This form of national snobbery and perverted patriotism is not confined to Europe. It is to be found everywhere, even in the democratic communities of the British Commonwealth and the United States. It confuses the paramount issues because men and women refuse to think and consequently become the victims of their emotions. They have been taught in their histories and through their educational systems, national

[2]Herbert Agar, *A Time for Greatness*, p. 32.

institutions and social environments to regard their own national sovereign state as the last word in political organization, and cannot conceive of any change which would not be a betrayal of their patriotism. Although they live in a world which is shrinking before their eyes, they still imagine that by adding to their citizenships and extending their loyalties they will lose their national identities. But do Scotsmen and Welshmen or New Yorkers and Kentuckians lose their identities by becoming loyal citizens of Great Britain or the United States? There are many people who still profess to believe that by entering into political partnerships with other democratic communities they will be dominated by one or other of their partners in the union. What! says the Briton, do you propose to convert this old country of ours into the forty-ninth state of the United States? What! says the American, do you suggest that the United States should revert to the position of a British colony? Both these die-hards will probably exclaim, "Perish the thought!" It never seems to occur to the antediluvians on both sides of the Atlantic that the members of an English-speaking federal parliament would be able to approach questions of common concern—foreign policy and defence, for example—from a common standpoint, because they would be impelled to do so by a common consciousness based upon the positive imponderables. They would soon realize that the communities they represented were all members of one body and that if one member suffers all the members suffer with it. This recognition of one supreme common interest is the principle underlying the Lend-Lease Act. We also see it in operation to-day on all the battle-fronts where American, British and Dominion soldiers, sailors and airmen are fighting shoulder to shoulder against the common enemy. One cannot help enquiring why these national communities, living in isolation a few years ago but now pouring their manhood and resources into the struggle, cannot stand shoulder to shoulder in times of peace in order to prevent the catastrophe of war and to ensure that the rule of law is respected and upheld.

XXI. SELF-INTEREST *v.* IDEALS

We may be told that an enlightened self-interest will suffice to conquer our preconceived ideas and enlarge our circumscribed outlooks. History, however, does not support this view. So long as each community retains its national sovereignty there is always the tendency to drift apart when the crisis is passed and the common danger has been removed. Hence the necessity of creating democratic institutions through which policies can be evolved that are neither American nor British but a combination of both. But to achieve this result it is essential to appeal not only to an enlightened self-interest but to the noblest instincts and highest ideals of the two hundred million potential electors in the new federation.

In a frustrated and disillusioned world, Hitler outlined his plans for filling man with "an anarchic passion, to smash and delete all the old institutions."[3] He mobilized the forces of a dynamic barbarism to loot and destroy what he described as a moribund civilization; in other words, a civilization based on economics and materialism which had no backbone and had failed to discover the inspiration of a higher purpose which it could serve. Hitler produced an "explosive idea"[4] which gripped the imagination of the discontented nihilist fraternities in every country. That is the reason why World War II is so often described as a gigantic civil war, because the nihilists, whether active or passive, are to be found everywhere. But apart from the natural and laudable determination of the democracies to save their own skins, what have they done, or what do they propose to do, to counter Hitler's destructive, base, negative, but nevertheless explosive, idea with a creative, noble, positive and explosive programme which will make its appeal to the good sense and goodwill of the common folk in all the freedom-loving and democratic countries? It is suggested that an integral part of this programme is the establishment of the rule of law which, as we have seen, involves the federation of the English-speaking peoples. To support or reject this explosive idea becomes the acid test of our determination to uphold and extend the traditional principles of liberty, equality and democracy bequeathed to us by our forefathers.

Surely this is "a time for greatness" and, having poured out our blood, tears, toil and sweat in a united effort to defeat the forces of evil, why should we refuse to enter into the closest political union in order to reap the fruits of victory?

XXII. WIN THE PEACE

When Nurse Cavell faced the firing squad, she said, "Patriotism is not enough." To win this war is not enough. Victory on the battlefield only creates the conditions which will present the United Nations with an

[3] *Cf.* Herbert Agar, *A Time for Greatness*, p. 72.
[4] *Cf.* Herbert Agar, *A Time for Greatness*, p. 76.

opportunity to construct the edifice of peace on a solid foundation. Whether they will seize this opportunity remains to be seen. They may do so, but, on the other hand, when the pressure of war is relaxed victory may be the signal for a general stampede. Licking their wounds, the sovereign states may return once more into their national enclosures —"back to normalcy," the fatal cry of the early 1920's—and our Western civilization, already "going soft" before the war and bereft of a higher purpose, will totter inevitably towards its final doom. Whether it can be rescued from its passive barbarism and materialism, whether it can be imbued with noble aspirations and ideals, and whether it is to be inspired by a higher purpose will mainly depend upon the degree of collaboration which can be achieved between the English-speaking peoples. In practice this co-operation can find its true and permanent expression only in democratic and federal institutions. This truth is exemplified by the experience of the U.S.A. Almost a century has elapsed since Abraham Lincoln, at a critical moment in the history of one branch of the English-speaking peoples, inscribed "One and Inseparable" on its banner. To-day all the branches of this scattered family of free nations are presented with the opportunity of becoming "One and Inseparable." The opportunity may not recur again until civilization has taken one more plunge on the downward path, and then it may be too late. It follows that the protagonists of liberty, democracy and federalism must nail their colours to the mast now, and there is no time to lose. Let them blaze the trail and by their example inspire other nations to pull down the barriers of national sovereignty and co-operate for the welfare of mankind. In the Soviet Union we find another example of federalism which enables two hundred million human beings of diverse races and religions and speaking different languages to combine together for their mutual advantage and, when their country is invaded, to fight for their freedom to the last ditch against the common enemy.

Then why should not the United Nations construct a World Authority or Confederation upon the ruins of the League of Nations? Within this circle the British-American peoples, speaking with one voice and united in one policy, will be able to assist in rehabilitating the oppressed and impoverished nations, take the lead in establishing the rule of law, and thus make the world a saner, safer and happier place for their children to live in.

XXIII. The Opportunity

Here, then, in the twentieth century of the Christian era we find two great democracies, the American Republic and the British Commonwealth, comprising about two hundred million people. Between them they control about a quarter of the earth's surface, and if they linked up in a federal union they would become jointly responsible for the progress and welfare of upwards of four hundred million human beings occupying colonial territories. Both America and Britain are highly industrialized countries. They command vast resources of raw materials and their standards of living are the highest in the world. Their ships sail on every ocean, and when victory is achieved they will find themselves possessed of almost a monopoly of sea power. They are developing the potentialities of the air, and at the conclusion of the war their combined air fleets will constitute the greatest concentration of power the world has ever known. It is to be hoped that in conjunction with our gallant Russian ally it may be possible to create an International Air Police Force under the direction of a United Nations Authority. Under this formidable umbrella the British-American Navy, acting on behalf of the Authority, will be able to police the seven seas.

Nature, science, industry, commerce and finance have vied with each other in pouring their resources into the laps of the English-speaking peoples. It follows that, with all these advantages, never in the history of mankind have two great nations been given such an opportunity of assuming its moral leadership, of guiding its destinies and advancing its civilization.

XXIV. Imperialism

But what is of even greater importance is that both have inherited traditions based on the principles of justice, freedom and democracy. Both have accepted the implications of trusteeship for the native peoples they now govern. No one can accuse them of fighting for territorial aggrandizement. The old imperialism has been replaced by a new concept based upon federalism and trusteeship. Federalism, as distinct from imperialism, implies an international organization founded not upon force but upon voluntary assent in which all the federated or confederated communities are equal in the sight of the law. A confederation of the United Nations must therefore be charged with the responsibility and equipped with instructions for codifying and, if necessary, enforcing the law. Such an International Authority must also be able to bring about changes in the law from time to time through a peaceful procedure, in order that the code may conform to new needs and conditions as they arise. Human society can never be static, and the law of change operates in the international, no less than in the national, community. The League of Nations came to grief because it was deprived of these necessary and elementary institutions and because it lacked effective leadership. It follows that if the union of English-speaking peoples becomes a member of the International Authority, there is every reason to suppose that it may develop into the sheet-anchor of the new Confederation. Living up to its traditional policy, based upon freedom, democracy, equality and law, it would contribute immeasurably to the stability and cohesion of the infant authority, and thus help to prevent the disintegration which paralyzed the activities of the League.

The English-speaking peoples should, therefore, not be deterred from joining together in a federal union by the fear that such a course might be interpreted as a threat of Anglo-Saxon domination over the rest of the world. To capitulate to this fear is a confession of our lack of self-confidence, and raises a doubt as to whether we sincerely believe in our traditional principles. It may also be regarded as a betrayal of democracy, the cause for which we profess to be fighting in this world struggle, because federation implies an extension of the democratic system and its application to international relationships.

No doubt the concentration of power under the control of a federal parliament might become a temptation to abuse it for wrongful and imperialistic designs. There are still imperialists everywhere; they are by no means extinct even in the democratic countries. But they are far less likely to dominate the policy of a federal parliament than they are to influence the governments of national sovereign states. Furthermore, democracies and federations can hardly be described as the most pronounced warmongers, nor are they conspicuous for their acts of aggression. The supreme test, however, for the English-speaking, as indeed for all other, peoples as to whether they have abandoned imperialism will be their readiness or refusal to co-operate with other members of the United Nations, including Russia and China, in establishing an international authority and inaugurating the rule of law. The Soviet Union, although it is not a democracy in the sense we understand it, has already been organized on federal lines, and there is every reason to suppose that the provinces of China will be federated in a democratic republic at the conclusion of the war.

The vital question, however, is this: Will the English-speaking peoples be prepared to join the other members of such an authority in endowing it with the control of the air? This explosive idea implies the creation of an Air Police Force and the international control of civil aviation. If such an arrangement can be agreed to, then the whole system of national sovereignty falls with a crash. Moreover, if the English-speaking peoples are willing to pool their air resources with those of other nations to maintain international order and to provide a sanction for the public law, then it is nonsense to suggest that a British-American union could possibly be regarded as a threat of Anglo-Saxon domination. On the other hand, if any countries refuse to enter into the Confederate partnership and insist upon retaining their national air forces, then it is more important than ever that the English-speaking peoples should unite and consolidate their resources. At the same time they should rally in support of the International Authority all those nations who are prepared to resist aggression from whatever quarter it may come.

XXV. LEADERSHIP

In the past many efforts to bring about changes in international relationships have failed for lack of a bold and courageous leadership. It will be remembered that in 1910 Congress passed a resolution demanding an International Navy. This proposal, however, was not pursued with vigour, and was finally torpedoed by the Kaiser and Admiral von Tirpitz. At a much earlier period Henry IV of France launched his "Grand Design" for the policing of Europe, but, as Rousseau pointed out, when Henry died his Grand Design perished with him. On the other hand, the brilliant advocacy and stern determination of Alexander Hamilton triumphed over all obstacles. His loyalty to democratic ideals, his unswerving belief in the good sense of the average citizen, his ability to distinguish between primary and secondary objectives carried the federal cause he had championed to victory. Well may we wonder whether the massive structure of the United States of America would ever have been built had it not been for the courageous efforts of Hamilton and his friends.

And where, in the English-speaking communities, are the Hamiltons, Lincolns and Gladstones of the twentieth century, men who will be prepared to forsake all else and devote their lives, careers and fortunes to the service of the higher purpose, men who will be inspired by the noblest traditions of their ancestors and by the political principles for which they lived, fought and died? Where are the men and women on both sides of the Atlantic who will be prepared to sponsor explosive ideas which will blow sky-high the apathy, ignorance, nationalism and materialism of their fellow countrymen? Where are the men who will challenge the nihilists, imperialists, isolationists, blimps and die-hards, and mobilize the ordinary folk throughout the English-speaking countries in support of a positive programme based upon justice and peace?

Perhaps that far-sighted statesman in Washington who has so patiently and successfully triumphed over almost insuperable obstacles and rescued his fellow-countrymen from the toils of isolation before it was too late, perhaps he will be prepared to sponsor the reunion of the English-speaking democracies. Is it too much to hope that he may be supported by those enlightened Republicans who still remember that at the beginning of this century it was their party, under the leadership of Theodore Roosevelt, William Taft and Elihu Root, that became famous throughout the world for its championship of international reforms? Some leading Republicans have already demonstrated their readiness to support the general interest—the cause of justice and the elimination of war—and to oppose the sectional and vested interests of the national sovereign states. Unlike their predecessors in 1918, they are not prepared to wreck the higher purpose or indulge in a new era of passive barbarism in order to promote what some of their short-sighted colleagues may imagine to be the prospects of their party and its triumph in post-war elections.

Perhaps on this side of the Atlantic the statesman who in the darkest hour of her history proposed to France the political union of the British and French peoples may be inspired by the vision of an English-speaking Commonwealth. At the conclusion of this world struggle in which he has played so conspicuous a part, perhaps he will be moved to collaborate with the President of the United States in achieving the greatest democratic triumph of all time.

No one can suggest, however, that the onus rests exclusively upon the leaders. They represent democratic communities and must be guided by public opinion. The main and ultimate responsibility lies upon the shoulders of every man and woman of the two hundred million citizens of the American Republic and the British Commonwealth. It is their "time for greatness," their opportunity to win victories not only on the battlefield but in the political arena, where their fate will be decided when the common enemy has been finally overcome. But unless they bestir themselves and are able to express an overwhelming public opinion in support of these explosive ideas, unless they insist that the plan for international reconstruction emerging from some new Philadelphia Convention is submitted to them for endorsement, they will run the risk of being thwarted by the vested interests. No doubt the latter "will flatter themselves with fairer prospects of elevation" by perpetuating the subdivision of the English-speaking peoples into several sovereign states "than by their union under a federal government."

Therefore, in this crisis of our common civilization, in this upheaval of humanity, in this hour of opportunity, the clarion call goes forth to all men and women of goodwill to support a cause which is essentially their own and thus hasten the coming of the Kingdom of God, "the day in whose clear-shining light all wrong shall stand revealed, when justice shall be throned in might and every hurt be healed."

IX THE WORLD IS ROUND

By Nora Waln

1. THE HOUSE OF LIN

FOR FIVE YEARS I have been living in England. As probably happens
to many others these days, my memory keeps bringing up to my notice
incidents which occurred at other times in my life. While I sat this
morning in a Buckinghamshire garden under the drone of warplanes,
rolling Red Cross bandages, a series of past events came to the fore
of my mind.

It was at my Pennsylvania home when I was not yet ten. My sisters
and I still had lessons at home. History was done for the day, and our
mother came in for geography and penmanship, subjects she liked to
give us herself. She already had her will set on the fact that we would
enter Swarthmore College and was more interested in our learning than
we were, then; but we were members of her family of children, who
came to number seven, and accepted her keenness about our
education as a mother's characteristic. Because she was beautiful, she
stirred me and held my attention in the way that which is lovely has
always done.

Standing by the schoolroom globe that afternoon, she cupped it
with her hands and said: "The world is round."

"We learned that long ago," mentioned Meg, the youngest there.

"That's good," smiled our mother. "All the frontiers and boundaries
you hear of in history are absurd and temporary. Always remember
that the earth is round and for ever connected together despite the
divisions people try to make."

She had travelled, and we hadn't yet. Some days she told us of places and people far away, her words bringing them near. Even then she was brief, planting the seed of one idea at a lesson, leaving us to search out more knowledge for ourselves when she had interested us. This day she gave no more of geography than a reminder of the shape of the globe we all inhabit, and passed our writing books.

With mother we had to copy what she had written for us until it was done in a clear hand and learned by heart. Her lessons were the last of the day. Each of us could go as soon as that was accomplished. The writing lessons were always quotations, prose or verse, sometimes serious and at others gay. This forenoon I had three to write and commit.

One from the Bible, "The spirit of man is the candle of the Lord." Then two from Englishmen who lived during the seventeenth century. From George Fox, "I have seen the Light of Christ shine through men." And from William Penn, "The humble, meek, merciful, just, pious, and devout souls are everywhere of one religion; and, when death has taken off the mask, they will know one another, though the divers liveries they wear here make them strangers."

Years passed. It was in China during 1921, and I was a guest at the Lin homestead, several days' canal trip inland from Tungchow. The world we live on, revolving about the sun in an elliptical orbit and twirling like a top as it goes, had brought us to the season marked on the Chinese Farmer's Calendar "Frost's Descent." The days were shortening. Twice there had been hoar frost on the roof tiles. This morning there was a thin layer of ice on the courtyard pool.

The flailing of grain was nearly finished. The larks had departed. The song of the countryside was now the sound of flour ground on stone mills and the call of the katydid. Walnuts had been gathered, and Mai-da, her mother, her aunt Shun-ko and I were in the sunny kitchen cracking nuts, taking care to keep the kernels in halves, as we made them ready to blanch and salt.

"Fen wu ch'ien jih hao, hua wu pai jih hung," said Mai-da, meaning "Man isn't always fortunate; flowers don't last forever."

"You speak as one who fears the falling leaves will break her head," responded her mother.

"Men of all nations make mistakes," remarked Shun-ko. "The time to test men and to save men is when life is difficult. Heaven has created woman able to share adversity and help through it."

They, too, spoke in Chinese. My puzzlement must have shown. Difference of language is a barrier. I know no easy way to remove it. The task is one for the mind, and the mind is lazy. Necessity is an effective goad. The barrier is not gone until one understands more than how to translate literally. I have come to be glad that in China, the first foreign land I visited, the Elders of the family who invited me decided that I was not to be spoken to, or heard, in any language except theirs, until I was able to use it as if born among them.

This decision for my education put on me the same necessity as the baby has in the locality where it comes to life. That morning in the Lin kitchen Shun-ko did not enlighten me by lapsing into English. She said the Chinese word meaning "politics," thereby opening for me a window through which I suddenly saw that Mai-da had not referred to the season but to the news, disturbing to us all, which her father and brother had brought home the previous evening.

The men were back from a business trip to Canton during which they had stopped at Hongkong, Shanghai, Tientsin, and Peking; and I was asked to join a family gathering in the library. When we were all there Mai-da's father had spoken first. He began by mentioning that at the close of the recent four-year war in Europe a more radiant hope of better relations with the Foreign Powers than had been experienced at any time since Western guns forced a trade treaty sprang up in China. He said this hope sprang from a deep-rooted faith in the people of the "government-by-consent" nations, which has persisted in Sun Yat-sen's followers, who include the Lin clan, even though frequently dashed. He longed for it to continue through the troubled years he foresaw.

On the journey they had met many of their countrymen and -women, of various walks in life, who felt a considerable distrust of the people of England, France, and the United States, due to suspicion that these nations were not only overlooking some of the Japanese Government's aggressions on China—while verbally censoring them—but jockeying to get Japan into the place here which had been held by the former German Government, doing this to secure Japan's assistance in holding on to what they had earlier grabbed, manœuvring under the excuse that order must be kept in China. My cheeks burned.

"Do these Foreign Powers desire order in our country?" the Family Elder asked. "And, if so, what kind of order?"

Mai-da's father glanced at his son, Peng-wen. Peng-wen rose, and just behind him was the family's collection of Western books. He stood straight as a lance. At the height of his shoulder were the works of Locke, Milton, Voltaire, Rousseau, Penn, a life of Roger Williams, the political ideas of Thomas Jefferson, and the speeches of Lincoln.

He looked sick at heart, but he kept his voice emotionless. He reported that not only were there men here and in Japan selling the tools of war wherever they could get the most money, but that some men who had been soldiering in Europe were entering the ports of China now that they were out of employment. These Westerners were from the defeated and the victor countries. They were seemingly without political principles. They were soldiers of fortune who gave their services to the highest bidder. Anyone with money could hire their help on any project. They were disturbers of the Chinese Republic's order, indirect promoters of civil war, yet until there was a strong central government there seemed no way of keeping them out. From reliable sources he had learned that such men were not unwilling to work for the Japanese Government.

The Elder halted Peng-wen and gave us a short review of the history of Japan since that country's contact with the West. He said it made him heavy because "it is right to consider another country as your own country, another family as your own family, another person as yourself," and all who observed could notice that civilization had receded there since Westerners pushed a way in.

Peng-wen turned to face the Western books. Touching the long row, he gathered strength, and these are his words as I wrote them in my diary later that evening: "Much darkness is on us. We must keep our vision clear. I have had the privilege of opportunity to gain knowledge of the West through attendance at a Christian Missionary School and through leisure to study abroad in more than one university. Life in our clan, which has stayed united during many generations of prosperity and adversity, has steadied me in my contacts outside. What I would offer for family consideration is that we do not abandon faith in the people of the 'government-by-consent' nations through whatever darkness we may have to pass. They have an inheritance of political wisdom similar to ours. I believe that inheritance will assert its compelling power. Then from our combined treasury we can together create a new essay in living, one better than East or West has achieved alone."

He sat down. The banker uncle spoke next, saying that he was of the opinion, gained by business experience, that exclusion is not right in this century but that there should be a reaching-out to understanding of other people. One of the children, a little girl, said in a clear tone that we should remember that it is the Law of Heaven that humans must be concerned to benefit each other, or all will perish, for all are one family. There was no dissent and the gathering dispersed.

And next morning in the sunny kitchen Mai-da's mother and Shun-ko talked to Mai-da and me of ways in which women could be of use. They explained the theory of Yin and Yang, or male and female principle. Yin and Yang must be in balance, or a family will not prosper. They are not the same. They are two different things and do not in any way rival each other, but neither is a whole. They complete each other. Woman is not wiser than man. Man is not wiser than woman. Wisdom is not achieved until the two have put their wits together. They felt that the House of Humanity needs renovating, and that this will not be competently done until women are less indolent than they have been about doing their share of mending and keeping it in repair.

Now in Buckinghamshire, England, more than twenty-one years later, I have remembered that autumn evening in the Lin library and the following morning when we cracked nuts. The part of China where I visited the Lins has been invaded by the Japanese. Some of the family's members are with Chiang Kai-shek's "workers-for-better-days" outside Japanese-occupied territory. But the homestead has not been abandoned. Through centuries it has never been left either in eras of civil war or foreign invasion.

"There is work for good which a household can do just where it stands," is a sentence from a letter they recently sent to me through the Red Cross, an organization all of us must indeed call blessed.

II. A FAMILY OF FRANCE

After China, France was the next foreign country I visited. My husband, our daughter and I lived there from 1932 to 1934. It was in France that we came to know Jacques and Yvonne and their children. They have three boys and two girls. When we first met them, Jacques was a young doctor, practising medicine with his father in the small town where both were born, living a pleasant life, devoted to his family, his work, and to music.

We knew them through music. My husband used to study with Yvonne's father. Now that he was old the music-master had left Paris, where he worked for many years, and returned to X, which was also his birthplace. Jacques plays the violin, Yvonne the piano, and they always brought their children to her father's musical gatherings. We took our child, too. The old music-master wrote simple parts, so that the little ones could play in his orchestra, if the original composer had overlooked them.

But it is not of the small town of X with its cobbled streets, square town hall, clear-belled church, and self-contained people, among whom we were so happy, that I would here tell. It is of Jacques in England during the summer of 1940 when he was brought over from Dunkerque with his legs broken. That happened to his legs while he was tending the wounds of machine-gunned children, whom nuns had carried to what they thought was a safe place—well over on grass—at the side of the road. A young German slowed the motor-cycle he was riding and deliberately swerved, knocking Jacques down, and the corps behind this leader, leaving the highway which was open to their passing, rode over his patients.

"Did you ever read the *Badouin de Sebourc?*" Jacques asked my husband and me after he had told us this.

We hadn't.

"It is an old tale of many parts," Jacques continued. "In it the hero, robbed of his inheritance through his own negligence, regains it by battling intelligently with his enemy Gaufrois, who has as his assistants the Devil and Money. I used to laugh at it as foolish when my father would quote from it to me. I was the fool, until I saw Gaufrois on that motor-cycle. I saw him as a doctor sees. He was a fair lad of strong physique, as were many of those who followed his lead; but he was afflicted with as grim an ill as the mind is heir to and unconscious of his own sickness—a paranoid. "

"What is a paranoid?" I had to question.

"A person so mentally deranged that he feels sudden urges to assert himself by murder. The paranoid is a slayer of life, the life of others or self. It is the most difficult of all mental diseases to treat. The germ of paranoia is probably latent in many people everywhere. Tribal taboos and social laws have been enacted to keep it in check since the beginning of history; eras of terror happen when it gets out of control."

We talked of other things. After a while my husband said, "You are staying with us?"

"I am with you," Jacques answered quietly.

"Our house is your home in England."

"Thanks—until I can walk again. Then I must go. I am a doctor. I have seen a disease. I knew it was being nurtured in Germany. I have been guilty of the sin of separateness. I did not strive to help cure or control that disease as I should have done, as I would have done had the menace been cholera or yellow fever. I paid my taxes and wanted it kept out of France. I have learned that evils cannot be kept away by paying taxes, combined with a willingness to go to the front at call. I must go back when I can walk."

He came to us from the hospital. He knew his mind, and we did not urge him to stay longer than until he had the use of his legs. "I am an average Frenchman," he would say, "and the average Frenchman has had little desire to travel, preferring to get his knowledge through books." He had visited no country before England. The Continent of Europe is such a small place. The nations there are not as large as our States, yet he had not been out of France to those that border France. He had not crossed his native frontier into Germany, Switzerland, Italy, or Spain, but he had read widely.

Events in France that summer humiliated and shook him to the depth of his soul. He was alert and quick of ear but he did not feel sure of the spoken English language, although he could read it easily. I would see him scanning *The Times* and often watch him listening carefully to remarks not addressed to him. When he could move about I noticed that he did not want escorting. He took to visiting round without us, making trips to London alone, buying papers and periodicals of his own selection.

"You will tell me the truth," he said finally, sitting down beside me one morning when I was mending socks. "I must know. Am I correct in assuming that here in England this summer I, a Frenchman, have met no flicker of contempt, no glint of mockery, no covered insult? Only deep compassion?"

I could assure him that, according to my observation, he was correct in assuming this.

"And no ill feeling toward your country, the United States, for slowness to help?"

"None," I could honestly answer.

A light came up in his eyes. "And I always thought that the British couldn't comprehend 'Liberty, Equality, Fraternity.' Thank God for England, Scotland and Wales. Let this community be the rock to which we anchor a world citizenship."

The last day he said, "I will teach my children that the good in France must not only become the living law of France but must be universal. With God's help it can be done."

"*Restons unis plus étroitement que jamais*"—let us remain more closely united than ever—is what he wrote on the card which came with his parting gifts of roses for me and a French song for my husband.

III. THE KINSHIP OF THE SPIRIT

Experience has taught me that my mother's instruction was founded on truth. I did not intend to travel. When a child, I loved my home-place, so that I thought I never could leave it. But ours is an age of movement. I made an exception just to visit in China, and there by chance was an Englishman who married me, a man whose avocation is music. And so after ten years of marriage I went to France to keep house awhile, and on to life among the Germans for four years. I've spent a glorious summer in Czechoslovakia and learned there what a true democracy can be. I have musical Russians and Poles as friends. I have been in Japan. The world is round, and in every land I have entered I have found people kin to me in heart and mind and spiritual outlook.

We went from France to Germany when the Nazis were already in control of the government there. Evil was enthroned. I would not minimize that evil. Nazism is a reign by the feeble-minded who are without knowledge of either the rights or the responsibilities of healthy humans. It is not a crop of tares suddenly sprung up to frighten and bewilder us. It is the harvest of seed that has been sown through at least three-quarters of a century.

A German, Professor Z, called my attention to this. A long list of mentally deranged writers have sown the seed, and unbalanced state administrators have harrowed the ground. Fichte and Spengler and Bismarck are among those behind Hitler. It is a madness based on the unsound idea that the many are here to benefit the few. He showed me how other writers and thinkers have stood against this evil; but not enough of them. In my own time I have seen men and women and children staunch against it, both German Jew and German Gentile, and yet go down. Even so, valiant Germans have helped to teach me that the spirit of man is the candle of the Lord, a light that cannot be dimmed by the firing squad, the beheading block, the hangman's rope, or any effort at false teaching.

As Nazism has spread, its evil has been carried into other lands. All who stand against this thrall, inside the lands they hold, possess a valour I would not comprehend if I had not lived in Germany from 1934 to 1938. It is the same of Japan. I have Japanese friends whose courage is such as few outside can realize. How many of our dear ones survive I cannot know. Nor can any of us who suffer this anxiety. But bonds of union do hold across the frontiers of strife. Also, occasional messages arrive letting us know of friends who are yet alive and want to hear that we are still all right.

We came to England from Germany. Perhaps only those who have been for a while in a place where all is denied, which we and our fathers before us have so long taken for granted, can really know what it means to see the white cliffs of England shining in the sun. Now every time I hear of a refugee let in, they shine for me with a special beauty.

In our century we have been shown by world-wide catastrophe that no one of us can enjoy a civilized order without keeping its foundations firm everywhere and being careful about what is built on them. For the second time in the life of those of my age, we are giving our all just for those who survive to have the chance to start building again. We differ among ourselves as to the way to rid our civilization of this menace, some putting their faith in the use of material arms and others in spiritual arms, yet we are united that the menace must be thoroughly got rid of.

And we all know the correctness of Sumner Welles's recent words in *The Atlantic Monthly*: "When this war ends, Europe and much of Asia will be grim places to live in or to contemplate. Starvation, hatred, and disease—the terrible camp-followers of war—will be more widespread than they have ever been before in modern times. The people who survive will face the job of making life tolerable again, or even possible."

We have many plans. Let us by all means discuss the pros and cons of various alternative plans, but in our discussions and possible disagreements let us always remember that for action, and much action is necessary, we must join forces, all the forces we have throughout the world. We will need them. With unflinching courage let those of us who have been shown it boldly urge on all of us who do not yet comprehend it the truth which has consistently and repeatedly been made manifest to humans on this earth through centuries in many places and languages.

This truth is that all of us born to life here, no matter how divers the liveries we wear, are members of one family, the family of mankind. None are *Herrenvolk*. Nor are any to dwell in ivory towers. There are no weapons the cleverest minds can devise which will not eventually explode on those who hope to dominate with them. There is no isolation which even the most cunning can achieve for themselves. It is not sensible to decide that some can live in cotton pants on a handful of rice while others must have finer raiment and a richer diet. Neither is it prudent to use superior talents for any other purpose than to promote the welfare of the entire human family.

This earth is our home for the years we are here, and the home of our children after us. It is a place of neighbouring courtyards. If there is a fire, an epidemic, or an evil of any kind in one part, the trouble will spread if not intelligently and adequately coped with. The more we discover, the smaller we find the earth to be. So we had best make a good home on it without trying to escape the conditions. It is a beautiful place really, interesting, varied, and fruitful. Our behaviour on it should show our gratitude.

To establish and maintain a good home it is necessary to have unity in essentials, clear decision as to what is to be done, and an honest carrying out of what is decided upon. Such a home prospers although things do not always turn out exactly as planned. The members of a family are never all alike, yet in a good home everyone contributes to the household, even the feeblest are encouraged, and sometimes their gifts grow to be of immense value.

We of the family of mankind differ in various ways, including the colours of our skins. I have known people in China who presume that they are superior because their complexion is yellow, and people in America who think they are superior because theirs is white. I am certain that the Colour Bar is an illusion. It is a sophistry to conclude: "Man is made in the image of God; since it is well known that God is not a negro, it follows that the negro is not a man." And just as much a mistake to twist this the other way.

Not all things are alike. Another countryside I see may be more beautiful than the landscape where I grew up, yet I find my native place dearer. The river there sings me the sweetest song, the trees are a pattern for all trees, and there is a flat grey rock that rests me more when I stretch out on it than any couch I've found elsewhere. For me there is no faith nearer the truth than the Quaker Faith, to which I was born. Nicholas and Jane Waln went out from Ribblesdale in Yorkshire with William Penn, pledged to help found in the New World a nation which would be a model to other nations, a place to which peoples from all the quarrelling nations of Europe might come and prosper; and the State they started became a part of the United States. When I am away from the United States I am always homesick. I miss our American brands of candour and humour. This hold, which my own has on me, has helped me to appreciate the love others have for what is theirs.

My husband finds England fairer than other places, and his home here better than any other house no matter how much more modernly equipped. Shortly before the British declared war on Nazism in September 1939, a telegram came asking if we could take two Czechoslovakian children, a boy and a girl aged three and five. Their names are Puffi and Sisi. On their arrival our daughter set herself to make them happy. They had been over the place, gathered eggs, picked peaches from the garden wall, and seemed all right. But when she was drying Puffi after his bath, she said: "You will like it here, won't you?" Bravely, through tears he could not control, he replied, "Thank you, it is all right *dukuo budov Nacisti v Praze*," which is his native speech for "until the Nazis leave Prague."

Once we have agreed to undertake world citizenship, I feel sure that each of us will proudly contribute our precious treasures to a world community; but I find myself very reluctant to have any World Committee peering into the dusty corners of my United States. We have much that I am more than satisfied to let anybody investigate, but there are some things I am touchy about, among them the relation of most white and brown Americans to each other and the dangerous trades by which much of our fine goods are made. I feel like a housewife who wants to clean before letting any neighbours in. Probably members of other nations are the same way about their shames.

Regarding a charter for our world's government, my idea is the same as William Penn's. He took care to make his Frame but cautioned, "Governments go from the motions men give them. Let men be good, and the government cannot be bad. If it be ill, they will cure it. I know some say, Let us have good laws, and no matter for the men that execute them. But let them consider, that though good laws do well, good men do better; for good laws may want good men and be abolished or evaded by ill men; but good men will never want good laws, nor suffer for ill ones."

X WORLD COURT

By Sir Cecil Hurst

———————— ◆ ————————

1. The Story of Arbitration

STATESMEN on both sides of the Atlantic in their speeches about war aims and about post-war reconstruction have made it clear that in their view there must be a court to adjust international disputes.

In his broadcast on March 21 of this year Mr. Winston Churchill, the Prime Minister, said: "I hope we shall not lightly cast aside all the immense work which has been accomplished by the creation of the League of Nations. We must try to make the Council of Europe, or whatever it may be called, into a really effective League with all the strongest forces concerned woven into its texture, with a High Court to adjust disputes, and with forces . . . ready to enforce their decisions."

Similarly, Mr. Cordell Hull, the Secretary of State, speaking on June 23, 1942, said: "Settlement of disputes by peaceful means presupposes respect for law and obligations . . . It is plain that one of the institutions which must be established and be given vitality is an international Court of Justice."

A moment's reflection will show any thinking man why there must be a court, and why that court must possess all the strength that can be given it so as to command the confidence of the world.

Peace is the aim—and to-day future peace is the chief aim—of the statesmen of democratic countries. There is a growing recognition of the fact that peace cannot be achieved merely by a determination on the part of individual States to keep out of war and to avoid provocation. States must stand shoulder to shoulder if peace is to be maintained.

There must be something in the way of collective security. Collective security entails an organization, but it entails more than that. It entails co-operation of a cordial kind. Co-operation will not be attained unless mutual rights and obligations are clearly defined; and cordiality will not be achieved if there are friction and disputings between the members of the organization.

There is no use in being blind to the burden of collective security. The advantages are obvious—if it works—but to make it work implies that each party will face up to its obligations, and the obligations will be heavy. In a democratic State they will be unpopular. They will cost money, they may block the way to needed reforms at home. They will be the bugbear of every Minister and every official responsible for finance: every effort will be made to limit and restrict the obligations. Every limitation, however, which is successfully introduced will weaken the security and alarm public opinion in the other countries which feel disquieted by the international situation of the moment and where the need for security is acutely felt.

Disputes about the meaning and effect of an agreement for ensuring collective security are more than likely, and machinery for settling such disputes is essential. So far as these disputes are justiciable in character, it is a court to which they must be referred.

It is not only disputes connected with collective security that render a court so necessary. International commerce will be more important in the post-war world than ever before. Commercial treaties and arrangements are a fruitful source of disagreements. Economic and financial co-operation will be helped by the existence of a court commanding such confidence that all states will resort to it, and functioning in a manner that will ensure an expeditious settlement of legal disputes.

In principle no one will contest the need for an international court. Thoughtful minds have been feeling after it for the last century. What many people do not realize is that for the last twenty years a court has existed possessing a jurisdiction wide enough to cover all the disputes referred to above. Confidence in this court has steadily increased. Like all human institutions, however, the court can be improved, but before any attempt is made to amend its stature, people should know more about the court and about its work. They should know also more about the efforts which preceded its creation, for those efforts began long before the existing court came into being. They were spread over most of the nineteenth century. The story is worth studying because it shows the difficulties which have to be overcome in connection with an international court, and it shows also the importance of Anglo-American co-operation. Most of the noticeable events on the road towards the judicial settlement of international disputes have been occasions on which the two countries were acting together. This is not unnatural. The points of contact between the two countries in the past have been numberless. Both countries like to see the rights of their peoples respected; both of them are peace-loving States, and though friction has been frequent there has been a will to find some peaceful means of solving particular disputes, and for the same reason there has always been a tendency to support machinery for facilitating the settlement of future disputes.

It is just over a century since the bickering over the boundary between Canada and the State of Maine terminated with the signature of the Ashburton Treaty of 1842, but there it was diplomacy which solved the dispute, not anything in the nature of judicial settlement. A few years later the Oregon boundary dispute was settled by a Joint Commission—just a step nearer to judicial machinery, but still a method which falls far short of the submission of the dispute to a court. In 1873 came the first of the classic arbitrations—that of the disputes arising out of the Alabama Claims. In 1897 the dispute over the Venezuelan boundary was in the same way submitted to arbitration, and in 1904 came the arbitration over the right of American fishermen to participate in the fisheries on the Newfoundland coast.

All of these were controversies which might have led to war if either party had been actuated by designs of aggression. As such they are good instances of the usefulness of arbitration as a means of settling a justiciable dispute by peaceful means, but they also show the shortcomings of arbitration as against judicial settlement by a court.

Arbitration necessitates the negotiation and conclusion in each case of a special agreement regulating the details of the submission of the case to the Tribunal. Such an agreement counts as a treaty between the States and entails all the long processes of the diplomatic method. The discussion about its terms may continue for years. Again, this special agreement must regulate the details of the procedure. Even if the parties to the dispute may agree to leave some of those details to the Tribunal itself to settle, it means that the arbitrators may have to meet in order to settle some unimportant point. A Tribunal composed of prominent and busy men might not want to have to make the journey to the meeting place of the Tribunal merely to make a decision on a point which might be settled without difficulty by a single individual permanently established at the seat of a court.

There are other difficulties, too, inherent in the system of arbitration of international disputes. There is the choice of the arbitrators. There have been instances in the past where attempts have been made to nominate mere politicians, whose chief concern would be to manipulate the decision, rather than jurists endowed with the capacity to give a judicial verdict.

Again, the cost of a great international arbitration was sometimes enormous. On the British side the expenses of the North Atlantic Fisheries Arbitration came to over a hundred thousand pounds, a sum which seems trifling as compared with the expenditure in war, but which in peace-time is enough to make responsible statesmen hesitate about plunging into international litigation.

It is not to be wondered at that at both the First and the Second Peace Conferences at The Hague efforts were made to introduce a simpler and more effective machinery for the peaceful settlement of international disputes.

II. Gropings towards an International Court

In 1899 the First Peace Conference adopted a Convention setting up a Permanent Court of Arbitration.

Though it is called a Court of Arbitration, it is in reality little more than a large body of potential arbitrators, four of whom are nominated by each of the states which are parties to the Convention. From among these arbitrators the parties to a dispute may choose their tribunal. Nevertheless, the conclusion of this Convention marked distinct progress towards the idea of a permanent international jurisdiction. The Convention contained a series of provisions on the procedure of an international arbitration, which were to apply unless the two parties agreed to substitute other provisions. The acceptance of the Convention also indicated unanimity as to the general principles on which arbitrations should be conducted.

The Second Peace Conference in 1907 marked a further stage in the progress.

Not only was the Arbitration Convention of 1899 enlarged and improved, but two schemes were launched for the establishment of real international courts. One was the proposal to set up an International Prize Court. The other was a scheme for setting up a "Court of Arbitral Justice."

Neither of these courts came into being, but the proposals show the steady progress which the idea was making that there must be machinery for the peaceful settlement of disputes.

The Prize Court Convention was intended to create an international court of appeal from national prize courts. It was concluded under the stress of the exasperation created by the decisions in the Russian and Japanese prize courts during the Russo-Japanese War.

The Convention was never ratified. This was, in part, due to the belief that the divergencies between Anglo-Saxon and Continental prize law were so great that the court could not function satisfactorily unless the States could first agree on a code of rules which the court should apply, and in part due to a special difficulty which was believed to confront the United States owing to the wording of the Constitution. Art. III §1 of the Constitution declares that for the United States the judicial power is vested in the United States Supreme Court and such *inferior* courts as Congress might establish. Could there be a *superior* court in matters of prize? An attempt was made to avoid the difficulty by a protocol providing that for the United States monetary compensation should replace the reversal of the decision in prize, if such were decreed, but the protocol was not proceeded with when the ratification of the Convention was abandoned.

The second scheme provided for setting up a "Court of Arbitral Justice." If this plan had ever come into operation, it would have established a World Court: it would have done what was only accomplished fourteen years later after the establishment of the League of Nations.

The cause of the failure in 1907 is interesting; it illustrates so sharply some of the difficulties surrounding the establishment of an international court. Two competing principles were involved—principles which no one would say were lightly to be disregarded. The first is that no court can or will be regarded as a World Court unless the Great Powers are solidly behind it. In 1907 none of the Great Powers would have rallied to the idea of a World Court unless it was certain that among the judges of the court would be found one of the nationals of each of those States. Is it likely, for instance, that the citizens of the United States would have accepted a scheme for a court which might have jurisdiction to decide a matter affecting—let us say—the Monroe Doctrine, without some guarantee that among the judges there would be a citizen of the United States?

The second principle is that international law proclaims the doctrine of the equality of States; this doctrine is one of importance to States which are fearful of being bullied by neighbours of greater size and power. Perhaps the doctrine seemed to be of greater importance thirty years ago than it does to-day, but who can wonder that in 1907 voices were raised in the Conference at The Hague to the effect that though it was quite reasonable that the Great Powers should always be represented, the principle of equality must also be allowed to operate, and this rendered it essential that the other Powers should be represented on the same footing.

Unfortunately, there were forty-four States represented at the Second Peace Conference and the prospect of a court comprising forty-four judges did not appeal to Western minds. The rule of unanimity prevails in diplomatic conferences and the result was that no convention for setting up the Court of Arbitral Justice was ever signed.

III. The Hague Court of Justice

So matters stood for the next few years, but the conviction was growing all the time in thoughtful and progressive circles that something in the way of a court must be set up if the reign of law was to be established in the world. Consequently, when schemes for the creation of a League of Nations were prepared as part of the peace settlement after the First World War, provision was made for the establishment of a court. The Covenant of the League (Article 14) lays down that the Council of the League shall formulate and submit to members of the League for adoption plans for the establishment of a Permanent Court of International Justice. No attempt was made to elaborate the details of the scheme in the Covenant: the duty was merely imposed on the proposed Council of the League of formulating a plan.

It may well be asked why it was assumed that it should then be possible to do what had proved impossible fifteen years before. The answer is that many things are possible in the peace settlement at the close of a World War which may not have proved possible at other times. The influence of the Great Powers is greater after a war in which it is they who have borne the burden and carried the war through to a successful conclusion. It was not unreasonable to assume that as part of the peace settlement which was being effected a scheme could be evolved which would command universal acceptance.

In 1920 the Council of the League set up a committee of jurists to elaborate a plan for the proposed world court. This committee was international in character; it consisted of ten men drawn from different countries, but it was dominated by the personalities of Mr. Elihu Root, the ex-Secretary of State of the United States, and Lord Phillimore, formerly a Judge of the High Court of Justice in the United Kingdom. It is to those two men that the ingenious plan was due which got over the difficulties as to the choice of judges in face of which the scheme of 1907 had had to be laid aside.

To comprehend the idea which they put forward it must be remembered that the Covenant of the League of Nations provided for setting up two bodies—the Assembly of the League, and the Council of the League. The first included representatives of all the States which belonged to the League—great and small alike; the second was to be more in the nature of an executive body—restricted in numbers and one in which it was assumed that the voice of the Great Powers would predominate: for each of them was given permanent representation and between them they were intended to constitute, and did at first constitute, a majority.

The point on which the 1907 plan for a Court of Arbitral Justice broke down was the difficulty of harmonizing the interests of the Great Powers with their world-wide interests and the interests of the smaller Powers with their belief that their safety would be imperilled if the legal doctrine of the equality of States was ignored.

The Root-Phillimore idea combined these two divergent interests by providing for simultaneous but wholly independent election of the judges of the court by the Assembly and by the Council. The list of candidates for election to the Court was placed before each: the Assembly elected men sufficient to fill all the vacant places, the entire court if all the places were vacant; the Council did the same. Only those who were successful in both the Assembly election and the Council election became judges of the court. Election by one body and not by the other was nugatory. At the end of the first ballot the two bodies compared notes, and where the results coincided the election was complete; where it did not, the places were still vacant, and a second ballot, and if necessary a third, had to take place. If, at the end of the third, there were still any vacant places, a new machinery came into play. A joint committee composed of representatives of the Assembly and the Council was set up, and this committee proposed to the Council and the Assembly respectively the names of sufficient candidates to fill the remaining places.

Cumbersome though this plan may sound on paper, it has worked well in practice. As often as not individual vacancies have been filled on the first ballot; and even when the entire court has had to be elected the three ballots have usually been adequate to provide for the election of all the members. Only once has it been necessary to set up the Joint Committee to propose a candidate, and that was at the very first election in 1921.

A permanent home for the court was already available in the magnificent Peace Palace which had been erected at The Hague for the Permanent Court of Arbitration through the generosity of Mr. Andrew Carnegie shortly before the last war on a site provided by the Government of the Netherlands. The committee of jurists which worked out the draft statute of the court recommended that the court should be set up at The Hague, where the committee had itself done its work. This suggestion was felt by the Assembly of the League to be appropriate and was unanimously adopted.

The election of the judges in 1921 enabled the court to come into being. It was formally opened in January 1922 and functioned as and when required from that date up to the moment when the invasion of Holland in 1941 rendered further sittings impossible. Theoretically the court is still in being, for though the mandates of the existing judges should have expired and their successors have been elected in 1939, it was impossible to hold an Assembly at Geneva at that date, and reliance had therefore to be placed on the provision in the statute that judges of the court retain their places until their successors are appointed.

IV. THE WORK OF THE COURT

The work done by the court is greater in volume than most people realize. In the first ten years of its existence the court held twenty-four sessions and gave judgments in sixteen disputes submitted by States. It also rendered decisions in the form of advisory opinions in twenty-two cases referred to it by the Council of the League of Nations. In the next eight years the work of the court was rather less in bulk. The political situation in Europe was deteriorating. The Nazis came into power in

Germany. German cases were withdrawn from the court and the tide began to set against the submission even of justiciable cases to the decision of the court.

It is not easy to appraise the importance of the work done by the court in the maintenance of peace. Two cases stand out prominently in its history as occasions when its decisions have calmed public opinion at a moment when that opinion was becoming so inflamed as to endanger those "good understandings between nations upon which peace depends," even if not peace itself.

The first was the Tunis-Morocco dispute between France and the United Kingdom in 1921 about the bestowal of French nationality on the British subjects living in Morocco so as to render them liable to French military service. Morocco was only a French Protectorate; it was not French territory; and the British Government resisted France's claim to incorporate in the French military forces men who were and remained British subjects. France, on the other hand, claimed that the matter was one which by international law was solely within her domestic jurisdiction and as such not a matter in which other States could interfere. The dispute became acute when individual British subjects who had failed to respond to the call to the colours were arrested and marched through the streets in custody. After the Government of the United Kingdom had brought the matter before the Council of the League an agreement was reached to ask the Court whether or not the French action was a matter solely within the domestic jurisdiction of France. The court's decision that it was not led up to an amicable agreement between the two countries which brought the dispute to an end. The tension was so acute between the two governments at the time that, if a solution had not been found, relations between the two countries would have been seriously impaired. Without the court's decision on the legal issues involved, it is difficult to see how matters could have been adjusted.

The second case was that relating to the sovereignty over Eastern Greenland in 1931. Greenland is a vast area which Denmark regarded as a Danish colony, and as subject, *in toto,* to Danish sovereignty. Greenland is almost all ice-bound, with only a coastal fringe capable of supporting human life. Norway claimed that the area outside the settlements was *terra nullius,* and proceeded to take steps to appropriate it for the benefit of Norwegian trappers and hunters. Fortunately, both countries had accepted the compulsory jurisdiction of the court, and Denmark set the court's jurisdiction in motion accordingly. She won her case after a forensic battle of some magnitude and Norway accepted the decision without question.

Neither Denmark nor Norway can be regarded as Powers of such importance that an armed struggle between them would have initiated a world-wide conflagration; but to the peoples of the countries concerned the maintenance of peace is equally important whether they belong to a mighty nation or to a small one. Nor is it easy to conceive any proceeding more likely to inflame public opinion than a violation by another State of what a country believes to be its national territory.

As compared with the two outstanding disputes mentioned above, the greater part of the court's work has consisted of deciding cases which attracted little public attention, though no doubt they related to disputes which it was all to the good to get settled.

On the other hand it must be admitted that the court's decision on the question submitted to it by the Council of the League in 1931, as to the legality of the *Anschluss*—the customs union between Germany and Austria—did nothing to help the cause of peace.

This episode in the court's history is dealt with later on. Its importance lies in the light which it sheds on the necessary limitations of the functions of an international Court of Justice. The court was struggling to deal with a political issue which should never have been referred to it.

V. THE SELECTION OF JUDGES

When first set up in 1921 the court consisted of eleven judges and four deputy judges. In 1931 the deputy judges were abolished and the number of judges increased to fifteen.

This number is too large. If the court is to play its proper part in the post-war world the number of judges should be reduced.

Compare it with the final courts of appeal in the Anglo-Saxon countries of to-day. The normal composition of the House of Lords when sitting for judicial business is five. The number of the judges in the Supreme Court of the United States is nine, but in that court if there is a vacancy or if a judge is ill or absent, his seat remains empty; no deputy takes his place.

The larger the number of judges in a court, the more there is a tendency to weaken the sense of individual judicial responsibility on the part of the various members. One must admit that on the Continent of Europe there are many instances where the number of judges in a final court of appeal is larger. The Chambers of the *Cour de Cassation* in France, for instance, comprise a President and fifteen judges, but abroad there may have been other difficulties of which account had to be taken, and there it may be wise to adhere to larger courts.

If the International Court is to command confidence in the Anglo-Saxon mind the number of judges should not exceed that to which the peoples of the Anglo-Saxon world are accustomed in their own final courts of appeal. The figure of nine which prevails in the Supreme Court of the United States should not be exceeded. Nor should the class of deputy judges be revived in the court at The Hague. Their existence in the early years of the court led to an unexpected and somewhat unfortunate result.

The climate of The Hague is trying in the winter. Some of the judges came from hot countries and found themselves unable to attend when a session of the court was held in the winter months. This led to deputy judges taking their places almost as a matter of course during part of the year, with the result that the idea began to grow up that the composition of the court varied with the season of the year at which it was convoked, an idea most prejudicial to its permanence and uniformity.

Even if the number of regular judges were limited to nine, the court must occasionally sit with more. This is due to the necessity of providing for what are known as national judges. These are appointed for the purpose of taking part in the hearing of a particular case in which a State is a party which has no national among the regular judges of the court. In such a case a State is allowed to appoint one of its nationals as a judge for that case. He sits and acts on exactly the same footing as the regular judges of the court.

Ardent supporters of the movement for a World Court have in the past questioned the need for having these national judges, but the feeling has prevailed that they were a necessity and must be provided for. So long as a court has to rely largely on public opinion and on the political instincts of the people for its support, national feelings must be taken into account. Is it likely that for some time to come the peoples of democratic countries would allow their governments to accept obligations requiring disputes involving what they might feel were issues of vital importance to the country to be submitted to a tribunal in which no national of the country sat as a judge?

There is also a feeling that it may be helpful to the judges to be able to get from one of their own number, and not merely from the arguments of Counsel, an understanding of the background of the dispute.

Another possibility to be reckoned with is that the case before the court may be a dispute between two States of which one has, and the other has not, a national among the regular judges. Equality must be obtained in such cases. The man in the street would never believe that his country got a fair deal if there was no judge from his own country, but there was one from the other. It is not likely that any proposal to abandon the rule allowing the appointment of a national judge where necessary would meet with general acceptance. In considering therefore what is the best figure for the number of regular judges in the court, account must be taken of the fact that the court may have to sit in particular cases with two judges more than the adopted figure.

At the time when the number of judges was raised from eleven to fifteen and the deputy judges were abolished, the idea was prevalent at Geneva that the work of the court was increasing steadily and would tend to increase still faster. It was a time when the more important powers in Europe were accepting the compulsory jurisdiction of the court— that is to say, they were accepting the obligations embodied in a separate protocol, dating from 1921, ancillary to the statute of the court, enabling any State to bring before the court unilaterally a dispute on a matter of international law or treaty obligation. The effect of this is to enable one State to cite another State before the court without obtaining the latter's consent in each particular case. It puts the court on a level with national tribunals. It was generally supposed that the more general acceptance of the compulsory jurisdiction would result in a substantial increase in the volume of international litigation before the court, and therefore it was considered expedient to make the number of judges large enough to enable the court to sit in panels. No such increase in the volume of work has occurred and at present there seems to be no need to contemplate a division of the court into panels.

VI. ADVISORY FUNCTION OF THE COURT

Article 14 of the Covenant of the League as to preparing plans for setting up the court stipulated that in addition to its competence to determine disputes submitted to it by the parties, the court might give advisory opinions upon any dispute or question referred to it by the Council or by the Assembly.

One of the points for consideration in connection with the future of the court is whether it will be expedient to maintain the jurisdiction to deal with matters on an advisory basis.

There is no doubt that the existence of this branch of its work has been a stumbling block to many people. The lawyer finds it difficult to reconcile his ideas about the nature of the work of a court of justice with the rendering of opinions upon an advisory basis. The business of a court is to decide cases, not to give opinions to executive bodies which are not themselves parties to a dispute and which have no power to enforce compliance with the opinion when it has been received. In the United States particularly, this jurisdiction to give advisory opinions has been looked at askance. It was widely thought there that these advisory opinions would be regarded as laying down the law like a judicial decision, and that the United States might be prejudiced by the decision without having had the opportunity of being heard when the case was under consideration, and without the benefit of the provision in the statute that the decision of the court, in a disputed case, has no binding force except between the parties and in respect of that particular case.

There are good arguments for and against the retention of the faculty for the court to give advisory opinions. If a change is made, it should be in the direction of restricting the right to ask for such opinions rather than of abolishing it.

Both the Council and the Assembly of the League can nominate committees of lawyers to give opinions on questions before them. There is no paramount need therefore for these bodies to be able to set the court in motion. The lawyers appointed to serve on such committees can be as eminent as the circumstances of the case require, and the procedure of an *ad hoc* committee set up in this way will always be more rapid than the procedure of the court.

Still more unreasonable is it to give the Council and the Assembly the exclusive right to ask for advisory opinions. Many of those given by the court in the past have related to the work of the International Labour Office, yet neither the Governing Body of the Labour Office nor the International Labour Conferences are given the right to ask the court for an advisory opinion. The request must come from or through the organs of the League.

In practice the court has carried out its duties in connection with advisory opinions in precisely the same way as it has done in cases submitted to it by a litigant State. The procedure is to all intents and purposes identical. There is therefore but little substance in the criticisms against the advisory jurisdiction made by the lawyers. They are apt to forget that the Act of Parliament which set up the Judicial Committee of the Privy Council in 1833 gave the Government of the United Kingdom the right to refer a question to the Privy Council in a similar way.

The existence and the occasional exercise of this power by His Majesty's Government has certainly not weakened the Privy Council. Within similar limits, it will probably be wise to retain a right to set the court in motion in order to obtain an advisory opinion.

It is sometimes said that it is unnecessary to provide advisory opinions because, if a judicial decision is wanted, it is always possible to arrange a test case, and to obtain a decision this way. In the international sphere this argument is not sound. The last occasion upon which an opinion was rendered by the Privy Council shows how useful this method of obtaining a judicial decision may be—for advisory opinions by the Court are, in fact, judicial decisions.

The case was that of the boundary between Canada and Newfoundland. It involved the control over Labrador, and the decision of the Privy Council awarded it to Newfoundland.

A test case has to be arranged between the parties, and must be founded on some act involving the infringement, or the alleged infringement, of a right. In a boundary dispute, such as the Labrador case, this would mean some violation of the territorial integrity of the State concerned. Once that has occurred, it would be difficult to avoid a clash of forces. Long before the decision of the court has been reached, the parties might be at war.

The power to give an advisory opinion in such cases renders the court as flexible an instrument for securing a peaceful settlement of a territorial dispute as arbitration. Certainly international arbitration rendered a service to the cause of peace in disputes such as those relating to the Alaska and Venezuela boundaries. The same may be said of the decision of the Permanent Court of International Justice in the advisory opinion rendered in the case of the boundary between Albania and Jugoslavia, relating to the monastery of St. Naoun. It is difficult to see how a test case could have been arranged satisfactorily which would have solved any of these disputes.

On the whole there seems to be a good case for retaining the power to call upon the court to render an advisory opinion, but it will probably be expedient to restrict it to disputes between States and to give the right to call for such opinions only to governments.

VII. The Procedure of the Court

The idea prevails in some quarters that it takes the court at The Hague an unconscionable amount of time to decide a case and that its procedure is unwarrantably cumbersome and slow. That the court works slowly must be admitted, but as a criticism the allegation is unjustified. The court's procedure is bound to be slow.

There is first of all the difficulty that arises from the fact that the judges are all of different nationalities, different languages, different upbringings. Their legal trainings have necessarily been diverse. Getting down to a common basis of understanding on the case before them is therefore bound to be a long process, and the output of decisions, even if the sessions of the court were continuous, would necessarily be smaller than in a national tribunal.

Another consideration is that the court must not only do its work with a single-minded desire to do justice to the States which are litigants before it, but it must be known to be doing so. It has not got the long periods of tradition behind it that a national court possesses. Even if in the future organization of the world some machinery is created for enforcing compliance with the decisions of the court, it will be on public opinion that for a long time to come the court will have to rely for its support. If public opinion is to support the court, the world at large must feel sure that meticulous care is taken in arriving at the decisions.

The criticism that the court is unduly slow over its work probably emanates from people who do not know its method of work. It may be well to describe it.

The statute of the court prescribes that in each case there shall be written and oral proceedings. When the written proceedings are completed, a day is appointed for the hearing of the oral arguments. They usually last more than a day, so it is really the day for the opening of the oral arguments. When the oral arguments are concluded the shorthand notes are circulated to each of the judges. A meeting is then held at which each of the judges in turn expresses orally a preliminary opinion on the merits of the contentions of the parties. In the light of this preliminary discussion each of the judges prepares and hands in a written note giving at length what he considers should be the judgment of the court. These notes are circulated for all the other members to read, and after studying their contents the President prepares and distributes a paper containing a series of questions covering every point which is germane to the final decision and on which therefore the court must make up its mind. The judges then meet again and in a more formal deliberation take decisions on every question formulated by the President and also on any other point which one of the judges may wish to raise. At the end of this deliberation the court elects by secret ballot a drafting committee and this committee prepares a draft judgment. The text is circulated and amendments may be proposed. The drafting committee is then given the opportunity to revise its draft, and when this has been done the text is again circulated to all the judges. After adoption in second reading, time is given to any judges who feel unable to accept the decision to write their dissenting opinions. These again are circulated and are considered by the drafting committee. If no alterations are thought to be necessary in the text the judgment is submitted to a meeting of the court for final adoption, and when passed a day is appointed, the parties are summoned and the judgment is read in open court.

Described in detail, the procedure may sound cumbersome, but if the prestige and the reputation of the court are to be maintained, it would be unwise to cut it down.

The peoples of the litigant countries must be in a position to know that every possible consideration has been given to the contentions put forward on their behalf. They must know also that no attempt is made by the judges who are nationals of the more important States to steamroller their colleagues, and above all that in the case of national judges appointed to take part in a particular case, they are treated on exactly the same footing as the full members of the court.

It is for similar reasons that the court has never attempted to curtail the length of the oral arguments, even though sorely tempted to do so in cases where for days together it may have been obliged to listen to speeches which did not seem to be either relevant or useful. One or other of the States in litigation before it has to go away defeated, and it would not render it easier for the defeated State to accept the decision if it could be said that its Counsel had not been allowed to put forward in full the arguments he desired to address to the court.

It must also be remembered that the language difficulty complicates the work of the court. The statute prescribes that English and French are the two official languages. Other languages can be used only by consent and, if used, are interpreted into one of the official languages and the interpretation becomes the official text of which alone the court takes cognizance. This means that only four of the fifty States which are parties to the protocol bringing the statute of the court into force can address the court in their own language.

As between the two official languages everything submitted to the court in one of them, whether orally or in writing, must be translated into the other for the benefit of judges more familiar with the latter than with the former. Interpreters must also be available for the private deliberations of the judges.

It is true that the parties to a case are given the right to agree that one or other of the two official languages shall be exclusively used in a case. Such an agreement, however, can only apply to the arguments; it does not affect the work of the judges.

Such conditions do not and cannot make for speed. The language difficulty must be a problem in an international court. Perhaps some improvement may be found if in the future peace settlement any changes are made in the statute of the court.

VIII. Suggested Amendments

That steps should be taken to introduce into the statute the amendments which experience shows to be desirable is clear. The future peace settlement will afford a good opportunity of doing so. The invasion of Holland has interrupted the work of the court, the mandates of the existing judges have expired and a new election of judges must be made. Owing to death and resignations, there are now three vacancies in the court.

Caution, however, is necessary. Ill-considered changes may do more harm than good. As regards the functioning of the court, it is only a very partial revision of the statute in the light of the experience of the last two decades that is wanted.

The desirability of reducing the number of judges has been urged in the earlier part of this chapter. It may be useful to indicate some other amendments of the statute which it might be well to make at the same time.

The clause which stipulates that every nine years all the members should go out of office should disappear. It destroys continuity in the court. Only in the exceptional case of the re-election of a judge is there any element in the court left to carry on the tradition of the experience gained in its previous working. The system adopted in the abortive scheme of 1907 was much better. There every judge was elected for a fixed period—twelve years under that scheme—and when an exceptional vacancy occurred, owing to death or resignation, the successor was elected for the full twelve years' period. Under the statute now in force a successor to a judge who has died or retired is only elected for the remainder of his predecessor's term. When once a man has been chosen as a judge, attendance at the sessions of the court should be a matter of course. Illnesses are inevitable, but no one should be given, or should retain, the appointment unless he is young enough and strong enough to stand the climate of the country where the court is established.

Election for a definite period, whether it is twelve years or nine years is immaterial, eliminates any difficulty as to fixing an age limit for the judges. It must rest with the electors to bear in mind that no one should be appointed unless there is reasonable expectation that he will be able to carry out his duties throughout the period for which he is elected.

The nomination of candidates for election as judges should be taken out of the hands of the national groups in the Permanent Court of Arbitration. The nomination should be made by governments. It is the governments which are really interested in getting the best men to serve in the court. If the Permanent Court of Arbitration disappears, as it well might do now, for it has served its purpose, the choice of candidates for the court must necessarily be made in some other way, and the natural course would be to impose the duty on the governments.

A matter requiring very careful consideration will be that of the extent to which the connection between the court and the League of Nations should be maintained. The plan for establishing the court prepared by the committee of jurists in 1921 made it a part of the organization of the League. Like the International Labour Office the court became an autonomous organ of the League. Election of the judges by the Assembly and by the Council, in accordance with the Root-Phillimore scheme, accentuated the intimate relations between the two. The court's budget was to form part of the budget of the League, and the practice has always been for the budget, after being approved by the League's financial commission of control, to be submitted to and passed by the Assembly. Similarly the staff of the court has been made interchangeable with the secretariat of the League, and its members are subject to similar terms and conditions of employment.

In the first few years of the existence of the League and the court the intimate connection between the two seemed natural enough. Of late a doubt has been growing up as to whether from the court's point of view the disadvantages did not outweigh the benefits. However much it incorporates the existing structure of the League of Nations, the postwar organization for the maintenance of peace and for ensuring collective security cannot hope, at any rate in the early years, to embrace all the States of the world. Some must and will be left out. So long as the organization is not universal it cannot constitute convenient machinery either for providing for the budget of a World Court, or for effecting the choice of the judges.

The tendency in the years before the outbreak of the present war for States to discontinue their membership of the League led to the financial burden of the upkeep of the court being borne by a steadily diminishing company. The result was unfortunate from every point of view. The budget of the court has always seemed heavy, if not excessive, to the financial authorities, and as the number of contributors grew less, the burden grew greater. It seemed unjust, too. The States which had withdrawn from the League still got as much benefit from the court as before. The court was open to them on the same footing as to members of the League. They could still bring their disputes before it if they so desired. They could still be subject to its compulsory jurisdiction and be brought before it by unilateral action on the part of other States because the Optional Clause (the special protocol provided for in Article 36 of the statute by which a State accepted the compulsory jurisdiction of the court) contained no stipulation enabling a signatory to withdraw. Again, judges who were nationals of a State which withdrew from the League were not affected thereby and continued to draw the emoluments derived from the contributions of other States. Where a State had withdrawn from the League because it was against the policy for which the League stood, the position of a judge who was a national of that State became anomalous; either he would be opposed to the policy of his own country, and thereby would cease to represent any connection between his own country and the court, or he would become a potential element of discord in the court.

On the other hand, States which had ceased to be members of the League, but which had ratified the protocol establishing the court, claimed to participate in the election of judges.

All of these were matters of inconvenience and some of them seemed to require adjustment. Accordingly arrangements were made at Geneva during the last few years before the outbreak of the war so as to enable States which were not members of the League to participate in the election of judges both in the Assembly and in the Council. They were given the right to send a delegate to sit with the other members and take part in the election on the same footing, but nothing could be done as regards contributing towards the expenses of the court except on a voluntary basis.

In the hope that the United States would become a party to the protocol setting up the court, a special agreement was negotiated in 1929 dealing with the points which were supposed to be the obstacles to the accession of the United States, but ratification of this agreement was refused by the Senate, and the United States still remains outside the list of States which are parties to the court's statute. Assuming that the co-operation of the U.S.A. in the post-war settlement is obtained, the opportunity should present itself of adjusting the difficulties resulting from the existing connection between the court as a World Court and a League which is not universal.

IX. LIMITATIONS OF A WORLD COURT

There remains the question: How much can a World Court do in achieving the preservation of peace? No one will deny that it can do something, but there are limits as to what a court can achieve, and this fact should be clearly recognized.

The court is not, and cannot be, more than a court of justice: it cannot by itself, however successful in its operations, achieve the permanent preservation of peace. To expect it to do so would be as absurd as to expect the national courts of justice to ensure industrial peace and to prevent workmen from ever going out on strike.

The business of a court of justice is to solve issues between parties by the application of a rule of law, to decide issues which are known as justiciable, that is to say which can be solved by the application of a rule of law. If they are not justiciable, they lie beyond the sphere in which a court of justice can operate usefully.

Unfortunately, the delusion is widespread that the field in which the court can operate is universal.

This mistake is partly due to the language employed in Article 14 of the Covenant, which said that the court was to be competent to hear and determine *any* dispute of an international character which the parties might submit to it.

It is not only the man in the street who makes the mistake of thinking that the court's competence is as wide as the desires of the parties. The French and the Swiss governments fell into the same error in the special agreement by which they submitted to the court their dispute about the Free Zones of Gex and Savoy.

These Free Zones were created after the Napoleonic Wars. By 1920 they had become an anachronism and a burden to France. The negotiations between the two States for the introduction of a new régime made no satisfactory progress, and ultimately France by unilateral action imposed her customs tariff at the Swiss boundary of the Free Zones, and included them in her general customs area. Switzerland challenged her right to do so, and the parties agreed to submit the dispute to the court. The special agreement between them provided that if the court held the French action to be unjustifiable, and if the parties could come to no satisfactory agreement, the court was to indicate the arrangements which should replace the régime which France had swept away. It was agreed that the *status quo ante* could not be restored, that some more up-to-date arrangement was wanted and the court was to prescribe what it should be. In effect the court was given the task of elaborating a new customs tariff. Mr. Kellogg, who was then a member of the court, annexed to the court's decision a special opinion emphasizing the limitations on the court's functions resulting from the fact that it was a court of justice, and as such could not deal with political questions; as he pointed out, the making of a tariff is a purely political function.

Given that the all-important question is the preservation of peace, it is well to remember that few of the aggressive wars which have disturbed the peace of the world in the last century found their veritable origin in an issue which a court of justice could have solved. The Franco-German war of 1870 is a good instance of this. Even assuming that it was Germany that was bent on aggression, there was nothing contrary to international law in her refusing to give France a general pledge that the King of Prussia would never allow a German candidate to become sovereign of Spain. It was her refusal to give this pledge which was made the pretext by France for a declaration of war. What help could the decision of an international court of justice have given to the preservation of peace on that occasion? If the issue had been submitted to a tribunal, it would have been Prussia, not France, who would have won her case.

The same lesson is to be learned from the reference to the Court by the Council of the League in 1931 of the difficulty that had arisen over the contemplated Customs Union between Germany and Austria.

In March 1930, Germany and Austria concluded a protocol by which they agreed to negotiate for the assimilation of their tariff and economic policies. The independence of Austria under the peace settlement of 1919 was to be inalienable without the consent of the Council of the League of Nations, and France, at a meeting of that body, attacked the legality of the Austro-German protocol. The Council of the League sought the help of the court, and requested an advisory opinion as to whether this instrument would be compatible with the Treaty of St. Germain, by which Austria had agreed to abstain from any act which might compromise her independence. Germany had already agreed in the Treaty of Versailles to respect the independence of Austria.

Customs Unions, such for example as that between Belgium and Luxembourg, had been concluded without imperilling the independence of either party, and yet there was an instinctive realization by everyone who studied the foreign affairs of Europe that the proposed Customs Union between Germany and Austria would be the jumping-off ground by the former for further measures for the absorption of the smaller country. Yet the objections to it were political more than legal.

The court was hopelessly divided. By the narrowest possible majority it held that the proposed arrangement was inconsistent with the treaty stipulations by which Austria was bound.

It was a decision that injured the reputation of the court, for it was generally regarded as a political decision: but the lesson to be learned from it is that the Council of the League should never have referred the matter to the court at all. It should have been clear to that body that the question was political and not legal, and therefore not one for the court.

The moral is obvious. A court of international justice cannot solve political problems.

Another reason for strengthening the court in every possible way is that the world is certainly moving in the direction of the general acceptance of the idea that States must be willing to subject themselves to the compulsory jurisdiction of the court in regard to disputes which are genuinely justiciable in character, disputes in which the parties are in conflict as to their respective legal rights. It is true that the present war has necessitated, on the part of the United Kingdom, a partial withdrawal from the acceptance of this compulsory jurisdiction, which she gave in 1929, but this is only a temporary set-back. In the post-war world different considerations will apply. The greater the need and the desire for substituting the reign of law for the reign of force, the greater will be the need for making the machinery for eliminating disputes run smoothly.

It may yet be a long while before the acceptance of the compulsory jurisdiction becomes universal, but come it will. There is something hollow and unreal about admitting the need for a court to settle international disputes and, at the same time, refusing to accept its jurisdiction except by consent on each occasion. It is a very human attitude, of course, and, for democratic countries where governments have to bear in mind the public opinion of their peoples, is not to be wondered at. Adverse decisions by the court must always be reckoned with as a possibility, and might be inconvenient, but they should not be allowed to constitute a bogey in the path of international progress.

Such is the tale of the Permanent Court of International Justice at The Hague.

To play the part in the post-war world which the court ought to play necessitates the fulfilment of two conditions: The court must be qualified to do its work properly; the world at large must have confidence in it.

There can be no such confidence in the court unless there is general understanding of the work that the court is doing and can do. It is for that reason that public interest in the court should be stimulated.

That the court should be qualified to do its work properly depends on others and not upon itself. It depends, first and foremost, on the choice of the right men to be judges in the courts. It depends, secondly, on putting the judges to work in conditions that will facilitate the successful execution of their task.

In the maintenance and upholding of the court in the post-war world will be found abundant scope for co-operation between the British Commonwealth of Nations and the United States, and not between them alone, but between all the United Nations.

XI THE SOCIAL SERVICES OF BRITAIN

By Megan Lloyd George

———◆———

1. Phases of Development

WE ARE NOT unnaturally, I think, proud in this country of our Social
Services. This vast organization built up in the course of centuries by the
united efforts of the philanthropist, the social reformer, and the politician, is a combination of individual and State effort. The foundations of
this great rambling edifice were laid in the days of Queen Elizabeth,
and were designed only to meet the needs of a purely agricultural community. As early as 1601, the needs of the poor were for the first time
recognized as the concern of the community, and not merely the responsibility of religious and charitable bodies. The simple and charming
Almshouses in villages and towns all over the country are an enduring
testimony to the first awakening of the social conscience of the nation in
this matter. The Poor Law of 1601 replaced the churches' control of
charity by the Municipality and Parish overseers. It made a distinction
for the first time between the vagrant and the "poor in very deed"; it
made provision also for work for the workless. Side by side with the acceptance by the community of this new responsibility, there were always
the humanitarian efforts of the individual, and of charitable organizations. In the countryside, there was the "lady bountiful"—sometimes a
woman possessed of genuine human sympathy who devoted most of her
time to good works and the relief of distress in her neighbourhood.
They were not all made, however, in that mould. There was the lady of
the manor who drove round in her carriage to distribute largesse and

"to dispense" charity. It is said that one old woman to whom the footman on his mistress's behalf had handed a loaf of bread, curtseyed, and said in her gratitude: "Bless you, milady, we shall meet in Heaven." "Drive on, John," said the lady of the manor, scandalized at the presumption. Charity was all very well—but social intercourse, even under such circumstances, was not to be thought of for a moment. There was also the patronizing and benevolent tyrant. Jane Austen epitomized the type, for all time, in the masterly drawing of the Lady Catherine de Bourgh: "Whenever any of the cottagers were disposed to be quarrelsome, discontented, or too poor, she sallied forth into the village to settle their differences; silence their complaints; and scold them into harmony and plenty."

The second phase in the development of our Social Services began with the gradual transformation of Britain into an industrial community, creating new conditions, resulting in new abuses. The industrial revolution became an all-absorbing process. Everything had to give way before it. The making of wealth, and that quickly, was the paramount consideration, and the worker was considered only as a means to that end. His remuneration, his conditions of work, the needs of his family, and the home in which he lived were of little concern. Science was harnessing all the forces of Nature and the mineral wealth of the nation to the production of a new and better prosperity; and all the time the conditions of the people were deteriorating at an alarming rate. The consequent evils were attacked by two sets of reformers—political and literary. The greatest among the first were Robert Owen, a cotton manufacturer, who strove for the health and education of the people, particularly the children, at his own mill; and Lord Shaftesbury, who fought and won some important victories in factory legislation in the political field. Amongst the men of letters were Charles Dickens and Charles Kingsley, who exposed the terrible conditions then prevailing.

The third period was initiated by the Education Act of 1870, which introduced National Education, and brought about a marked change in the outlook upon social reform. The new far-sighted reformers fighting a lone and uphill fight against ignorance, indifference, and the opposition of entrenched vested interests grew into an army of men and women possessed not only of vision and enthusiasm, but of the ability to frame and administer social legislation. The year 1908 saw the beginning of a social revolution in the attitude of the State towards the individual, who through misfortune, ill-health, old age, or unemployment found himself faced with the refuge only of the Poor Law, and what were virtually starvation conditions, when a Liberal Government carried a great succession of measures, beginning with the Old Age Pensions Act of 1908, and culminating in the National Health Acts of 1911. The passing into law of these bills involved also a constitutional crisis of the first magnitude which gave the House of Commons for the first time complete control of finance.

After the Great War the clearance of the slums and the rehousing of families in decent homes that conformed more properly to the standards of a civilized community became a matter of great urgency. Under the Coalition Government, for the first time the State subsidized on a large scale the housing of the people. This responsibility was extended under Labour and Conservative administrations. The rising tide of unemployment immediately after the war also made it necessary that adequate provision should be made for the maintenance of the unemployed, and a wider measure of insurance to provide for the large number of workless was passed, again by the Coalition Government. Successive governments extended these measures, and later a Conservative Government passed a bill to make provision for widows and orphans. In order to give some indication of the increase in the scale of these services in the last fifty years, it is interesting to note the difference between the amount of money spent by the State in 1891 and in the years immediately prior to this war. In 1891 the State expended on Social Services about £20 millions, and in 1900 £36 millions—sums which included Education, Health, Housing, Poor Law, and Lunacy; in 1910, with the addition of Old Age Pensions, they rose to £55 millions; by 1935–36 they had risen again to the annual sum of £500 millions. In all some thirty-five million people were covered.

This slow, natural, but sporadic evolution, so characteristic of British methods, has its advantages, but it also has its drawbacks. Like the old manor houses, such a distinctive feature of the English countryside, the original building of one period, a wing added at a later date, a second or third in yet another period—each part was admirable in its day, the whole making a harmonious pile, but unwieldy, cumbersome, and wasteful to manage. It became increasingly clear that a comprehensive scheme for the co-ordination and development of these Services under one national authority was essential. In 1941, therefore, Sir William Beveridge, at the request of the Government, made an investigation into the Social Insurance and Allied Services of the country. The report which he produced as a result of this exhaustive enquiry has been universally acclaimed as a valuable and historic document. It is certain that no proposals have been more discussed or have aroused greater interest in every section of the community. Sir William postulates that the five giants on the road of reconstruction that have to be faced and overcome are Disease, Ignorance, Squalor, Idleness and Want. He claims only to attempt to deal here with Want. It is to be done, he suggests, by insuring in one all-in Insurance Scheme, the whole population, man, woman, manual worker, black-coat worker, more adequately against the risks of ill-health, accident and unemployment, providing for their dependants —in the case of the death or incapacity of the breadwinner—by providing in addition a minimum income of £2 a week for man and wife, apart from the entirely new and important development of children's allowances. The main principles of the report have been accepted by the Government. It now remains to be seen whether the country and Parliament will insist upon the early implementation of the proposals. That, in brief, is an outline of the history of the Social Services of Britain.

II. THE FIVE GIANTS

(a) Want

The first primitive attempt to banish Want was, as I have said, the Poor Law of 1601. It was the beginning—albeit a miserably inadequate one—of State provision for social security. After that, for over 300 years, the relief of the destitute in the country was the responsibility of the local Poor Law Authorities. The first real breakaway from the Poor Law came with the passing of the Old Age Pensions Act by the Liberal Government of 1908. The fear that had haunted so many throughout their lives that, in old age, the only refuge open to them would be the workhouse—that the only alternative was that they should be an embarrassment and a burden to their children—embittered and overshadowed the lives of hundreds of thousands of honest and hard-working men and women.

Sir George Newman, for many years Chief Medical Officer of Health to the Board of Education, has said of this Act that "it brought inexpressible joy, comfort, and a sense of security to a million homes in England." There were no compulsory contributions under the Act. The State became responsible for providing pensions of from 1/- to 5/- a week at the age of 70—subject to a Means Test. The anxiety lest the granting of services of this kind should sap the initiative and discourage the thrifty instincts of the people was expressed in those days as it has been to-day about the Beveridge proposals. A responsible leader of opinion in those days—Lord Lansdowne—went so far as to say that he was much afraid that it would "weaken the moral fibre of the nation, and diminish the self-respect of the people." This was a few years only before the British people gave an example unequalled, perhaps even unrivalled in their history, of steadfast courage, endurance, and resolution. As for the suggestion that it would encourage improvidence, the very opposite has been the case, and the increased security gained has resulted in an enormous increase in the invested savings of the people.

In 1925, Mr. Winston Churchill, then Chancellor of the Exchequer, brought in the Widows, Orphans and Old Age Contributory Pensions Act. Old people who had been insured under the National Health Scheme became entitled to a 10/- weekly pension, if over 70 years of age; and, from 1928 onwards, each insured person on reaching the age of 65 could draw the pension. To-day, a woman receives the pension at the age of 60 if contributing, or when her husband reaches the age of 65, if not herself contributing. For old people who are not within the insurance scheme, there is a pension of ten shillings available at the age of 70, following a Means Test. Great hardships still existed. Due to the rising cost of living, there was much distress among pensioners, who were forced to turn to the Assistance Board for relief. Supplementary pensions were introduced in 1940 by the late Government to eke out the Widows and Old Age Pensions in case of need. They have removed the main cause of outdoor relief, but there are still a large number of old people on relief, mainly those who, as a result of not being insured, are forced to bridge the gap between 65 and 70 to qualify for the non-contributory pension. That is the situation to-day.

Before the war, when unemployment figures were stabilized at a high figure, there was a consensus of opinion in favour of Retirement Pensions in order to make way for the younger generation in industry. The Beveridge Report, on the other hand, stresses the fact that the population figures make it clear that in the near future "persons past the age of what is now regarded as the end of working life will be a much larger proportion of the whole community than at any time in the past." The report goes on to say that it is "therefore necessary to find ways of postponing the age of retirement of work rather than of hastening it." It adds that to give a full subsistence income in the future to every citizen on his or her reaching the age of 65 or 60 would impose an unjustifiable and harmful burden on all citizens below that age. Therefore Sir William suggests a transitional scheme, covering a period of 20 years (from 1945–65) when full Contributory Pensions will become payable at the rate of 40/- weekly for man and wife, or 24/- for a single person—with assistance pensions granted in the transitional period to ensure that no aged person is in want. Pensions proposed in the Beveridge Scheme are Retirement Pensions and *not* Old Age Pensions. Should a man or woman continue to work after reaching the age of 65 or 60, they would be entitled to have their pensions increased for each year of postponement.

(b) Disease and Idleness

The National Health and Unemployment Insurance Acts of 1911 constituted another revolutionary change in the Social Services of the country. Their objects were to provide for insurance against loss of health; for the prevention and cure of sickness; and for insurance against unemployment in a restricted number of industries. This last form of assistance was extended in 1920 to cover all industries with the exception of agriculture. Up to 1911, if a workman broke down in health or was unable to obtain work, he had nothing to fall back upon except Parish Relief, and that was nothing more than a miserable pittance. The probability was that, in the end, he and his family would be driven to the workhouse, and that was a prospect which the British workman with his sturdy independence loathed and abhorred with his whole being. A hundred years before, Charles Dickens in *Oliver Twist* had painted a grim and terrible picture of the workhouse, where paupers were treated not so much as human beings but as a race apart to be used and abused, and downtrodden; where children—little bags of skin and bones—were stoned, bullied shamelessly, and beaten to a sullen, soulless submissiveness. This powerful and remorseless revelation by Dickens did much to kill Bumbledom. And then came the Act of 1911. Under its provisions every man or woman over 16 years of age employed under contract in manual labour (non-manual was included for earnings which were less than £250 a year) must be insured against sickness or unemployment. They were to pay 4d. a week. The employers the same, and the State an additional sum. It was from this calculation that came the cry of the day: "Ninepence for fourpence." There were to be five medical benefits: free medical treatment, sickness, disablement, and maternity benefit;

with additional benefits that included amongst other things, dental, ophthalmic, convalescent homes, and surgical appliances.

This measure was at first received, as the Beveridge Report has been, with general approval, but as time went on, and the liabilities it imposed became clearer, the opposition developed and became both strident and strenuous. It became known among certain sections as "The Malingerer's Millennium."

My father, its author, was dubbed "a tyrant attempting to do what the worst of the kings in the darkest ages in British history failed to do." The doctors of the country united in resisting it. This was indeed a formidable challenge to meet, for they threatened at one moment to hold the whole country up to ransom; and if the measure were continued with, to go on strike. The challenge was accepted. The Chancellor of the Exchequer was equally resolved not to give way to "stand and deliver" threats of this kind, and he organized third- and fourth-year medical students in various parts of the country who undertook, if the strike were called, to maintain and carry on the medical services of the country. I remember well—although I was very young at the time—telegrams coming in, day by day, and hour by hour, announcing that the resistance of the branches of the British Medical Association in the great cities had been broken and that they were prepared to come in and work the scheme.

The other strenuous opposition outside Parliament came from the mistresses, who would be compelled under the new bill to insure their domestic servants and stick stamps upon the insurance cards. They said that they were being asked to become tax-gatherers. They vociferously resented the indignity and organized protest meetings all over the country, declaring that they would not co-operate. The Act brought the whole country within the State service of health. About 150,000 a week received benefit. But the scheme has proved its value not only in providing a health service for the people; it has had besides an educational value which has been incalculable. It established the Medical Research Council and Industrial Research Council, and led to the creation of the National Tuberculosis Organization, of Tuberculosis Officers, Dispensers, Sanatoria, Clinics and Hospitals. The establishment of the Ministry of Health in 1919 brought all these Services under one Government control and supervision; and in 1929 Mr. Neville Chamberlain transferred the care of the sick from the Guardians and placed them under the County Local Authorities. It is naturally difficult for me to say much about the part my father played in these years. I would like to quote, however, the words used by Mr. Churchill in a speech he delivered at the time. He was commenting on the fact that Germany had taken ten years to establish their system of Insurance: "We have stood looking at it for twenty years, and we should have been looking at it now, and making speeches about it, and shaking our heads over it, and appointing drowsy committees of inquiry, and dealing with mountains of musty blue-books, if one man had not come along." In all these controversies my father had the powerful support of the Prime Minister, Mr. Asquith, and a great body of radical opinion in the country who fought with him through thick and thin.

Another aspect of this problem of making provision against ill-health concerned the workman who was fatally injured in an accident and whose dependants were left unprovided for; or who was injured in such a way that he would not be able to carry on his occupation. The first measure to deal with this was passed in 1897. It is interesting to note here that this bill was drafted, not by legal experts, but by men of commerce, so that all the world might understand; and yet there is no Act of Parliament which, line for line, and word for word, has been the subject of so much litigation.

These Services have been extended by successive governments in successive acts. Sir William Beveridge proposes that Workmen's Compensation should be a part of the general security plans.

One of the most pressing and urgent problems which the new Ministry of Health had to face was the reduction in the rates of maternal and infantile mortality. Early in the nineteenth century, in spite of the efforts of social workers, the maternal death-rate had declined only 6 or 7 per thousand mothers. This figure remained tragically constant for a number of years—in spite of the splendid work done in voluntary provision for the care of expectant mothers, and babies and young children. It was not until 1918 that these Services were consolidated in the Maternity and Child Welfare Act, again the work of the Coalition Government. At the end of the last century 140,000 infants died each year. By 1940 that terrible national loss was reduced to 35,000 a year, which means that, whereas in 1900 there were 150 deaths per 1,000 births, in 1939 there were only 50. This remarkable result is a combination of the efforts of the mothers themselves, aided by skilled advice and State assistance. Pioneers like Robert Owen and Rachel McMillan had begun and developed the idea of the Nursery School, where children might be left under the care of trained personnel for the day. Welfare Committees were set up in each area; Crèches, Day Nurseries and Convalescent Homes were pushed forward. The employment of women within four weeks of childbirth in factories or workshops was prohibited.

Important developments have taken place within recent years in the supervision and care of the child in school. This School Medical Service has been described as one of the most far-reaching social reforms in history. It provides for a medical inspection of every child attending State schools. Children from 100,000 homes are examined throughout England and Wales by doctors and dentists, and school nurses. It is estimated that more than a quarter of a million defects require immediate treatment every year, which is provided by private practitioners, hospitals or school clinics. The crippled, the blind, the deaf or the mentally defective child have been cared for in special schools. Among the leaders of this particular form of rescue work was Sir Robert Jones—known as "Bone Jones," because of his marvellous skill as a surgeon. He was famed for the miraculous operations he performed on the mutilated and maimed in the last war, but his greatest work perhaps of all was in restoring the joints and muscles of children by massage manipulation.

There are no more tragic figures among all the toiling, suffering victims of the industrial revolution than those of the children compelled by the economic circumstances of their parents to earn their living and to work unbelievably long hours under indescribable conditions. Southey, speaking of labour in the factories, said: "Though the majority of the children employed were 9 years old and over, it is not uncommon to find in the mills children of 6 years of age. There were some under 7, and still more under 8." They worked often 15 or 16 hours a day. Punishment, such as sousing in water, was not infrequently used to keep the children awake. A gradual improvement in the hours was brought about in the first place by that great and courageous reformer—Lord Shaftesbury—who, against the opposition of powerful commercial interests, initiated a number of Factory Acts which regulated the hours and conditions of those unhappy children.

Parliament decreed in 1906 that children must not only be medically supervised but must also be fed, and so a scheme for meals at school was launched. It is generally agreed that it has been one of the most beneficial changes that we have seen in our time. Since the beginning of this war a scheme has been initiated which provides for a supply of free or cheap milk for every expectant mother, and child under 5. Where the joint income of the parents is not more than £2 per week, the milk is provided free. The latest available figures show that over three million expectant mothers, and children—that is, almost 90 per cent of those eligible, are benefiting under the scheme. Further, our Minister of Food, Lord Woolton, has followed an enlightened policy in this as in other respects, and has not only consulted doctors and scientific experts like Sir John Orr, but has followed their advice and carried it into practical effect. Two years ago he launched a scheme for the free distribution to expectant mothers and young children of fruit juices and cod liver oil— for which a small charge is made, except in necessitous cases.

Lastly, there are the Hospital Services of the country. They are divided into two, those maintained by private donations, and those by public funds. There is no doubt that the Voluntary Hospitals have rendered a great service to the community. In the past few years they have been facing a growing financial problem, and some adjustment in their management will have to be made. It is unlikely that public funds will be voted for their maintenance without some form of control and supervision being exercised—either by the Local Authorities, or the Ministry of Health. The Beveridge Report suggests closer co-operation and co-ordination between the two systems in order to secure a National Hospital Service.

(c) Ignorance

It would be quite impossible in a brief summary of this character to do more than outline here the history of the educational services in Britain. Up to the end of the nineteenth century, Education was either in the hands of the Church, or dependent upon the generosity of individual benefactors who endowed schools and colleges in both the ancient universities. The quality of the teaching was poor. The curriculum was restricted. Even science was not taught. The main study of the child was the dead languages of Greece and Rome. Dr. Arnold, the famous Headmaster of Rugby, the father of the modern public school system, said: "Rather than have physical science the principal thing in my son's mind, I would gladly have him think that the sun went round the earth, and that the stars were so many spangles set in the bright blue firmament." Such a restricted background was hardly likely to fit a man to earn his living in a hard, competitive world. Grammar schools were founded at an early date, and it was estimated that they covered 6,000 of the population. Winchester and Eton provided a few places "for the poor and indigent"; but in the main, until the Act of 1870, only a small fraction of the children of Britain received an education worthy of the name. That Act, and the Act of 1902—known as the Balfour Act— established a national system of Education. Children were compelled to attend. And now the Council Schools are instituted, and Education is practically free for the child without means. School and travelling fees are paid by the State, and meals are provided at a minimum cost for those who can afford to contribute; and free for necessitous children.

Welsh and Scottish Education have distinguishing features of their own. Mr. Kenneth Lindsay, in his book on English Education, says that "much virtue is attached to Scottish Education which in truth should be ascribed to the home and to the kirk." Wales, like Scotland, has found her main formative and educational influences on the hearth and in the Sunday school. Another remarkable feature in my country is that the universities were built, in the first place, by the pennies of the poor— although they are now assisted by grants from the State. Both countries have peculiar historical and traditional characteristics of their own which, if the variety that has contributed so much to the rich texture of British civilization is to be preserved, must be maintained in their integrity. To Wales this is a matter of even greater significance in one respect, for she has a language which is spoken as their mother tongue by close on a million people, and which is the key to a remarkable and beautiful literature.

It is an interesting fact that at the most critical moment in the Great War of 1914–18 when the military fortunes of the country were at perhaps their lowest ebb, the Government introduced a great Education Act which, although it has been on the Statute Book for over 20 years, has not yet been fully implemented. It was introduced by Mr. H. A. L. Fisher, one of the greatest figures of Education. It was an inspired declaration of purpose, enlarging the whole horizon and giving a new meaning and significance to Education. It provided for the raising of the school age, for compulsory Continuation Schools up to 18, and it brought hope and encouragement into the ranks of the teaching profession. The Act is still virtually a dead letter, but its spirit has inspired many changes. It was the leaven which produced a few loaves. Now the Government is considering, so we are told, a new and comprehensive Educational Policy. It is to be hoped that it will, in the main, carry on the Fisher tradition in its outline and in its practice. There are one or two issues which, if not properly handled, would revive old controversies and create new ones.

A question which is arousing considerable interest is the future of the public schools in England, such as Eton, Harrow, Winchester, Rugby. In spite of the fact that scholarship facilities are available for children of working-class parents, in the main these schools are regarded as the exclusive preserve of the upper, middle, and professional classes. On the credit side they have made a great contribution in various ways to British life. They do encourage qualities of self-reliance, loyalty, and a sense of responsibility, which are all vital qualities of leadership. They do lay great emphasis—more emphasis than on learning, the criticism sometimes is—upon the development of character. On the debit side, the public school exclusiveness fosters the class system and produces all too often that most obnoxious of all weeds—snobbishness. It is not enough to enlarge the entry to the public school so that more children of poorer parents could enter. It is also necessary to introduce a more democratic basis to the whole system.

(d) Squalor

The industrial revolution left us with a serious problem. The population had migrated and redistributed itself. The agricultural workers had surged into the cities. New towns were built in the vicinity of the factory, and hovels—for one can hardly dignify them by the name of houses—were built higgledy-piggledy, without thought for the health or the well-being of the workers who were to live in them. The health of the nation was naturally seriously affected by these terrible conditions, so that by the end of the last century and the beginning of this, the housing problem had become a formidable one indeed. Early legislation in this country was due to the initiative of individuals and progressive industrial towns. But there was no national attempt to tackle the housing of the nation; but as the relation between housing and public health became more recognized, other legislation followed, culminating in 1890 in the housing of the working classes. In spite of this, housing development generally was still left in the hands of private enterprise and the more progressive Councils. Under all these schemes the rents remained relatively high. The total number of houses built did not appreciably reduce the shortage. At the end of the Great War private enterprise was completely unable to cope with the acute housing shortage owing to economic circumstances, and the abnormally high building costs. The Coalition Government was therefore forced to step in with State subsidies. The 1919 Housing and Town Planning Act gave housing subsidies to Local Authorities, divided the country into regional areas, and appointed Housing Commissioners for each area—and further-more undertook a National Housing Survey. In 1930 the Labour Govern-ment brought in what was known as the Greenwood Act—a measure for housing and slum clearance under which the Local Authorities classified the number of houses unfit for habitation in urban and rural areas, and began their demolition and replacement. In addition there were measures designed to deal specially with the problem in the countryside, where the lower wages paid to workers on the soil necessitated a more generous subsidy. By 1938, 800,000 people had been transferred from slum areas to decent houses and overcrowding had been to a considerable extent relieved. Since the war we have, of course, been faced with a special problem—that of the repair and replacement of houses damaged in the Blitz. But over and above this there is a very considerable housing programme that was in process of being carried out, and which will have to be resumed and intensified when hostilities cease. Standards have changed and been raised even in the last two or three years, and we are all hoping that the new post-war houses will be very different from the pre-war ones; that they will be fitted with all the modern conveniences and amenities so that the housewife both in the town and the countryside will be able to have more leisure from her domestic duties.

Without decrying the work and vision of men and women of all parties and of none, in the field of social welfare, the Liberal Party has the proud and proved claim of being the chief influence in improving the general conditions of life in this country during the past hundred years. Liberalism emerged as a definite political party just over a century ago; during these hundred years Liberal governments held office ten times, covering in all some forty-nine years. During those forty-nine years it was Liberal governments who were responsible—among other social measures—for the first organized scheme of universal compulsory educa-tion, the earliest effective factory legislation, the chief Trade Union Acts, the first provision for Workmen's Compensation, Old Age Pensions, National Health Insurance, Unemployment Insurance, the first State guarantee of a minimum living wage. Each item is symbolic of the aims of Liberalism—liberty, more liberty, and liberty for more people; each new piece of legislation added something to the personal independence of the common people by breaking down ancient privileges and restrictions, and by creating new conditions which made freedom and self-reliance possible. Standing for the equal right of every citizen to personal liberty, Liberalism works to bring the practical affairs of the State—laws, administration and customs—into harmony with that principle.

XII WHAT THEY THINK OF EACH OTHER

A Mass-Observation Report

━━━━━◆━━━━━

1. THE COUSIN-COMPLEX

Mass-observation has made a study, throughout the last six years, of the feelings of the British public on the subject of the United States, and of differences between feelings about the American people and about American institutions. Any survey of present feelings on these subjects can best be interpreted against a historical background, and a brief summary of main trends up to 1941 is therefore given below.

The most significant feature emerging from the Mass-Observation data is that the Americans have never been looked upon wholly in the light of foreigners. This is no doubt to be accounted for by the fact that the two nations speak the same language, and it has had important effects upon the whole question of British feelings about the Americans.

It is generally held that the Americans are a people related to ourselves—distant cousins of a sort—and criticism of things in America has often been considerably more outspoken than might have been expected if this were not the case. Just as, in families, relations are often judged more critically than strangers, so the Americans have to a large extent been measured against what may be called a standard of British behaviour, whereas other nations have been judged against a standard of foreign behaviour, which, rightly or wrongly, is far less exacting.

President Roosevelt has always been popular in this country, and in the years leading up to the outbreak of the present war came to be regarded as one (if not the first) of the leaders of the opposition to

Fascism. A week before the Fall of France in June 1940, the President's historic speech attracted much notice in this country, and Roosevelt became more popular than ever.

Through the summer of 1940, a considerable body of opinion expected immediate American entry into the "shooting war," and, when this entry was not forthcoming, dissatisfaction began to make itself felt in some quarters. American aid to Britain at that time was not apparent to the so-called "man-in-the-street," and doubts began to be expressed as to whether the United States were really helping us as much as they could. As a part of what may be called the "cousin-complex," there has always been a tendency to credit the Americans with more talk than action, and this tendency was encouraged by what the average Englishman heard during the months of the Battle of Britain.

The news of the transfer of the fifty destroyers brought an immediate increase in confidence in the United States, although a minority pointed out that "the ships are out-of-date anyway, and we're giving up valuable bases for them." A further, and more marked, increase in confidence came with the news that both of the major candidates in the Presidential Election were strongly pro-Allied in their feelings. In spite, however, of the feeling that Willkie was as much anti-Nazi as Roosevelt, the latter's re-election brought with it a further increase in confidence in the part which the United States would play in the development of the war.

The feeling was often expressed, from this time right up to December 1941, that Roosevelt was ahead of Congressional opinion—indeed it was sometimes suggested that he was ahead of public opinion in any quarter. A belief grew that the President was very skilfully manœuvring the reactionaries and isolationists into a position in which they would, at some not very distant date, have no option but to endorse American entry into the war. In contrast to this, another minority continued to express the view that American aid was not what it might be, and that the Administration might reasonably be expected to move more quickly.

This latter point of view, however, was checked when the Lend-Lease agreements became law in April 1941. Criticisms that the Americans were trying to make money out of the war (as they were often accused of having done out of the last war) rapidly became no more than a very small minority attitude.

What little criticism of United States policy there was in the summer and autumn of 1941 was centred mainly on the allegation that American help was still not as great as it could, or should, be. It was recognized, however, that a very considerable amount of aid was by now being given, and, in fact, another minority held that more material was now being received from America than we should be able to expect if America were to enter the war on a shooting basis, as in that case her own war-needs would have to be given priority over the export programme.

II. AFTER PEARL HARBOUR

A profound change in public feelings about America was brought about by the Japanese attack on Pearl Harbour. The most important feature of the change was one which did not appear at first and became a really significant trend only some weeks later. This was the view that the Americans had been caught napping. The general opinion, before, had been that the Americans were supreme as regards efficiency when once they undertook a job, even if they might be rather over-given to much talking. It was a severe shock to the British public to find that the United States were apparently no more prepared in 1941 than we our-selves had been in 1939.

Satisfaction with the American war effort, through the early months of 1942, was very low—in a typical London count there were four people dissatisfied out of every nine questioned. Feelings about our own war effort were at the same time less favourable than at any other time of the war, and this feeling that our own conduct of the war was unsatisfactory may have been to a large extent responsible for the blame handed out to the Americans. This conclusion is confirmed by the fact that when, in the last week of February 1943, the American Forces suffered a reverse in central Tunisia, little or no anti-American feeling was expressed: the general attitude was rather that it was a good thing for the Americans to suffer a little reverse in Africa, as it would make them realize some of the difficulties with which the British are confronted. But matters would not have been taken in this way had the progress of events on other fronts also been unsatisfactory at the time.

Through the second half of 1942 confidence in the American war effort revived steadily, largely as a result of General MacArthur's defence of the Bataan peninsula and his organization of the Allied strategy in the south-western Pacific. General news-reactions became at the same time more cheerful than for many months, and the expected duration of the war began to decrease fairly rapidly. Thus the more favourable feelings about America were symptomatic of a general increase in cheerfulness.

The campaign in North Africa affected public opinion about the Americans less than might have been expected; and, while there is no doubt that people's views were to some extent modified by the American attitude towards Darlan, this modification was much smaller than was made to appear by certain sections of the Press at the time. It soon became clear that there was no wide divergence between American and British Official Policy with regard to the ex-Vichy men in North Africa, and criticism was directed (when it was present at all) against the general line of policy—not against the Americans in particular. The general trend of opinion was that, in matters of long-term strategy, expediency must be subordinated to political principles, but that expediency might be made the final test if the question were one of securing an *immediate* military or tactical advantage. This explains why (as was found by Mass-Observation) distrust of Darlan was comparatively restricted during the first fortnight after the Allied landings in Algeria, but rose to a peak towards the end of November. There was no change in fundamental viewpoint; but as it became more clear that the North African campaign was not going to be a walk-over, so it became more widely felt that co-operation with the former supporters of Vichy was a measure of expediency which our political credit could not afford.

There is at present a considerable difference of feeling between attitudes towards the American Government and those towards the American people. Of the latter, only half as many have nothing to say as have 1 o settled opinion about the American Government.

About the American people, one in every three expresses vague favour in the most general terms, while about one in five expresses a more specific type of favourable opinion. Specific disfavour is slightly less frequent than specific favour, but there is little or no disfavour in general terms, and the amount of such general disfavour would furthermore appear to be on the decrease.

Liking for the American people is largely on the grounds of their friendliness, or other similar qualities, such as generosity, frankness, etc., though miscellaneous grounds of various kinds are becoming more frequent as the Americans in this country become better known.

Dislike of the Americans, as has been pointed out above, is mainly centred on the allegation that they are "all talk and no deeds," and in fact generally on their alleged trait of boastfulness. But here, too, specific points are becoming increasingly diverse, and the proportion referring to this particular trait (though still the largest single group) is rapidly falling, and is now barely half as numerous as was the case just over a year ago.

There is evidence that as the number of Americans in this country has increased, and as the Americans have become better known in Britain, so opinions about them have become steadily less generalized and more specific. At first this trend resulted in a lessening of favour towards the Americans, as preconceived ideas, mostly favourable, were dispelled. By now, however, the increase in specificness is accompanied by a resurgence of favour towards the Americans—as they become better known, so particular points of likeability about them have come more into the public eye.

Present feelings about President Roosevelt show a very high degree both of interest and of favour, and indeed feelings about Roosevelt and Churchill have of late been very similar. A considerable body of opinion likens Roosevelt to Churchill. Apart from the President, few people in this country have anything very definite to say about American politics, or political figures. Such few feelings as are expressed are evenly distributed over the range from praise to condemnation. There are, however, slightly more mildly unfavourable comments than any other sort. Opinions are well summed up by the following remarks, made by a middle-class man aged 40 and an artisan class woman aged 35 respectively:

"Well, politics are much the same in any country, you know, really. There's a lot of shady business goes on there that nobody is ever told about. Now the Americans, they are more open in their graft than we are here—I suppose they do actually have more graft, though when you look at the —— borough council here in London that seems hard to believe. Anyway, they're not as bad as most foreign countries, like the way that kings of Yugoslavia get murdered when they come to Marseilles."

"I don't like the things that go on in politics in America from what I hear of them. Their political parties seem both to stand for exactly the same things, so that they are fighting only for places and not for principles. And they have people in American politics that no right-minded person could approve of. Not that there aren't people just as bad in this country. Russia's the only place where they don't seem to have any Fifth Columnists—and the only reason for that is that they were all shot before the war."

It is noteworthy that among those who have been to America, or who claim any real knowledge of conditions there, opinion of American politics is more favourable than among those whose opinions are based only on hearsay. In particular, American films would appear to give a highly derogatory impression of their politics.

The proverbial hustle and efficiency of the Americans comes out most strongly in feelings about American industry. Here opinions are for the most part fairly definite, and more strongly favourable than those on any other aspect of American life. Nevertheless, the verbatim comments recorded show that praise is given for quantity of production rather than for quality—and the favourable view now taken of American industry might be much less strong if it were not for abnormal war conditions. It is a common generalization that there is, in industry, an "American way" of doing things as opposed to a British way, and this American way, though it is recognized to provide more and cheaper goods, is not considered to give better quality, or even better value for money. This feeling is strongly brought out in many references to American cars, wireless sets, and other manufactured products.

iii. American Troops in Britain

Feelings about the American troops in this country include all shades of opinion. Points of friction arise most often out of the alleged tendency of the Americans to be over-ostentatious, a tendency which manifests itself in boastfulness, in "behaving as if they owned the place," and in being more lavish with money than British soldiers could afford to be. In reply to a direct question, it was found that the majority of the public said that they liked the American troops. Thus dislike of them is a minority feeling, though the minority often feel much more strongly than the satisfied majority, many of whom have never met any American troops.

Americans are widely believed in this country to hold patronizing opinions about the British people, although women's ideas of the attitudes held by Americans on this subject are much less critical than those of men.

The Americans are also generally thought to hold a low opinion of the British Empire—and particularly of the British treatment of the Indian problem. Often, however, it is made clear that this imagined American disapproval is considered justified—as for example in this comment made by a lorry-driver:

"Well, I don't think they give us much credit for the way we've let things go in India. Mind you, I'm not saying this against them—in fact, I think it is a good thing of them not to approve. Of course, the way they treat the niggers isn't anything to be proud of either."

We referred above to the fact that the Americans were judged in this country by a standard higher than that applied to other nations. There would appear to be an implicit recognition, in many of these comments about American views of the British, that the Americans have an equal right to judge us by these higher standards. Occasionally this recognition is even made explicitly, as by this housewife:

"Well, of course they'd expect Germans or Frenchmen to treat their colonies like we've treated the West Indies, and so probably they wouldn't mind. But they know that the British have a better tradition to live up to, and naturally they don't like our setting a bad example right on their own doorstep."

IV. WHAT THEY THINK OF US

Mass-Observation has also made a study of the feelings of American soldiers in this country on the subject of Britain and the British. There is great difficulty in obtaining really genuine expressions of feeling, as it is well instilled into the Americans not to take part in careless discussion with strangers. It is often necessary, therefore, to use roundabout methods in order to obtain the material required, and what follows has been collected entirely by indirect and conversational methods.

Rather less than a quarter of the remarks recorded contained definite favour of the British, and almost as many implied some degree of resentment at the British attitude towards Americans. In particular, the alleged habit of the British of sending their children out to beg candies from the Americans was unfavourably commented upon on several occasions. The British social system was also mentioned several times as being definitely inferior to that in the U.S.A.

"My grandfather was Scottish, and I like this country. I feel I belong to it more than some of the boys feel. But I don't care for the way the children behave, begging from the troops. The kids themselves are nice enough kids, and they're very polite—much more so than American children. But there's this one thing we don't like—it's not what we expected of English children."

"There's a lot of things strike us as a bit queer. For one thing, the desserts are *hot*. In America they're always cold, so we keep getting a surprise. And a thing that none of our boys like much is the way the kids are sent out to beg all they can from us. They're nice kids, and they oughtn't to be sent out that way. If we had the candies and all we wouldn't mind, but it's hard enough to get them ourselves. Oh, sure it happens—it happens too much— any of the boys will tell you the same. It's one of the things that made us kinda disappointed about this country."

"Before this war I used to be in a night club back in N'York, and when an English ship docked and the English boys were in town, we treated those boys pretty well. Maybe they didn't think we did, but we didn't do the almighty guts out of them the way some of our boys are being done here."

"About your taxis: the U. S. troops always pay too much. We don't see why fares should be so high just for us."

Apart from these more specific points, a general impression was gained that Britain was looked upon not only as backward compared with the U.S.A., but as being definitely impecunious and without much of what even the poorest people in America take as a matter of course:

"In America even the poorest people can afford a car. And then we have central heating in our houses and bathrooms." (Our investigator remarked that all modern houses have bathrooms.) "Not many of your houses are modern."

"Is it on account of the war you never have eggs? Did you use to have them? I had grown to suppose England had always been an eggless country."

The favourable comments were often of a far-reaching nature, and evidently sincere. The following is a small but fairly typical selection:

"I like England for its compactness. You could never be far from a town— wherever you might be. The people are grand—treated me fine. I'm intrigued by the way you speak over here—sure I've spoken to Englishmen before, but not *en masse*. The food of course could be better, but I guess that's due to the war."

"I like the English humour—and I like the Scottish better still—it's dry— it's the sort I like. And the Scottish hospitality is the best in the world—I never saw such hospitality—even in the U.S.A."

"On the whole, I like your people. I don't think they're so slow—though some of the boys think that."

"I had an English friend before I came over, and I stayed with him last week-end at his place near ——. My, we had a swell time. They were real good to me. I went out last Sunday with his two kids into the woods, picking primroses, and I thought England was sure a beautiful country. It makes it all seem different if you've a friend living in the country. You see it all differently. I think maybe the boys would all like it better if they could see it the way I saw it last week-end."

"I sure do admire your taxi-drivers—they drive—my, *can* they drive! But they *chisel.* As soon as they see our uniform up go the prices."

"We're getting along swell with the English, and don't let nobody tell you different. Some of our boys have too much to say about it. But we feel more democratic than you are, as well as more modern in every way. . . .

"The English are more quiet and refined in their ways than we are; our boys raise hell wherever they are—even back home; they're not so refined— that's how I'd put it. When we first came over, one of our boys said to a girl in a restaurant, 'How are ya, babe?' and, my, if looks could kill!"

"I do like your taxi-drivers. Those boys sure can drive. The way they get around in the black-out's wonderful to us."

"England isn't a democracy, the way *we* understand democracy. Churchill has no feeling for the working classes; he's on the side of the Tories who want to hang on to what they've got. Still, there's a lot of good things I like about England. You don't know crime over here, the way we know crime back in America. Your bobbies don't need to carry arms. You haven't the gangster stuff over here that we have—that's one of the best things about England."

Minor grumbles, such as licencing hours and the weather, are referred to fairly frequently, but usually only when those interviewed were made to feel that criticism was being asked for. These lesser criticisms should be to some extent discounted on this account.

We conclude with a random selection of comments from the material collected by Mass-Observation's investigators, which gives a good picture of the general impression of this country at present (March 1943) existing in the minds of the American soldiers here.

"Well, I'll be frank with you: I was here in 1937, and the difference in London is terrific. I mean the difference in the tradesmen most of all. They used to be proud of their businesses, proud of their craftsmanship, proud of what they were selling you—and much too proud to do you down. That's all gone. They're all on the snatch now; they don't seem to care any more. I don't like the attitude of the shopkeepers or the hotelkeepers or the taxi-drivers to us either. They're all as indifferent as hell, and apt to do the living lights out of you. And the English still think themselves top-dogs everywhere."

"The English are O.K. I haven't found anything wrong yet. In the provinces they live almost like cavemen—but I suppose that's England. I prefer to be an American and live in the States—but I like it here fine."

"In London they're not so bad—England's a pretty backward country. But after the war I'm convinced it'll start going places! Some of the people here are rather mean—don't seem to like us boys much. Considering we volunteered at the very beginning of the war for the [*Canadian*] army, they've nothing to complain about." [*U.S. Soldier in Canadian Army.*]

"I think education ought to be free over here the way it is in America. It costs too much over here, and it isn't fair on the poor person.

"And I can't understand why you British weren't the pioneers in central heating, the way your climate is. You need it far more than we do, but there isn't so much of it here. But I like England pretty well; I like to go walking in London—a lot of it's pretty and quaint. And it's amusing to us—all this old-fashioned stuff. Maybe you figure you British are amused at the Americans. But how I see it is, it's more amusing to look back on things the way they used to be: new things aren't funny the way old things are. If England is twenty per cent amused it us, we're eighty per cent amused at England."

"One thing has struck me a lot: your civilians are pretty decent in helping us out about the exchange. A lot of times when one of our boys has been in a jam and couldn't figure it out about your money, some civilian has stopped and helped him out, and they've never done one of them a dirty deal yet. But they're slow in giving change in the shops, and the tradesmen are surly—they don't seem to want to serve you—you'd think they wanted to keep their stock to themselves."

"The best thing I ever saw in England was Bournemouth. My, that's a fine town—a marvellous town. I like the southerners better than the northerners, but I don't like the way they overcharge the American troops in the off-licence places."

"I like to go visiting into English houses—the people are very kind and hospitable. But they ask too many questions. They want to be polite and to draw you out, but it gets tiring answering questions, they ask so many. But I like England very well. I wouldn't mind living here and bringing my wife and children over, if the war finished this year or next, and if the weather was like it's been this spring."

"What I like about England is the cleanness of the streets in the little towns and villages. And the way the English soldiers are so generous with their cigarettes, when they cost them two bob for twenty. They never think twice before handing a packet round. And I like the pubs. They're the most wonderful atmosphere for drinking I ever met. But I don't think you English ought to put so much blame on our boys for being wild. Of course we're wild. A lot of us are three or four thousand miles from home, away for the first time—it's the chance of our lives. It's just the same with the English sailors when a ship docks at a foreign port. An English ship pulls into Boston—plenty of fights then—wild?—they're just the same as us."

XIII AMERICAN MEDLEY

An English Girl's Impressions

By Antonia Bell

---

1. THE YOUNG IDEA

IF YOU want to know what young Americans are like, read the papers, for they are typical of America, and especially of American youth, in a way that ours are not typical of England. Journalism in America is more democratic and more general in its appeal. A Sunday paper has forty-six pages and five supplements, including a coloured comic. *Life* and *The Saturday Evening Post* have the glossy paper, wide margins and full-page advertisements that Americans love, and are read by everybody from college boys in Massachusetts to farmers' wives in Nebraska. Even *The Atlantic Monthly,* supposed to be highbrow, is good to look at and easy to read.

Americans like to know about everything that is going on without making a labour of it. I was surprised to find how much they had read of the happenings in England, and how anxious they were to know more.

"What do the English think about Russia?" small boys in Buffalo asked me.

"How do they like our President?"

"How does our Curtiss P-40 make out compared with your Spitfire?"

A small schoolgirl in Dallas, Texas, wanted to know if we had much "goofer-trouble" in raids. A goofer, she explained, is one who stands staring with his mouth open.

Several times there was flung at me—"When are you British going to abolish your Caste-system?"

The moment I stopped speaking, I was always bombarded with questions. Children jumped to their feet and waved their hands in the air, each frantic with anxiety to be heard first. I have never met a shy American. In England, when you finish speaking and ask for questions, every single head turns round to see if anyone behind is brave enough to lead off.

Our national disease of shyness makes Americans ascribe all sorts of nasty qualities to us that we really don't possess. They call us cold, "high-hat," "stuffed-shirt," or just plain rude. And the more strongly we feel anything, the more afraid we are of showing it.

Least of all can Americans understand how proud we are of England, because we carefully avoid saying it—heaven knows why. Americans know America is the finest country in the world, and they don't mind telling you so. Some of them are just beginning to realize that there are other countries. They could not believe that I wanted to go back to England because it was England. They kept assuring me that I was going from a sense of duty, to share the horrors of bombing with my family. America is so huge and diverse a country—you can find descendants in it of every European nation, as well as black, yellow and red—it is amazing how they are all held together by their pride in being Americans. Their worst word of abuse is "un-American." The advertisement of a super brand of tinned peas is headed, "How *American* it is to want something better." They believe that the American way of life is the most progressive, free and democratic in the world, and the Stars and Stripes hangs above every school platform.

I have often thought that boys and girls in their teens have a happier time in America, where there is a definite place for the awkward age. In England you are kept a schoolgirl as long as possible, and then expected to grow up with a bump. In America the "Sub-deb" and her brother have a special life organized for them: instead of taking a girl of sixteen to a grown-up party, you arrange a party for boys and girls of sixteen. You may not approve of a fifteen-year-old schoolgirl wearing a sophisticated dress in the evening, and having her hair "permed" and using lipstick and nail varnish, but it makes her a lot happier. A girl who has grown to the size of a woman feels absolutely miserable in the kind of clothes designed for children. And as for boys at English public schools, they often never meet any girls and have to learn later how to get on with them. Some never learn at all.

American boys and girls are encouraged in every way to be independent. I remember well the disgust of a ten-year-old boy from the Middle West when he came to England and was taken out for a walk in the park with his little cousins, for at home he used to drive the wagon to market. Boys in America who want some extra pocket-money go out and earn it. Even the son of a rich man will deliver newspapers or serve as a soda-jerker behind a drug store counter, so that he can buy himself a new boat for the holidays. There is no snobbery of "it isn't done." In fact, America has no class-distinctions in our sense, except perhaps for some survivals in old cities like Charleston, or Philadelphia or Boston. The hotel porter speaks to you as an equal, and the taxi-driver joins in your conversation. All the same, it is ridiculous to say there is no snobbery there; snobbery is to be found in every country where some people live better than others.

II. Coloured Folk

What we find hard to understand is their attitude to negroes. In theory, negroes are citizens with full rights, but in every city they have to live in a separate quarter. In the South they have separate schools, theatres, restaurants, separate seats in the buses and separate coaches on the trains; and they never, never meet the white people socially.

A woman from the North came to live in a Southern city and invited a distinguished negro lawyer to dinner. Her own negro servants refused to wait on him, muttering, "We don't wait on no coloured folks." That is one side of the picture. On the other, here is what a friend in New Orleans told me about a coloured porter at a New York station:

"I knew he was a Southerner, he was so nice and helpful in getting my bags on the train, so I said to him:

" 'You come from the South, don't you?'

" 'Yes, ma'am, I comes from Alabama.'

" 'Do you like it here?'

" 'No, ma'am, I don't like it at all. I can sit where I like on the street-car, but nobody talks to me. You're the first person that spoke to me since I been working here.' "

Another friend, who lives in the North, said:

"On buses and subways I always sit down next to a negro, so they shan't feel they are being avoided."

Well, it is an American problem, and the less advice we give, the better.

III. Contacts

Americans are not only free from shyness, they love to meet new people and make new friends. There can be no country where a stranger feels a stranger for so short a time. Everywhere you go you are welcomed like a long-lost cousin. An American told me how surprised he was that English people in the trains did not talk to each other. "That would never happen in the States," he said.

Indeed, on American trains no one waits to be introduced. I remember when I was on the Cleveland express, the conductor came into our car, and bent down and said something to each person in turn, and in turn they rose and followed him. I was new to America, and when he came to me I could not understand what he said, so I got up and joined the procession. We went through car after car towards the back of the train and at last, growing worried, I asked the girl in front of me, "Do you know where we are going?"

"Oh," she said, "didn't you hear? There is a *very* fat man on the train. He comes from a circus, and he weighs three hundred pounds, and we're all going to have a look at him."

It is because Americans find it so easy to make contacts that they are master salesmen. Selling, and being sold to, is one of the national pastimes. There are college courses in High-Pressure Salesmanship and books on the Psychology of the Customer. "He sold me the idea" is a common phrase, and to make a good impression is "selling yourself." Advertising in the States is a science and an art. They have a hundred different ways to make you read the advertisement. You see a picture of a little girl in a pink dress gazing at a sunset above the words, "What can a child believe in?" You read, to discover that it is Spink's Household Magnesia. Few can resist reading right through the sad story of the girl who neglected to use Brown's Antiseptic Soap, or making the discovery that Bob left home because his wife did not make her gingerbread with Sweetie-Pie Molasses. Radio programmes break off every fifteen minutes or so while a cooing voice asks you intimate questions about your liver, and begs you to win success in life by taking So-and-So's Health Salts. You may not like it, but you can't help hearing it.

America gaves tremendous scope for salesmanship, being the richest country in the world, with the highest standard of comfort. In spite of the depression, she is still the land of security and opportunity. Those in England who grew up between two wars have never known care-free security. Over their glad, confident morning loomed the knowledge that the world they had grown up in would not last very long, and it did not seem much use making plans which war was bound to over-throw. When war did come it was almost a relief and spirits rose in the face of actual danger. Our hope is that the generation after this will grow up as Americans do, or rather did before Pearl Harbour, and as all children should, feeling that the world is safe, beautiful and good.

The first thing we can do to make it so is to strengthen the under-standing between young America and young England. That is easily done if the two meet, as can be seen from the few English children who were lucky enough to be sent to American homes. The need is for hundreds of others like them to stay in American homes, and for Americans to stay in English homes. Surely a scheme like this can find a place in the many plans now being laid for the post-war world. Boys and girls of the two nations will then grow up to like and under-stand each other and, looking on all that has to be done, will say, "Let us go forward together."

XIV FREEDOM OF THE SKIES

By Air-Commodore P. F. M. Fellowes

I. INTERNATIONAL CONTROL

To ESTABLISH in the world-consciousness a proper sense of the urgency for action now, it must be universally recognized before the end of this war that the newest creation of humanity—Mastery of the Air—already far transcends in importance and power any previous human innovation. This statement applies both in a good and evil sense. Conceive the difference in status between a walking and a flying bird, and that is something of the change humanity is to undergo.

At the end of this war will arise a great moment for action. If we are not prepared and let this slip by, such a moment may not arise until the end of another war.

World opinion is so fluid and changes so rapidly that the moment of writing this must be fixed in some way. A good way is to quote the contemporary opinions of leading men and of the most weighty organs of the Press. I will therefore quote shortly the sayings of the Air Minister, the Vice-President of the United States, a debate in the House of Lords, and *The Times*.

At the presentation of the Air Estimates on March 12, 1943, Sir Archibald Sinclair shows that he has an open mind. He says, "Though Air Transport is a young industry and its potentialities have everywhere fired the imagination, its organization cannot be considered in isolation, but must be framed as to be consistent, *in spirit and in truth,* with the principles which should govern the international economic policy of the United Nations after the war." He ends by saying, with reference to our national method of developing civil aviation: "The policy of a chosen instrument remains the policy of the Government now, but when they were thinking of the future after the war, everything must remain." He presumably meant "must remain open." He also announced the formation of an Air Transport Command formed to work in close collaboration with British Overseas Airways Corporation, with which it would be integrated. These two organizations during the war would organize and control strategic air routes for all oversea ferrying, and for reinforcement.

In the House of Lords, on the same day, the Government spokesman, Lord Cranborne, accepted a motion by Lord Londonderry to secure for this country a due share of world Air Transport, but rejected an amendment by Lord Davies that Civil and Military aviation should be considered from a standpoint of the general interest, and that the United Nations should constitute themselves into an International Authority, charged with the duty of drafting a code of regulations governing the employment of aircraft, and controlling an Air Police Force to ensure that this code was respected and upheld.

On the day previous, a *Times* leader—and *The Times* on this question is doing a great work in leading, and not following, world opinion—quotes Mr. Wallace, Vice-President of the United States, as saying that the United States will renounce world rights over aviation gained in the war, and that he warned his countrymen against the danger of the grabbing of air rights over other portions of the world and denying equal rights over their own territory to other nations. To quote from *The Times:*

"Mr. Wallace, the American Vice-President, said: 'We do not want imperialistic American supremacy in the air and on the sea.' He was referring to the campaign conducted by a section in his own country which has been suggesting that while other skies should be open to American aircraft in the world after the war, American skies should be closed to foreign aircraft. As he said, imperialistic supremacy in either field would be only too likely to make a third world war certain. The Atlantic Charter rightly includes freedom of the seas among its cardinal principles. Freedom of the skies will be equally an asset of victory and a pledge of unity for essential international purposes. The two freedoms are in fact complementary. In both fields supremacy must be international. But freedom of the skies is a phrase that requires definition and application. How it is to be achieved and sustained is a problem that the interested nations are required to approach and to solve. The time to act is now. A right solution will be one of the assurances that the United Nations, who have entered a partnership dictated by the necessities of war, will be no less able to preserve and develop it for the organization of peace.

"Given the vision to see the opportunity and the vigour to use it, co-operation in the air after the war offers the prospect of most fruitful international action. The aeroplane has so conquered time and space that the setting up of a World Authority assuring freedom of the skies and exercising responsibility on behalf of the United Nations on all issues of the organization of international air transport ceases to be Utopian. It has indeed become inevitable; for unless the victorious nations are determined to plan together for the future, and to maintain their co-operation on this vital matter, the whole framework of a new ordering of the world by the United Nations is likely to prove fragile—if only because the international control of civil aviation is inseparable on any conceivable view of the needs of security from the international organization of military power in the air. The scope and powers of an international authority will admittedly have to be defined with care. But this is not the only sphere in which some modification of old sovereign rights, and some dovetailing of purely national enterprises into a larger conception of international unity, has become imperative. Nothing could be worse than a return to the policy of 'closed skies' and unregulated international competition. . . .

"Victory will be fruitless without pooling for peace. But this pooling will not be achieved unless the foundations of agreement are laid now. . . ."

Now this extraordinarily far-sighted statement of policy, advocated in *The Times,* it will be noticed, asks for international supremacy, and not only in the new field of the air but also in the long-established field of the sea. This is remarkable and world-shaking in import. If it is followed through and carried out, it might lay the foundation of a permanent safeguard of peace by an international control of sea and air, the two elements open to common use.

II. THE SHRINKAGE OF SPACE

The attitude of mind represented by Lord Cranborne in the House of Lords is exactly analogous to that of the pre-war governments of Messrs. Baldwin and Macdonald, dangerously parochial and cautious to the point of madness, and would, if maintained, secure for the world certain war with the shortest possible interval of peace. The world has now reached the stage of development in shrinkage where only the boldest and most constructive policy can save it from a period of successive wars. The popular British pre-war policy of *laissez-faire* and safety first is the certain way of obtaining such an appalling future, and no person, whatever his eminence and position, has the right to remain in office and to sacrifice the common people to another holocaust, due to his ineptitude and this passive attitude of mind. The Government must realize their responsibilities to those they govern. They must understand that, as the world gets smaller and smaller, and people get closer and closer, the causes of friction become more and more pungent and frequent, and therefore new and urgent measures are required to meet this new menace to peace.

To say that people are getting to know each other better because of flying facilities, and therefore peace will become more secure, is denying facts. Why do the Germans hate the French, the Russians the Germans, the French the Italians, and *vice versa?* Why is it that we have never found it possible to dislike anybody very strongly? It is because hitherto we have not been too close to anybody. It cannot be emphasized too strongly that the world is shrinking so fast and we are all becoming so intimately in contact one with another, that new measures must immediately be devised to safeguard against this new and menacing state of affairs.

Peace, if it were merely static, would make war essential to the maintenance of the health of the world (Mussolini's theory), but peace can never be this: the rate of invention, the spread of education and the shrinkage of the world will maintain and ever increase the dynamism of peace. The effort to keep the peace in the future is going to become ever more intensive; past wars will be looked back upon as comparatively restful periods of defined activities. The spread of education is increasing the number of thinkers at a higher rate than ever before, and this, added to the rapid shrinkage of the world, is producing a force of immeasurable and unknown dynamism for which we have to evolve new methods of control.

Fortunately for the world the four great national aggregates, the British Commonwealth, the Chinese Republic, the Russian Republic, the United States Federation, are all led by men of outstanding quality. If these four men will take upon themselves personally the responsibility to the helpless multitudes of humanity, that at the end of this war they will so organize the armed forces policing the world to secure permanent peace, then out of this terrible holocaust good will have come. But if on the contrary the responsibility for the future controlled peace is to be shelved and allotted to international committees requiring unanimity of voting to settle an issue, then we had better prepare now for the next war.

Plans for peace must be made now; to await the end of the war to make these plans is to leave it too late. It is up to the four great world leaders to insist upon the formulation of these plans now and to lead their own nationals along the right mental paths so that their own national committees, with the full assent of the people, can agree upon schemes for initiation immediately on the declaration of peace. This is a greater and far harder task to achieve than the winning of the war, and will stand out as such historically. If these four great leaders rest content in merely winning the war they will have failed their trusting peoples most lamentably and incidentally destroy their own historical reputations.

III. THE FUTURE OF AIR TRANSPORT

When the moment comes to consider how the future of air transport will be decided—and to be of real value it must be soon—it is assumed that this decision will rest entirely on an agreement made between the four principal Allied Powers, and that in making their decisions they will have two primary objects in view: the maintenance of the future peace of the world, and the setting of the scales to allow for the growth of the greatest efficiency in the use and development of air transport. If the longest and strongest view is taken, that is the view which does not include another world war, as an essential to meet the world conditions induced by a further world shrinkage, then the Allied Powers will have to decide on the formation of a supernational directive World Air Board to control the principles and policy, and some of the practices of both civil and military aviation. Incidentally, if they do so decide, this will be the first and obvious step in world federation, a process which has to be brought about by evolution, if the world is to be spared a further awful spasm of world-diminishing pains.

It may be argued that a World Air Board could not control both civil and military aviation, on the analogy that navies and the Mercantile Marine have largely remained separate. This is not altogether true in history, although it may have been true recently.

In any case, the unity of the air, as opposed to the separateness of the seas, speeds of movement, conditions of operation, and the ultra-rapid shrinkage of the world all tend to modify this argument.

There are certain outstanding principles and rules which the Allied Powers will have to settle. The principal one is as to whether freedom or not of the entire air should be internationally accepted. If not, what limitations are to be set upon this freedom?

The probability is that the limitations set will be that internal passengers, mail and freight will not be allowed to be carried by extra-national aircraft, but that all aircraft will be allowed free access to certain aerodromes and seadromes throughout the world.

On March 20 the joint Air Transport Committee of the Association of British Chambers of Commerce, Federation of British Industries, and the London Chamber of Commerce, laid down three definitions, as follows:

Freedom of Passage: This would permit aircraft to fly over any country without landing.

Freedom of Facilities: This entails the use of airports, weather reports, radio control, and other services of all States, "provided that the aircraft did not engage in any Trade arising from, or in relation to, such landings."

Freedom of Trade: This would permit aeroplanes to operate for hire or reward into, out of or within any other State.

Assuming the International Air Authority to have been established, it will be for them to advise the Allied Powers as to the powers that it will be essential to delegate to them.

IV. RULES OF THE AIR

On the civil side these will include the right to draw up general regulations governing the Rules of the Air and control of unfair or dangerous competitive practices. This power of control would have to include the right to reduce the status of international air lines from passenger to mail service, or to freight, or to cancel their international status altogether. It is probable also that the Air Board would be granted powers to negotiate with national governments on all the needs for the efficient conduct of international air lines, such as the laying down of standards for the inspection of aircraft, including engines, instruments, etc., in construction and maintenance; inspection both in construction and maintenance, standards of flying skill, navigational knowledge, wireless technique, etc. They would also need to establish a uniform world method for blind flying technique, including radio beam flying, blind approaches and landing, and clear weather approaches. Similarly they would wish to lay down international standards of fuel and lubrication oils, both as regards purity, methods of supply and refuelling arrangements; all meteorological information and communication systems would also need to be standardized. The question of which, and how many, aerodromes and seadromes should be under the authority of the World Air Board would need clear and definite settlement.

It is probable that in each country a certain number of these air bases would have to be made extra-national. In the latter case it would, of course, be within the power of the Air Board to lay down the dimensions, etc., of the runways on these air bases, but it is possible also that the Air Board would seek powers, by agreement with National Air Boards, to control the dimensions and equipment of many other air bases within the national control. In fact, an agreed standard for different categories of air bases would have to be universally accepted eventually.

The International Air Board would no doubt need to set up its own International Ground Services to man the various administrative, executive and servicing branches managing the extra-national airports, etc., and it would seem easy and natural for the meteorological and communication services throughout the world to come under their control.

Private flying, as such, would have to conform to the international rules of flying, and would either have to come closely under the control of the I.A.B., or each National Air Board (N.A.B.) would have to agree the rules controlling their own nation's private flying, with the I.A.B., and give a guarantee that these would be rigidly adhered to. The effects of collision in the air, even between quite a small aircraft and the largest types, can be so calamitous to the large aircraft as to put the control of private flying in a category apart from all other forms of private transport.

The difficulties of this question are immense, as discipline of individual owners is very hard to apply and will have to be drastic to secure safety.

As a result of the full activity of such an authority as the I.A.B. it would soon become apparent that they would need many subsidiary services. To mention only a few, which immediately come to mind: Rescue Services (both sea and land transport is involved); Health Services (doctors, hospitals and nurses involved); Civil Aerial Police Service; Aerial Survey Service; Works and Buildings Service; Catering Service; International Currency; Accountancy, etc., etc. How far some of these services would interblend with the military side of their responsibility, conveniently, could be discovered only by experience. It may prove that a great deal of the ground services of the I.A.B. could be militarized, and thus the strictest discipline in standards and service be secured.

They would have to control, in addition, the policy question involved in the design of the right types of aircraft for the various world air routes, whether flying-boat, aeroplane, or both cum-glider, and also, later on, that of the helicopter and gyroplane, and possibly other types.

The I.A.B. would need to have some directive control over the trend of development of aircraft, not only because they would pass types as suitable for use, but also because one of their main functions is to safeguard peace.

It is probable that the I.A.B. would not seek to interfere with, or control, any training schools whatever, either flying, navigational, meteorological, wireless telegraphy, aero-engines, or ground service training in general, but it is certain they would have to lay down standards of skill to be originally attained and maintained through the active life of any personnel employed by air lines operating internationally.

Equally, they would not seek to control any manufacturers in their methods, but here again they would have to lay down and enforce compliance with their standards of manufacture and inspection, as far as the aircraft for use internationally were concerned.

It is highly probable that, in the cause of the maintenance of peace, they would have to demand the right to inspect and be informed of all manufacture of aircraft wherever or whatsoever taking place within the world.

In all such matters of control and direction, it is safe to assume that the I.A.B. would not only make their directive control as elastic as possible, so as to avoid unnecessary interferences, accompanied as they always are by inevitable friction and delay, but also that one of their secondary objectives would be to safeguard initiative and individualism, and national rights over internal flying, as far as it was compatible with their two primary objectives.

v. An International Police Force

It will be seen from the forecast of the general lines on which it is believed world air transport will eventually have to develop that the control of flying between international and national is likely to be fairly sharply divided. Because the actual control is so divided it need not, however, be accepted that there will not be close collaboration and consultation between the I.A.B. and N.A.B.s; in fact, so far is this from the case that it seems probable that the I.A.B. will have to have a separate liaison officer with each important N.A.B., and a composite liaison officer with the less important N.A.B.s.

From the military aspect it is necessary to elucidate how defined is the split to be between the control of civil and military aviation. This must rest, to some extent, on the solution decided upon for military aviation. Is it to be left as national, international, or to be partly national and partly international? And again, is it to be mainly military or punitive in character, or is it to be primarily policing in function and preventive in character?

On the basis that the long and strong view is taken, it is necessary to predicate a force which is eventually to become an International Police Force in function because, if war is not to be catered for, national fighting forces will eventually lose their purpose. Assuming this to be the case, there can be no reason against—in fact every important reason for—placing the force under the I.A.B. and gradually cutting down the National Armed Forces to the character of National Police Forces.

This assumption inevitably brings up for discussion the question of the need of national navies, armies and air forces. If there are not to be any more wars, then national navies, armies and air forces plainly are redundant. At the same time, if war is to be abolished, we have had clearly proved to us that force is needed to safeguard peace. This means that the International Police Force would have to embody in itself not only Air Police but also Naval and Military Police Forces, and furthermore, that these Forces would have to be at the call of nations when needed to stabilize their governments under conditions where their own Civil Police Forces are powerless. Such conditions may arise in any nation, even the most phlegmatic.

To reach such an ideal in world government is a very long step, but if such an ideal state is ever to be reached, preparatory thinking and planning must be initiated. The enormous vested interests in the national navies, armies and air forces, to say nothing of the great business interests which depend upon them, have all to be brought into line before any useful advance can be made at all.

The present moment is particularly suitable for this planning, as the end of this world war should provide an opportunity for the reorganization of world forces, which it is hoped is unlikely to occur again for some time.

On general grounds it seems very unlikely that it would be possible to secure the complete elimination of National Armed Forces until a considerable period has elapsed after peace is declared, even if this is accepted in principle and ever proves possible.

A great deal will have been achieved if some beginning can be made in the organization of an International Force of all three arms—Navy, Army and Air Force—and as a start it would probably be necessary to incorporate whole ships' companies, regiments and squadrons from every National Force, and later, on this basis, to build up a truly International Force. Meanwhile, during the growth of this Force, the guardianship of the peace of the world would have to rest on the power of the Allied Armed Forces, but the fact that, with the common consent of the world, an International Armed Force had been set up would be a tremendous step forward to the establishment of a permanent world peace.

The purpose of this International Armed Force would be, during the period in which National Forces continued, to act as a reserve of strength for the forces of any nation or nations. Thus, to secure peace it would be necessary for the International Force to be immensely greater than any National Force. Such a scheme, if peace was successfully maintained for a long period, would gradually induce that confidence in the world which would admit of a gradual reduction, by mutual consent and agreement, of National Armed Forces, and thus the purpose in view—controlled peace—would gradually become more secure.

VI. INTERNATIONAL ALLEGIANCE

These suggestions, together with a proposed form of international oath of allegiance to such a Force, are incorporated in a pamphlet entitled, *Air Force for the Peace Front,* published by the New Commonwealth Society. The oath is as follows:

" 'Knowing that the Force I am joining is instituted to check war between States by reinforcing the victim of aggression and attacking the aggressor, I undertake to serve to this end in the Force until relieved of duty in accordance with its rules, to renounce my national allegiance while my service lasts, and to carry out the orders given me by the constituted authority of the Force without partiality or preference.

" 'Provided only that I may make an express reservation to the effect that, if my own country of origin is declared the aggressor, I shall not be ordered to attack it actively in person.'

"Use of the proviso would be permitted only to those available for service in the air. Each individual would decide whether he took the oath with or without the proviso."

It is a most important and interesting fact that Great Britain by the enlistment of the Americans, the Fighting French, Dutch, Norwegians, Belgians, Poles, Czechoslovakians, Slavs, Greeks, etc., in the Royal Air Force has not only established a foundation for the future World International Armed Police Force but has also proved the sanity and feasibility of the original proposal to do so.

It is true that this force has not been asked to take an international oath, and that they have a common concrete and immediate enemy, but it is not believed for one moment that the oath as set forth in the New Commonwealth's proposals would be a stumbling block if the nations believed that it would secure the peace of the world, nor is it believed that mankind has such a poor imagination that it has to know its enemy before it can subscribe to such an idea as an International Police Force for the maintenance of permanent peace.

Incidentally, the formation of an International Police Force inevitably *involves* the foundation of sea, land and air Training Schools and establishments and Staff Colleges; these, in their turn, necessitate the acquisition of extra-national areas for their accommodation. To avoid international jealousies and uneven economic impositions these schools, establishments and colleges will have to be spread, equally as far as this is possible, between the interested nations.

Exactly the same arguments apply to the positioning and setup of the executive and operational branches, sea, land and air, of the International Police Force, subject to any modification "strategy of control" may enforce. The harbours containing the sea forces, and dockyards repairing them, their refuelling bases will all have to be allotted between countries with great care and circumspection to avoid slights and friction. The same thing will apply in the distribution of ground and air forces, in regard to their barracks and airports, manœuvring grounds and exercising areas, technical and experimental establishments, technical equipment, servicing units, etc. Originally, use would no doubt be made of existing national establishments, bases, etc. Later, some of these bases would be permanently transferred to the I.A.B. and would represent a contribution by the country concerned.

The equipment would no doubt in the first instance be the best product and surplus of the present hostilities. Later this would be replaced by more modern equipment of a sort the use of which would be denied to National Forces as long as they continued to exist. To enact this measure would speed the disappearance of National Armed Forces and it might be reinforced by a world measure prohibiting the manufacture of new types of armament for any national force whatever.

If it is now agreed that an institution such as a Directive World Board, for the immediate control of the policy of international air lines, and the advisory control of the policy governing all internal civil aviation, and the eventual control of an International Police Force or Fighting Naval, Military and Air Force, is a desirable and feasible idea, it can now be discussed in greater detail how such a state of affairs can be most speedily brought about.

VII. A SUPREME COUNCIL

The first step to give such a project the necessary authority would be for the four major Allied governments—the United States, Great Britain and the Dominions, the Soviet Republic and China—to meet, discuss and agree the need in principle of such a Board. The next would be for each government interested to appoint a small committee to clarify their ideas, both on the civil and military needs of such a project, and generally to draw up the lines, only on broad principles, on which each individual government considered the development of such a scheme should be initiated and controlled. The next step would be for each of the four major Allies, and those of the minor Allies interested—e.g., France, Holland, Belgium, Norway, Brazil, etc.—and certain neutrals, such as Sweden and Turkey, to appoint members of an International Committee to secure a very broad and general agreement between the different ideas of the four major Allies, and to make an omnibus report on the agreed principles to the four major Allies, with copies to all other nations interested. Speed in decision is essential, so detail must be entirely avoided and a majority decision must be accepted, otherwise nothing would be achieved.

It is because of the World War that a situation will arise in the coming of peace whereby such a scheme may be able to be inaugurated, and therefore the responsibility for all but the principles must rest on the shoulders of the four major victorious Powers. In theory it may seem fair to give all nations, large and small, victor or vanquished, an equal say in the details of such a scheme; but in practice no decision could ever be reached in such a way, and let us not give way to hypocrisy and make-believe on this vital matter.

Where equality can eventually be given will be in the running of such a scheme; but the decision as to the lines on which this great organization must be built up must rest on those responsible for world order when it is initiated, and while it is being developed. The four great Powers, it is hoped, will be wise enough to recognize from the start that any scheme based on national selfishness and advantage can only be self-destructive. The self-seeking nationalism of the pre-war era, with its terrible consequences, has proved this clearly enough for all to see. The chances of the four great Powers taking this very strong and wise path will be greatly enhanced if the four great leaders—Messrs. Roosevelt and Winston Churchill, Marshal Stalin and General Chiang Kai-shek all live to see the peace well inaugurated.

In advocating the formation of an International Police Force it must not be lost to sight that in so doing a great risk is run. In the hands of the wrong people such an organization might become a terrible menace. To safeguard the world against this menace—gangsterdom in international control—it will be necessary to lay down very strict rules as to the periods for which individuals may be elected to seats of power, either on the International Air Board or to the higher posts of the International Police Force Staff in Command. The period of an appointment, it is thought, should not exceed two years for any one person, and careful safeguards should be instituted to see that people cannot move from one high post to another. In fact it is essential for mankind to safeguard itself with the utmost rigour against the formation of rings, parties, or vested interests, even of the most gentlemanly types.

VIII. RISKS AND SAFEGUARDS

History has clearly shown that humanity's capacity for self-deception is almost unlimited, and that ridiculous as it may appear in a historical sense, individuals have been genuinely convinced that they themselves were indispensable in certain offices. Otherwise honourable men have resorted to fundamentally venal practices to keep themselves in power in certain offices and positions on this justification, and therefore this human weakness must be most rigidly guarded against. If we did not thus safeguard ourselves, it would be one of the most certain ways of allowing Bernard Shaw's dictum that humanity has failed to be proved true.

The end of this war will not be the moment to seek national, much less personal, gain, but world advantage, perhaps a truism, but one that will have often to be repeated with great courage and determination if it is to receive anything more than lip service.

Having cleared the ground as to the objective to be sought, it will now be seen that within the limits of the control of the policy and principles governing flying generally, and Air Transport in particular, it should be possible to allow great freedom in the initiation of private companies to promote Air Transport.

Certain nations may wish to own and control their own National and International Air Transport Companies. Russia will certainly do so as her economic system does not allow of anything else, but that need not prevent any other nation from allowing her nationals to develop their activities under private auspices.

In the case of such nations, the I.A.B. would probably have to have the power of investigating the scale of national subsidies, and of controlling those subsidies to prevent unfair and cut-throat competition as between nations. They might, for example, have to request Russia to increase the charges on international Russian-run air lines to the point where those lines were securing a profit, and equally they might have to ask the United States to decrease their subsidies so as to secure fair competition between private- and State-run lines. To enable them to do this, the I.A.B. would have to have the right to audit the accounts of all international air lines, and it is probable that in the long run the I.A.B. would have to have a large staff of travelling auditors constantly at work to check the initiation of wrong policies before they could take firm hold.

As a result of experience it may even prove that the I.A.B. will themselves have to lay down the rates to be charged per mile for passengers, mail and freight.

There may be other forms of economic control which the I.A.B. would find it necessary to introduce as time went on, but it seems improbable that they would actually have to interfere in prices paid for aircraft, or wages paid to employees, or dividends paid to shareholders, always provided cut-throat or unfair competition was avoided.

Presumably services common to all, such as communication, radio beams, teleprinters, meteorology, fuel provision, maintenance of extranational aerodromes, languages, housing, etc., would come under the direct control of the I.A.B. and be paid for by them.

To cover all these costs they would either have to be subsidized by all participating nations, or else they would have to be allowed to levy charges on all air lines for services rendered. They would have to start on the former system, even if later they converted to the latter. Therefore there will have to be an agreed proportional levy on all nations in the world, probably on a basis of population to maintain the international activities of the I.A.B. It may be that some nations would have to borrow in order to pay, but as all nations will benefit, and particularly the undeveloped areas, this is a burden which all should gladly shoulder. In any case, if the I.A.B. is to operate with the requisite authority, the victor nations would have to be firm on this point, and secure the agreement of all nations, including any neutrals which have not participated in the World War.

IX. PLANNING FOR THE FUTURE

In the laying out of the air routes, the I.A.B. would only gradually take control. Many of the routes existing at the end of the war will no doubt be allowed to continue, and possibly even develop during the period in which the I.A.B. is taking over and planning and apportioning world air routes between the various national and possibly even private companies.

National interests will not alone govern the routing of these air lines, as if they were to do so the stronger nations, despite all precautions, would inevitably have their interests served first and best. The I.A.B.

will have to look far into the future and plan the world air routes to suit the world interest in commerce, for police, for World Federal Government requirements, for pleasure travel, and economy of effort. They will also have to foresee which areas of the world will benefit most by a major development of air travel, e.g., it probably will happen that property and amenities in the Polar regions will suddenly develop in value and amplitude respectively, in which case they would have need of more and better air connections, etc. The Polar regions have been used in this war to shorten communications, and probably will also be used in peace.

In the beginning the I.A.B. will no doubt make use of existing airports, and meanwhile they would be collecting data for the laying out of the ideal airport to suit the then existing type of Air Transport. Air Transport is not at all likely to remain static; not only speed, but size and types may alter greatly. For example, the uses of glider air-borne trains have not yet been tried out commercially, although they have been in war, nor have helicopter or high lift wing aircraft yet been tried out for taxi work from internal city airports. The uses of these types of aircraft, except for gliders, are unlikely to affect the types of aircraft used over the world air routes, but they very probably will affect the lay-out of airports and buildings servicing these airports.

Gliders, because of their lack of noise and the elimination of fire risk, may, if they are found to be economical, come into very wide use for all transport purposes, both military and civil. For internal use, for passenger, mail and freight carrying, a great future for gliders is foreseen.

On the general question of the need for an International Police Force to guard against the gangster type of nation, it is thought wise to emphasize a peculiar paradox which the recent shrinkage of the world has brought about. It is that the more powerful and richer a nation is, the less chance has that nation of making a profitable war. At this moment of world history, the United States of America is generally acknowledged to be the most powerful unified State, both economically and militarily, and her power to wreck the world by the use of either her economic or military power, at the end of this war, would be very great. However, in this highly unlikely event, were she to attempt to use her power militarily, her economic hold on the world would be automatically cancelled, because all nations would revoke their debts to her. We can therefore assume that any pressure she might exert on the world to secure her nationalistic aims would be economic pressure, supported by military power in being but not in use. But it will be found that even in the highly unlikely event of her wishing to, she really can do nothing on these lines because of the very fact that she is so economically dominant; anything drastic she does must echo back on herself to her own detriment. Her Lease-Lend policy has in effect placed the world in mortgage to herself, and to that extent the world is definitely safe from the United States turned imperialistic. This example is quoted because it is safe to do so without offence, because it is so highly improbable. It thus becomes clear that no State, however powerful, can wreck the world without wrecking itself, unless it can completely conquer and enslave the world, and fortunately no State, as we are now proving to Germany—a strong military, but economically impoverished Power—can yet, and, we hope, never will be able to do this. But it is now clear that had Germany prepared its onslaught more thoroughly, it is conceivable that she might have succeeded in her aims of enslaving the world. Such a possibility must be envisaged in the future, because it is profitable to such a State to do this, since she stands to lose little and gain all. For this reason it should become obvious to the Powers that will be in control at the end of this war that they in their own interests must take all steps, at any cost, to secure world peace for as long as possible. To secure freedom from global wars for ever is the ideal to be aimed at.

The Prime Minister in his broadcast on Sunday, March 21st, said: "We must try—I am speaking, of course, only for ourselves—to make the Council of Europe, or whatever it may be called, into a really effective league, with all the strongest forces concerned woven into its texture, with a High Court to adjust disputes, and with forces, armed forces, national or international, or both, held ready to enforce these decisions and prevent renewed aggression, and the preparation of future wars." He hinted that a Council for Asia would be required later.

XV INSIDE ISOLATIONISM

By Robert Waithman

1. First Causes

You have to begin, I think, with the understanding that during all but a negligible part of the time which has passed since the adoption of the Declaration of Independence in 1776 it has been the instinct of the American people to believe in what is now called isolationism. The American people have been—and to an extent often forgotten still are—a nation of immigrants from Europe. At one time or another their families were Germans or Poles or Italians or Greeks. Either they were ambitious or restless, or else some sort of persecution or poverty, or the sense of hopelessness in some other form, became more than they could stand, so that they sold what they had and embarked on the anxious adventure of crossing the Atlantic in search of a fresh start. At one time or another these families pulled up their roots and staked their future upon America.

Most of them found America bigger and richer than anything they had thought possible. America took them in without asking questions and gave them freedom and space and opportunity. And this family adventure has happened too recently to have been forgotten by most of the Americans who are living now. If it is not their own story it is likely to be the story of their fathers and grandfathers. The American frontier was not officially declared to be at an end until 1890, and for long after that there was unoccupied land to be had free. Thirty years ago the immigrants who built America were still arriving from Europe on the steerage decks of liners. Well over 1,000,000 immigrants arrived in 1914;

between the beginning of this century and the date of America's entry into the last war more than 14,000,000 people came and began to make the fresh start that America was offering.

Their children, and the grandchildren of men and women who pushed the American frontier westward across the virgin continent, were in the last convoys to North Africa and the Solomon Islands, or India or Australia or the United Kingdom. Those who are left at home, the fathers and mothers who took out American citizenship papers only ten, twenty, or thirty years ago, or who were born American citizens, are not disposed yet to take their nation for granted. There has not been time for that. There are people of every kind in the United States, some intelligent, some stupid, some greedy, some generous, some who think for themselves calmly and some who believe anything they are told and get excited about it. There is no exclusive vice and no exclusive virtue in the American people. But there is among them all an under-lying awareness of America, a deeply buried and often incoherent grati-tude for their country.

The thing we ought not to forget is that the immigrants who came to America to make a fresh start never ceased to be conscious of the need to stay an ocean away from war and persecution. This cornerstone of American foreign policy was laid by the instinct of the people. The preservation of the America they knew never ceased to be a personal anxiety, something that mattered to every farmer and drug store clerk and taxi-driver. There are other contributory explanations why isolation-ism has been the hope of Americans for two hundred years, but this is the one to remember all the time. It is the most cogent single reason why some Americans doggedly pursue this hope now.

For anyone who is trying humbly and fairly to comprehend the roots of American foreign policy the most vivid document in the record is the farewell address which was written in 1796 by George Washington, hero of the Revolution and first President of the new and still shaky nation which had been called the United States of America. George Washington, counselling the people to avoid both excessive partiality for one foreign nation and excessive dislike for another, wrote:

"The great rule of conduct for us, in regard to foreign nations, is in ex-tending our commercial relations, to have with them as little *political* con-nection as possible. So far as we have already formed engagements, let them be fulfilled with perfect good faith. Here let us stop.

"Europe has a set of primary interests, which to us have none, or a very remote, relation. Hence she must be engaged in frequent controversies, the causes of which are essentially foreign to our concerns. Hence, therefore, it must be unwise in us to implicate ourselves, by artificial ties, in the ordinary vicissitudes of her politics, or the ordinary combinations and collisions of her friendships, or enmities.

"Our detached and distant situation invites and enables us to pursue a different course. . . ."

There seemed to be such sound sense in this advice that it could never be seriously open to question. It was enshrined with Britain's blessing in the Monroe Doctrine in 1823. At all times of international crisis since then it has represented the steady, fixed course which successive Presidents and governments have been expected by the people to steer. For as a policy it met the two most important conditions: it was aimed at the objective the people held most highly, and it worked.

No political ties: no entangling alliances. These phrases, and others that meant the same thing, dogged President Wilson before the United States entered the war in 1917; and when the boys came home from France the same phrases rose to a crescendo. They went on echoing through the 'twenties and in the 'thirties: they were woven into the American creed on which the temple of neutrality was erected. They inhibited the United States Government from proposing or carrying out joint action with any foreign government or governments. Instead, the State Department had always to speak of something called "parallel action," so that there should never exist any condition which could be represented as the beginning of an entangling alliance.

Munich came and went, and the fatalistic march went on in Europe; and there was no effective promise and no effective threat that President Roosevelt or anybody else could make on behalf of the American nation. The nation at that time would not merely have disowned any leader who proposed to them any sort of alliance with any Power in Europe: they would have thought him mad. Long after 1939, when it had been so conclusively demonstrated that the President could not fashion American displeasure into a weapon strong enough to change Hitler's and Mussolini's plans, the isolationists in Congress and among the Press retained the power to rouse the American people with charges that the Administration was secretly helping Britain with her Atlantic convoys or had reached some secret and entangling naval agreement with Britain in the Pacific.

Right up to the moment on Sunday, December 7th, when the Japanese attacked Pearl Harbour and the naval alliance with Britain in the Pacific was revealed to be too hastily improvised, too little entangled, the counsel of George Washington had prevailed. Less than a month after the bombing of Pearl Harbour, Winston Churchill was in Washington. He went up to the United States Capitol and addressed a joint session of the Senate and House of Representatives; and towards the end of his speech he sadly told the Congress:

"Five or six years ago it would have been easy, without shedding a drop of blood, for the United States and Great Britain to have insisted on the fulfilment of the disarmament clauses of the treaties which Germany signed after the Great War, and that also would have been the opportunity for assuring to the Germans those materials, those raw materials, which we declared in the Atlantic Charter should not be denied to any nation, victor or vanquished. The chance has departed; it is gone. Prodigious hammer-strokes have been needed to bring us together to-day."

A year later the alliance of America with Great Britain had become wondrously comprehensive and efficient, and there was immense comfort in it for both Britons and Americans. Then there was, as there had been in the last war, much earnest discussion of the virtues of alliances on this pattern when the war would be over. But the echo of the prodigious hammer-strokes which had brought us together were not enough even now to drown out the other, older echo.

In March 1943, when the United States had been actively at war for sixteen months, a group of four Senators sought to secure a declaration by the Senate that it was in favour of participation by the United States in the administration and rehabilitation of the re-occupied countries and in the ordering and policing of the post-war world. Among the published comment on this proposal was a statement by Senator Burton K. Wheeler, Democrat of Montana, a leader of the Senate "isolationist" group. Senator Wheeler said:

"Generally speaking, of course, we can't live within ourselves but we should enter into no entangling alliances."

II. THE OLD INSTINCT

The main reason for American isolationism is that it has long succeeded by the grace of God, the Monroe Doctrine and the British Navy (which has made the Monroe Doctrine feasible) in satisfying the instinct of Americans who have an honest love for America and are grateful for America. So that it will be an egregious mistake for any Briton now or in the future to think of all American isolationists as ignorant and hysterical reactionaries. It will further be worth while not to fall into the error of accepting at face value the easy legend that has grown up to the effect that the Mid-West of America, being remote from the better-informed Eastern cities and inhabited largely by simple farmers, is the most backward area of the country. The Mid-West was predominantly isolationist before America entered the war, and it may be true that the fact that the people who live there are a thousand miles or so farther away from Europe and Asia helps to give them a sense of additional detachment and security. But if you have ever seen the Mid-West—if you have ridden or driven through it or even flown over it—you will be less likely to ascribe the feeling which its people evince to stupidity or ignorance. You are more likely, I think, to feel that isolationism was stronger here because the sense of the blessed peace and space and glory of America was stronger, and because the people longed more to save it as it was by following what almost everybody agreed to be the only course to salvation.

The truth is that up to the end of the nineteen-thirties there had been only one short period when the faith of the mass of American opinion in the no-entangling-alliances doctrine had been seriously shaken. That was during the period of controversy which, roughly speaking, began with the enunciation of Wilson's Fourteen Points in 1916 and ended some time after the final refusal of the Senate to ratify the Versailles Treaty. This was the time when there was a chance that the course of American foreign policy would be changed by the only force which could or can change it—the American people themselves. The circumstances in which they refused to make the momentous change that Wilson recommended have since been examined to the extent of several millions of words.

Most of the later American writing on Wilson's times has reflected the view that it would have been better for America and the world if Wilson's ideas had prevailed; and much of it has come around to the opinion that the peace of the world might well have been secured if America had put her weight into the League of Nations.

Now, when the new challenge to the old instinct is being shaped, it is probably encouraging to know that a large majority of the American people has come around to the view that Wilson was right, and is expressing itself in public opinion polls as overwhelmingly in favour of American participation in a system of collective security after this war. But this is almost certainly not a good enough indication that the American people are therefore bound to go along with the next advocates of collective security when the time for the hard, practical decision arrives. In plainer language, the American belief during the war that a system of collective security *should be* devised for the future is not a guarantee that the system of collective security projected when the war has ended or is ending will be acceptable to them.

When America was last at war there were no public opinion polls which arrived at their results by the careful and, as I think, accurate sampling methods now employed; but if there had been, they would have been unlikely to make any decisive contribution to the outcome. It is interesting and valuable to know the present cast of American thought; but what in my opinion is more interesting and more valuable is to know the larger, longer and more durable background to American thinking, and to realize how consistently and with what reason it has followed the isolationist line.

There is one more truth which it seems to me to be useful now to extract from the American record. It is important to know why the only serious previous challenge to American isolationism did not succeed.

To the question why the American people refused twenty-five years ago to abandon their belief in the efficacy of their old policy there might be one of two broad answers. It might have been that the people judged the new policy proposed by Wilson to be directed towards a wrong objective. Or it might have been that the people judged the new objective to be right but in practice unattainable.

I believe that the American people from 1917 to 1919 were attracted to Wilson's ideas, and saw clearly the benefits to America of the world without war which he was proposing. I think that, even in the period of post-war let-down during which the issue was fought out, the people would have made themselves so plainly heard that the Senate never would have rejected the treaty—if only enough of the people had believed that Wilson's plan would work. But they never were convinced that it would work. So they turned back to isolationism, which *had* worked before. Partly it was Wilson's fault: he was too preoccupied with the plan, and too forgetful of the roots of American thinking, and too late with his effort to change that thinking. Partly it was the fault of the events themselves: the daily story of the Peace Conference reawakened suspicions and built up disillusionment in America. It came to the point where the American people had to decide either that Wilson was right when he told them the new plan would work, or that the political opposition to Wilson was right when it told them the plan would not work. Some Americans believed Wilson; but there were many more who believed the opposition. When the substantial majority of the country came to the conclusion that the new plan would not work, or at the least that the risks to America, which would be involved in an attempt to make it work, would be too heavy, Wilson's chance of success had gone for ever.

We are now substantially at a point where the same mistakes *could* conceivably be made again. The first dangerous mistake now would be to fail to understand that isolationism in its most real shape is not a plank in the platform of some political party but an American instinct rooted deeply in the character and national desire of Americans. The second and disastrous mistake would be to present Americans once more with a fresh plan for collective security which they can be persuaded to believe to be unworkable.

III. GENESIS OF REACTION

It is certain that attempts will be made in the United States to represent as unworkable whatever plans may be proposed for the future. This attempt will be made in the main by the men whom I and other newspaper correspondents in the United States usually call "isolationist leaders." I have known for a long time that the phrase is not a sufficiently accurate one, but I have not been able to think of a way of projecting the fuller truth in another phrase as handy and space-saving.

"Isolationist leaders" sounds as though it refers to men who habitually and conscientiously express the will and thought of those Americans whose belief is that a policy of isolationism will serve the highest interests of the nation. But while there are such Americans, it has long ago become clear that they are in less single-minded company. "Isolationist leaders," in fact, can mean anyone of prominence who has consistently expressed isolationist views; and this is a large and catholic classification.

Isolation is the old, conservative doctrine in America. Every old and conservative doctrine in any country eventually comes to number among its exponents not only men who believe in it on the ground of conviction, but also men who have found that advocacy of the doctrine has increased their political popularity and advanced their personal fortunes. It has been observed by members of Congress and others that exposition of isolationist views has yielded rich rewards in the currency which has counted—in votes at election time. Politics in America is a highly competitive business: you cannot stand still. It always has been an asset to be known to the voters: to be recognized, for example, as a forthright, outspoken, realistic man. And foreign policy has always been a subject upon which the electorate has particularly appreciated forthright speaking. You cannot often, however, establish a reputation for forthright speaking upon advocacy of a middle-of-the-road policy. If you are to compel attention you must be forthright either along radical lines or along conservative lines. It is obviously much safer to be forthright along conservative lines.

This is perhaps the genesis of most reaction. You take a position which you believe to conform with that of the majority of the people to whom you are appealing; and as time goes on you are compelled to elaborate upon it and make it sound stronger. One conservative view leads to another. It is a fact, and there is no surprise in it, that many of the Senators and Representatives, the political candidates and ex-office holders who take the most reactionary line on foreign policy are men who are notorious reactionaries on social and economic issues. They took a position long ago, and they improved upon it and committed themselves more and more deeply until, as Walter Lippmann has said, they have a vested interest in their past mistakes. Moreover, the zest with which some of the opponents of President Roosevelt have seized occasions to assail him by indirection and have tied their political prejudices to their adopted stand on foreign policy is a factor which has constantly obtruded itself in the last few years.

I think that this is the basic explanation of some of the wild, unreasoned, isolationist talk which you used to hear reported from America in the 'thirties, before the war began, and even in the two years which elapsed between the beginning of the war and the entry of the United States into the war.

You can turn back the files of American newspapers now and read statements spoken by isolationist leaders in that American twilight era which sound strange indeed now. For example:

"The Administration's policy has . . . set the course for total annihilation of our magnificent modern civilization. . . ."

"Why all this sudden talk about war with Japan? What is America's stake in the Malay Archipelago, in Burma, in Indo-China, in Siam, in Singapore? . . ."

"France has been defeated, and despite the propaganda and confusion of recent months it is now obvious that England is losing the war. . . ."

"The German Fleet to-day is inconsequential . . . German submarines are small. They were designed to operate close to their bases—within a few hundred miles of England. . . ."

"There is here also the element of Japan. She is 6,000 miles away from continental United States and conclusive grip at each other's throat is even more improbable. . . ."

"Sending an army from America to the Continent of Europe itself to-day would not be like that of the First World War. . . . This time we would have to land overpowering forces all at once. For us to do that we would need prepare 5,000,000 to 8,000,000 American boys in addition to the British. . . . To land a force of a few hundred thousand Americans in Persia or Africa or other places would simply invite another Dunkerque. . . ."

"My position is that this is not our war. This is Europe's war. . . ."

These are statements made not by small-time hacks without political influence. They were uttered at public meetings by men of substance and reputation. I think it is unnecessary to identify them: I want merely to show that some of the great and respected isolationists have made formidable mistakes. The mistakes of lesser "isolationist leaders" have been many and spectacular. You can spend gaudy evenings re-reading the Congressional debates on such issues as Lend-Lease, Conscription and Neutrality.

Nor were the political personages who were making this sort of contribution to American national sentiment on the war without support outside Congress. It is probably sufficient to mention that a very prominent industrialist, whose plants later began to turn out in great quantities some highly efficient weapons, said early in the war that it should be the policy of the United States to give both England and the Axis Powers "the tools to keep on fighting until they both collapse"; and that one of the isolationist newspapers printed an editorial on November 11, 1941—less than one month before the attack on Pearl Harbour brought America into the war—saying:

". . . The main cause of this war is the same as the main cause of the last one. That cause was and is that the Germans are a virile, warlike people who want more room, food and glory, and that the British, Russian and United States Governments want to thwart that ambition. . . ."

The sources of these quotations have taken a modified line since Pearl Harbour; but they are still in existence, and with some exceptions they retain a vested interest in their old mistakes. Since the United States began to fight, moreover, many of them have drawn rather heavily upon their political futures and invested in a series of fresh positions.

They have taken an early and positive stand against the philosophy with which a number of Administration speakers have approached the post-war world. This conflict in its early stages became crystallized in the alignments of those who were for and those who were against the concept advanced by Mr. Henry A. Wallace, the Vice-President of the United States.

IV. ISOLATIONISM *v.* IDEALISM

When Mr. Wallace made his "Century of the Common Man" speech in May 1942, several days passed before any real notice was taken of it. It was only after some of the columnists subsequently read it and announced it to be one of the great speeches of the war that it was "taken up," discussed, praised, and denounced. In the months that followed it began to appear that the adverse comment upon it was growing, and that a great many people were taking their notion of what the speech was about not from the speech itself, but from hostile interpretations of the speech.

Mr. Wallace is a thoughtful man whose mind is still largely conditioned by the solid, careful habits he has acquired during the study and mastery of the agricultural sciences. Because he is not a glamorous figure, and because he conspicuously fails to give the orthodox impression of drive and efficiency, he has much less political influence than his friends hoped to see him amass after President Roosevelt had selected him for the Vice-Presidency in 1940. There has been an idea that the President employed him to try out upon the country, at no serious political risk to the Administration, the "extreme" liberal view of America's potential responsibilities in the post-war world. If such an experiment was ever consciously planned by the President, Mr. Wallace must have been a very ready collaborator, for there has never been any doubt that he spoke, and continues to speak, with the most sincere conviction. Some of those who incline to the more cynical reading of the situation hold that the

Wallace speeches were a mistake in that they created a bitter, nation-wide opposition to the liberal objectives toward which the President and the Administration are steering. There is, however, another view which I believe to be nearer the truth. It is that, at the cost of this indubitable opposition, Mr. Wallace contrived to shock the American people into their first real contemplation of the post-war world.

It showed up the incipient conflict between the American instinct for an isolationistic foreign policy and the wistful desire of Americans to seek and promote the humanities and the Christian decencies. This same wistful desire is often called American Idealism. It is what Wilson (as someone has said) put his shirt on. It is what has made some of the speeches of American statesmen, from Thomas Jefferson to President Roosevelt, sound sometimes naïve to calloused political ears in Europe. It is the simple American aspiration which, in its perpetual struggle with and frequent retreat before the shorter-term expediencies and in-surances, has baffled, irritated and defeated those abroad who have sought to discover in advance what the American position is going to be.

Mr. Wallace spoke simply of the hope of a better world where the common man would not be held down by poverty but would get his chance to educate himself and to make the most of his life. Searching for a phrase which would sum up the world he was envisioning, Wallace said:

"Half in fun and half seriously, I said the other day to Madame Litvinoff: 'The object of this war is to make sure that everybody in the world has the privilege of drinking a quart of milk a day.' She replied: 'Yes, even a pint.' The peace must mean a better standard of living for the common man, not merely in the United States and England, but also in India, Russia, China and Latin America—not merely in the United Nations, but also in Germany and Italy and Japan."

The language Wallace used was not as fine as that which President Roosevelt had earlier used when he defined the four freedoms—freedom of speech and expression, freedom of every person to worship God in his own way, freedom from want, and freedom from fear. But all Wallace was trying to do was to translate the conception of freedom from want into terms which would give it meaning to the common man in America.

But the speech produced in America a torrent of scornful criticism. "It means," a commentator wrote, "that hundreds of millions of Chinese,

Japanese, other Asiatics, Esquimaux and whatnot, whose ancestors have never tasted milk from the hour of their weaning to the grave, and whose stomachs would revolt at the smell of it, must learn to like it—or else." Someone invented the phrase: "Wallace's milk for the Hottentots," and it had a wide and exuberant circulation for a while. So America was to feed and educate the world—teach African bushmen their alphabet, go out on a global missionary jaunt "to make everyone else just like us"? One of the better-known isolationist journals printed an editorial saying:

"We can assure the talkers and dreamers . . . that when and if they try to bring these dreams into cold solid reality after the war they will fan up a fight in this country which will make the recent isolationist-interventionist fight look like a mere warm-up."

In a later speech Mr. Wallace said: "We can have full employment in this country without destroying private initiative, private capital or private enterprise. Government can and must accept the major responsibilities for filling in whatever gaps business leaves." This did not sound like a terribly radical statement. But a few days later Alfred M. Landon, former Governor of Kansas and Republican opponent of President Roosevelt, found in it evidence that Wallace's aims were comparable with those of Hitler. "By the use of Nazi Trojan horse methods," said Mr. Landon, "a small but dominant group of Nazi New Dealers, who seek to establish here what Hitler described in his early days as the National Socialist State, have seized control of their Party." Some time after that the President of the United States Chamber of Commerce, Mr. Eric Johnston, declared that unless the free enterprise system was allowed to function without government interference "there is some danger that our country may go totalitarian."

Mr. Wallace proposed that aggressor nations which in future begin to rearm must be first served with a "cease and desist" order, then warned of the consequences, and then, "if economic quarantine does not suffice," must be bombed by a "United Nations peace force." The *Wall Street Journal* objected that this was as bad as Nazism because "domination by the threat of force" was wrong.

Mr. Wallace suggested that supervision of education in enemy lands might be necessary after the war. In the outcry which followed even Wendell Willkie joined. He said: "Alien ideals superimposed by force will only produce resentment and hatred."

Mrs. Clare Boothe Luce, in a glossy maiden speech in the House of Representatives, contributed *globaloney,* the new word to describe the language of Henry Wallace and others who advance the liberal conception of a better world. Wallace was cartooned as a missionary who, while stewing in a cannibal's pot, was writing out a plan for a beautiful new post-war world and saying: "A pint of milk for all the kiddies, a Sunday school in every block, free vitamins—now let's see, what else?" Or he was shown riding on his donkey with rolls of specifications labelled "How to Make Our Pants Fit an Arab" and "Plans for Giving Our Shirt Away." And that was the real meat in the case which was presented against Henry Wallace. As many a critic said in a speech, or in an editorial, or in the bar, or at a dinner-party: what Henry Wallace was trying to do was depress the American standard of living for the benefit of foreign nations.

This was the real anxiety: that Wallace's better world would bring down the standard of opportunity and comfort which the American people had built up for themselves out of the rich land they had found and developed. Public opinion polls made the point crystal clear. Americans were willing, the polls showed, to lend-lease, to give, to feed the starving peoples. But when they were asked if they would be willing after the war to lower tariff barriers so that cheaper foreign goods should compete with home-made goods they always said no.

v. Insurance against War

The talk in America of post-war responsibilities is now—in the second year of the American war effort—as earnest and as honest as it has the chance to be. No foreign policy can be sound which is not based upon the real interests of the nation which espouses it; but the time is past when it is necessary to demonstrate to Americans that a stable Europe and a stable Asia, from which the recurrent threat of major wars will have been removed, will serve the best interests of every American everywhere.

From day to day fresh news of the Americans is helping to show how now, at this moment, when it is happening, Americans are feeling and reacting. It is conceivable, for example, that a Senate declaration in favour of the assumption of post-war responsibilities by the United States might be a cardinal factor in the eventual result. It is conceivable that, if those Americans who nurture and propagate whenever possible an

old and bitter prejudice against the Soviet Union and a continuous fear
of communism were able to impose their predispositions upon the
nation, the hope for the future might be blighted. It is conceivable that
circumstances might arise in which opinion in America would be close
enough to enable the Senate to make or break a peace treaty, and that
the issue might then depend on whether the present rule by which two-
thirds of the Senate must vote ratification of a treaty is still in existence
at the end of the war, or a new rule has been voted providing that ratification could be secured by a simple majority. It is conceivable that one
or all of these conditions might decide the outcome; but it does not at
present seem likely. What seems likelier is that the state of mind of the
American millions at the time when the peace comes to be written will
have most to do with the policy the United States will pursue.

There is no way of guaranteeing in advance what the Americans will
have felt, thought and decided by then. They will still be under the influence of the instinct which was formed in George Washington's time.
On the other hand, it is almost certainly true that, as has been said by
Professor Allan Nevins, a great authority on American history: "To
some extent every war begins where the last great war left off." Americans are in a frame of mind which reveals that the lessons, disillusion-
ments and emotions of the last war have left foundations of understanding which did not exist before.

Watching the scene close up, you find yourself able to produce strong
arguments both that the Americans will advance in a liberal new world,
and that the Americans will apply the conservative brake. Myself, I return to the conviction that has grown upon me ever since the grey,
nervous days of the Neutrality Act, Cash-and-Carry, and State Department negotiations with the Japanese.

There is the profound, understandable, human desire of the Americans to keep their plenteous country out of trouble, and there is in the
background the instinct to do it with an isolationist foreign policy which
has long succeeded and only lately failed. There is the other instinct that
we call American Idealism, a thing which, though it has been badly
mauled since Wilson's time, retains its connotation and means as it
always has done that the American people are at heart the same sort of
wistful Christians as we are.

I return to the conviction that the ultimate issue, the degree of American participation in the international future, will be decided by the extent to which the American people from now on become convinced that

a system of collective security which will work is being devised. They would like to take out insurance against war—who wouldn't? They are disposed to go along with the British, the Chinese and the Russians. They have entered a full alliance this time: they never went so far last time. But you are apt always to encounter in and not alone among those Americans who are labelled isolationist a sentiment which reflects no more of the hard-headed talk of the business men's luncheon club than of Wilsonian idealism. It is the straightforward feeling that international insurance, like insurance for fire and theft, will require the payment of a premium, and that before you pay a premium you should take the precaution of looking to see whether the company issuing the policy is a sound one and will be both able and ready to meet the possible claims upon it.

It will not be possible to convince the American people, I think, that any Balance of Power scheme is good enough by itself. It will be similarly useless to base any peace upon a plan in which the Atlantic Charter has to be ratified as an act of faith alone. But if there can be accomplished a peace by which the nations' trust in God is seen to be supplemented by stocks of dry powder, the American people will be as grateful as anyone else for it and will put their heart into it.

XVI AMERICANS IN ENGLAND
By Colonel Elliott C. Cutler

---

1. REACTIONS AND PREJUDICES

THE ADVENT of an American in Britain provokes in this visitor much the same initial reactions as would occur to anyone on arriving in a strange country. A newcomer, be he immigrant, traveller or soldier, cannot help but be struck by the apparent variations in customs and manners, the modifications in dress and habits, which serve to remind him that he is a visitor, not a native. But in addition to these sensations common to all visitors, the advent of an American in Britain is complicated by the fact that both visitor and native speak a common language. This commonness of speech simplifies intercourse. The American, therefore, is much more rapidly inducted into the customs and manners of those he visits, and more rapidly learns that they are far different from his own folk at home. Man being by nature conservative, these differences seem great. The very slowness of speech and action of the British as compared to the Americans is rapidly appraised and usually criticized. Thus, the new arrival, instead of being grateful that he can talk to people and bridge the gap of loneliness, finds through the very commonness of speech an implement which separates him rapidly from his hosts. He hastily judges the reserve of the British as haughtiness or "softness," and this widens a breach he should lend every effort to close.

Moreover, when the American comes to Britain, he comes with prejudices and preconceived notions. He has been brought up to think that the "Red Coats," who fought his antecedents at Lexington and who were defeated at Yorktown, were his enemies then, and on occasion imagines that they might, even to-day, be a threat to his freedom and existence. Such may be the pernicious influence of schoolroom textbooks. Also, the American, from his years of isolation, is apt to think any trouble in a locality reflects the type of people there. He is hasty in his judgment and feels that, having helped to settle one quarrel in Europe, he should not have to come here again, that people who continually quarrel are not really worth saving and that had the people here made a small effort since 1918 this would not have arisen. This feeling is not so strongly anti-British as distaste of war, a feeling that somehow or other America is being pulled into the war to help others out. One sees this in the greater amount of homesickness among Americans here than during the last war. One feels it in the smaller amount of singing among troops and in the lesser degree of fraternizing between the forces. Perhaps the American is just taking out on the British his antipathy to war; indeed, it is not only peculiar to the Americans, for long before America entered the war, signs that the general attitude towards war was peculiar led to the common saying that this war was a "phoney" war.

II. Young America Sums Up

But the anti-British feeling exists and can be read between the lines of the following note written by an American youngster of eighteen to his mother whilst in training at a camp in Mid-Western United States.

"They [his barrack mates] don't think it would do any harm if America pulled out of the war, for they believe this war is being fought to protect Big Business and England. In a way both these parties have perhaps the biggest stake in the war—the most to lose. Whether these men are right or wrong is beside the point—they will fight and fight well along with the great majority of enlisted men who fight because they were drafted and feel they have a disagreeable job to do before they can get back to their families again. Only a few, I believe, realize the great stake which America has in this war and are therefore anxious to do all they can to win. We ought to take a leaf from history and notice that all really great armies have been officered (and soldiered) by the so-called fanatical few who believed heart and soul in their cause. The French armies which Napoleon used to such brilliant success were composed of Revolutionary 'fanatics.' It was when this faith in their cause died out among the French officers that they were finally defeated—by 'fanatical' Spaniards and Russians whose homes were at stake and English nobles whose way of life was at stake. In 1870 the Germans marched through Austria and France because of the new Nationalistic spirit that permeated the Junker officers. In 1914 the same spirit almost won the World War, but a glorious British and French nobility, seeing their world tumble around them, hung on until the new American Democracy—eager to show the world what they could do—came in and brought them a hollow victory—for all that was left of France was the hollow wreck that fell in pieces at the first blow in this war, and a muddled, confused Britain, incapable of any consistent policy and unable to take any offensive action again. Out of the ruins there rose two small fanatical parties—the Communists and the Fascists (Nazis)—who whipped the stolid leaderless peoples of Russia and Germany into line, dominating their Gorts and their armies and created thereby the two most powerful countries in Europe—the world, perhaps. Whatever may be said, it is *still* the Communist Radical who whips the Red Army into repeated attack in spite of tremendous losses! And it is still the true Nazi spirit which makes the far outnumbered but élite Afrika Korps hold out in Tunisia—for the Afrika Korps men are young and enthusiastic. What makes the British 8th Army so effective I do not understand, unless there is some truth in the theory that out of the ruins of London there arose a new British spirit typified by the dogged middle-class solidity as represented in their Prime Minister. Or perhaps some of the spirit of 1914–18 was preserved in the terrible years of the Great Depression and has been relayed on to the British Army by the small, élite R.A.F., whose biggest gift to the British people (the 'so many' of Churchill's speech) was the spark of pride, the 'something to shout about' that the aristocracy—hungry Britain—needed so badly.

"In America the situation is entirely different in some ways but alike in others. America was disappointed, disillusioned by the last war—result: a mob of isolationist Middle Westerners who are ruining America. The Great American Public is not all out for the war, and Washington is filled with bumble-brains. It is up to the American Aristocracy (and I don't mean the moneyed class—you realize) to pull our country and our way of life through this war or else we shall be subdued by the aristocracy of brute-force and intellectual regimentation which characterizes Nazism. That is why I feel it is my duty to fight and not just sit around. . . ."

The above letter reflects both the education and the thinking of Young America. It must be reckoned with. It reveals a proud young spirit eager to offer his all, but a little critical all the same. Perhaps this young soldier forgets the century of peaceful amity during which the natural common viewpoint of the great Anglo-Saxon peoples, their way of life, their sense of fairness and love of individual liberty, have merged them into the greatest force for democracy this civilization has given rise to. The American also forgets that each generation is different from its predecessor and that change is an essential characteristic of Nature's recurring phenomena. These initial prejudices on the part of the American must be looked at with similar natural prejudices on the part of the Britisher, who has a perfect right to say that the United States of America of Revolutionary days was just a crowd of undisciplined rowdies, and can point out with historical accuracy that many of the "solid" folk were "Tories," who left the colonies when war was declared. Moreover, the Englishman resents the rapid judgments his American Allies often make and retires into his taciturn shell as a matter of defence at once; thus we see our desire for Anglo-American amity beset by two difficulties—firstly, the common speech which makes for a rapid separation of the people; and secondly, the prejudices evoked by past, not present, experiences.

What do we Americans actually know of the British to-day? If one lives here a little while, one is impressed beyond words with their uniform discipline as a people, and their ability to continue each day much as they did before. This equanimity and solidarity of the people is stupendous when carefully studied. The "black-out" of a great metropolitan area like London is an immense and startling tribute to the discipline of the people, and when we look at the ability of the English to withstand the war thus, we must marvel at their consistency and purpose, and wonder whether we ourselves could "take it." It must appear that the very ability of the Englishman to go perhaps a little slowly, to do each day's job as well as it can be done, irrespective of whether it is sport, love, work or war, is the very thing that has saved this land from extermination. The more mercurial people, amongst whom the Americans must count themselves, who enter with terrific pace into the initial effort, may more easily burn out, get tired, and at the end of a year need a vacation or a rest in order to carry out the day's duties. We have much to learn from our English friends.

III. Our Common Purpose

And before we close, let us see two statements by young representatives of Britain and America. The first quotation is from a letter written by Flying Officer H. C. Carpenter, R.A.F., to his mother and later published in the *Daily Telegraph Third Miscellany;* the second is from a letter written by a young American boy of eighteen in a U.S. Army Air

Force Training School to his mother. Their spirits seem to soar in the same *milieu*.

"This is something far greater than anything that has ever threatened civilization: it is the Armageddon, perhaps, that seers told of, the final struggle between justice and injustice. If we fail now, we fail our children, our children's children, and we bind countless generations to the brutalities of a fanatical and impossible creed of the worst kind. As I watched the pitiful flight of refugees in Belgium I realized that no sacrifice was too great to rid the world of this accursed evil. And so I shall fight this time in the air: however small in the eyes of the world is my success—for myself, and through myself to you, it is a victory."

"And, mother, there is no easier way to live or die than in a bomber, so do not think I am looking for glory or excitement. I just want to get in the war and do my best for those people whose lives are broken up by this war. My life is very little weight in the scale and its loss would mean very little to anyone except you and Daddy and my brothers. There are so many men who have wives and children whose lives would be ruined by their loss. . . ."

If now we look back at these views and recognize the common purpose of our people and their desire to live, love and work untrammelled by too much direction, and not desiring regimentation too greatly, we can evaluate them, and the qualities of each may implement and supplement the other. We can see that the pace of the American wedded to the solidarity of the British should be able to weld this fabric into a lasting form of civilization, one in which the quickness of one partner may institute the movement, but one which will last more surely because of the steadfastness of purpose and durability of the other. Thus we must turn to the larger responsibility which now confronts the Anglo-Saxon race. All who speak this language find themselves with an ever-growing concern that they may have a major responsibility for the civilization of the future. If they neglect this responsibility, then their children and children's children will suffer. If they neglect it, the sacrifice made by brave young men, both British and American, in these days will have been in vain. The battle for Britain will be just a note in history playing a minor rôle in the world to come, and the lives lost in the Atlantic will have amounted to nothing and be considered as pure waste.

XVII THE SPIRIT WITHIN US

By Ulric Nisbet

---

1. In the Light of Experience

At the end of 1939, when this Second World War was being waged mainly with words, a relative of mine in the course of a letter gave me news of a by no means unprosperous solicitor, who had been at school with us: "J., whom you regard as True Blue, is helping to train Territorials. However, he finds the war very inconvenient and would much rather it hadn't occurred." And he added, "By the way, what do you believe in? A facile pacifism such as 'if people had behaved in a different way, there wouldn't have been any war' isn't any use against continued Nazi aggression."

Relatives have a habit of being candid with each other, and in our family the result of such candour has in the past produced somewhat heated correspondence, followed by temporary estrangements, comparable in the personal world to Anglo-American relations in the international world of the 'twenties. But with the passage of time we have learnt to live and let live, and during our infrequent meetings limit our discussions to topics about which we share similar views. This particular relative had never shown any sign of caring greatly about the things in which I believe most, and as I had no illusions about my ability to convert him, I did not attempt to reply to that part of his letter quoted above in more than a sentence. What I said was, "I think the individual must work out his own point of view, his own salvation."

Nevertheless his question and the attitude behind his subsequent remark cannot, so far as I am concerned, be disposed of in a sentence—a sentence moreover that lends itself too easily to wrong interpretation. Now that we are being so thoroughly deprived of individual liberty in order to effect a more vigorous prosecution of the war, it may seem ridiculous to talk about working anything out by oneself. It may also seem, while the full outcome of the struggle is hidden from us, a selfish and disloyal thing to do. The past is past; all that matters now is victory. Together we stand; divided we fall.

I appreciate this point of view only too well, for once upon a time I shared it under very similar circumstances. If now I express a different one, I can only say that it is not due to selfishness or disloyalty, it is due to what war and peace have taught me. If *the soul* of Western civilization is to be saved, the individual must have the courage to stand alone, "to behave in a different way," and he must keep his faith in his ultimate usefulness irrespective of the attitude of his contemporaries. By this I don't mean that he should avoid allying himself with others who seek to build and to share a more recognizable heaven upon earth. Like must help like, so that out of individual thought and experience there may develop collective progress.

Here, then, is one reason why, when I was offered the privilege of contributing something of a spiritual nature to the cause of Anglo-American relations, I accepted. For I know no other way by which we can realize the ideals of fellowship and love, either personally or internationally, than by the way of conscious individual effort and faith. The world, in very truth, is an extension, a projection, of ourselves. What happens within us is repeated on the stage of the world outside us. As we have got to free ourselves from our own jealousies and hatreds and littleness, so we have got to free ourselves from the "unconscious" and superficial viewpoint of life, increasingly thrust upon us by materialistic conditions, and win back the deep power of subjective and inner vision. All the propaganda and intellectual arguments on earth won't suffice to bring us together and keep us together under the strain and stress of historic revolution, if we are, in fact, spiritually separated, spiritually impotent.

It is necessary to look at the past, the present and the future from this different angle and in the light of our own experience. I am going to try to do so, even though briefly, in the hope that it will help to bridge the difficult and often lonely waters between—in two very different senses—the Old World and the New.

II. THEIR WORLD REMADE

First, what do I believe in? When I ask myself that, I am conscious of the tremendous difference between my outlook now and my outlook twenty-five odd years ago; that is to say, between the one that I have worked out myself and the one that I was brought up to have. And because of this I realize that while people of my age or older might very well be likely to think as I do now, I would not be justified in expecting the younger generations, who have not gone through our experiences, to do so. Yet, owing to the opportunity that came my way in pre-war days of talking to hundreds of thinking young men and women from many countries and from many walks of life, I discovered that their general outlook was far more akin to my own than was the outlook of the great majority of older people with whom I had been associated. If Youth were not being called upon to fight and die again in war as a result of the outlook of its elders and fundamentally, whatever may be pretended to the contrary, in support of that outlook, I might not feel so keenly about this, for time would be on the side of Youth, and Youth with its courage and vitality would have a fair chance to remake the world.

During the last war I believed that my elders would remake it so that Youth would never have to go through such an experience again. But the world that they brought back into being after that war is not the one that I want Youth to fight for in this war. After all, what is the value of any world, or any outlook, that within the space of a single generation produces a great war, a disastrous peace, and a second great war? To those who fear change because they fear for their wealth, their prestige, their power, there is no doubt considerable value in keeping things as they were. But to Youth, which has to pay the heaviest price for this inertia and selfishness, there is something better to work and suffer for —a new world, a world in which ordinary people are not called upon to slaughter each other every twenty-five years.

What about it? To which the very powerfully organized forces of the old world—as opposed to the far weaker vanguard of the new world —will still retort in one form or another: "Hitler and his gang have got to be smashed. That's all that matters at present. Anything else that is controversial and likely to disrupt national or Allied unity must be put aside. There'll be plenty of time for such things when we've won the war."

It sounds reasonable enough on the surface, doesn't it? And it might be reasonable enough if exactly the same opinion had not been expressed during the last great war (with the Kaiser in place of Hitler) and proved utterly false. We in Britain and you in America did help to win that war at the cost of a multitude of dead. We did have time, and we should have had plenty of it, to get down to the making of that new world "fit for heroes to live in." In fact, there was a very great deal of liberal-progressive planning beneath the surface *before* the war ended. To quote Michael Straight:

"Where, in the Atlantic Charter, or the master Lease-Lend agreements, or the speeches of our leaders, is there anything to compare with the words of Woodrow Wilson before the first plenary session of the Congress when he said: 'We are here to see . . . that the very foundations of this war are swept away. Those foundations were the private choice of small coteries of civil rulers and their military staffs. Those foundations were the holding together of legions of unwilling subjects by the duress of arms. Those foundations were the power of small bodies of men to work their will upon mankind and use them as pawns in a game. And nothing less than the emancipation of the world from these things will accomplish peace.' "

And in England, "when . . . Ben Tillett won an all-important by-election at North Salford in November 1917, Webb wrote, in *The New Statesman,* one of the most moving documents of the war, 'The Vision of North Salford': 'The old politics are dead. Not the workmen only, but also the great mixed membership of the industrial co-operative societies and a considerable section of the shopkeeping and professional classes with a sprinkling of manufacturing employers, not to speak of the young men from the universities who are now in khaki, have lost faith in any more "reconstruction" of the England of 1913–14. The demand is for a new social order.' "[1]

But something went wrong, didn't it? Do you know what it was? If not, let me recall once more the damning indictment of a man who put truth and good faith above honours and expediency—Lawrence of Arabia:

"We lived many lives in those whirling campaigns, never sparing ourselves: yet when we achieved and the new world dawned, the old men came out again and took our victory to remake in the likeness of the former world they knew.

[1] *Will We Lose the Peace Again?* by Michael Straight. (*New Statesman*, Jan. 30, 1943, reprinted from the *New Republic*, Nov. 30, 1942.)

"Youth could win but had not learned to keep: and was pitiably weak against age. We stammered that we had worked for a new heaven and a new earth, and they thanked us kindly and made their peace."

"The old men came out again and took our victory to remake in the likeness of the former world they knew." And while they sat and schemed and argued with each other, millions of ordinary people, believing and trusting in them and in their desire for a new and better world, turned to the difficult task of finding a peace-time job and to the happier task of raising another generation of Youth—a generation that would never have to go through "that," never have to kill or be killed in order to "make the world safe for democracy." *Never!*

Well, public opinion, what about it now? Do you still think that the only thing that matters is to get rid of Hitler and *his* gang? Do you still think that there'll be plenty of time to begin making a new and better world when we've won *this* war?

III. IT DEPENDS ON OURSELVES

It's no use any of us pretending that the disastrous peace and this second great war are entirely the result of Hitler's machinations. Nazism wasn't built upon hot air any more than Fascism or Communism was. Like all social revolutions, not forgetting the French and American Revolutions, it was built upon conditions that were ripe for it—injustice, instability, disillusionment, despair—undergone by ordinary people like you and me. Hence it isn't enough to wipe out Nazism; we have got to wipe out the conditions that permitted it, and not only in Germany. Unless we are agreed upon this and make it a cardinal point of our peace aims despite all the propaganda of the old world, the peace will be lost for ordinary folk everywhere just as certainly as it was lost for them before.

Nor is it any use saying, as some people will, "Well, what can an ordinary person like me, or you for that matter, do about it, anyway?" There isn't one of us who can't do something about it—if we want to. Such negative attitudes denote the hypocrite, the fool or the moral coward. Those of us who take refuge in them are, whether we know it or not, almost as much responsible for the present chaos as are the mandarins of the old world whose supreme energies were devoted to the personal and national pursuit of wealth, prestige and power. For without the hypocrite, the fool and the coward as their pawns these men might have been prevented after the immense suffering of the last war from using the victory and the peace to re-establish their world, and from betraying principles and pledges and peoples for the purpose of maintaining it.

I say, "they might have been prevented." But did not World War I kill the very men who would have prevented them? And will not World War II do so also unless there are enough of us who, in the light of our experience, are prepared to devote ourselves to the task of ensuring that what Youth is supposedly fighting for and dying for is not this time an empty dream?

"Peace, and with it happiness. Life, and with it love. Justice and freedom for all men." Are these ideals impossible of attainment? Yes, absolutely impossible, unless we, *as individuals,* are willing to work and suffer for them, and unless we, *collectively,* choose leaders who will value them above wealth and prestige and power. There can be no new order in Europe or anywhere else so long as people think, or pretend, that it can be brought about at the top without any change of outlook or without any renunciations on their part. To achieve it we have got to renounce practically all our traditional ideas about nationalism and patriotism and class and wealth—all forms of snobbishness, all causes of war—and regard ourselves as members of humanity, sharers of the world's wealth and the world's problems in common. We have got to break through the false veneer of our too complex and already obsolete civilization and establish a simpler existence based on an altogether truer understanding of the meaning and value of love. It is only thus, by revising our own personal outlook and choosing leaders who are motivated by the same ideals, that we can help to create social, political and economic conditions that will function for peace instead of for war.

With the radio, the aeroplane, and other instruments of our time Science has broken down the old frontiers between nations and brought them together. Surely it is obvious that what Science has accomplished technically mankind must accomplish spiritually, or survival is impossible. In other words, the peoples of the nations have got to get together of their own free will or be forced into slave-union by a conqueror nation. The only alternative is extermination by means of a series of world wars scientifically fought out by evenly balanced groups of nations.

We cannot escape our responsibility as individuals. Each of us must answer the question: How much of our national wealth and prestige and power; how much of our own too, if we have any, are we prepared to sacrifice for the sake of our children and for the sake of common humanity?

"But what use is all this," you may say, "against the menace of Nazism?"

It's no use at all, unless it is the cause for which you are fighting, working, suffering. If it is, it will give you greater inspiration and courage than any other man-made cause can give you during this period of wholesale destructiveness and in the years to come. For it is the cause of Youth and of the ordinary man not in one country or one Empire but everywhere.

IV. REALISTS AND RENEGADES

On the British Victory Medal of 1918 these words are inscribed: "The Great War For Civilization." Millions died in that war, and the men of the old order had their opportunity to build the new world they had promised to those who fought for them. They did not build it, because they did not want it. Why, then, should they want it now? Was not Lord Derby expressing their real aims when he said to the boys of Rossall School in November 1940, "You must fit yourselves for the commercial battle for the world's markets that will follow the war"?

The seeds of World War III are being sown already. Only the spiritual unity of all of us, who call ourselves progressives, can prevent them from germinating. And one of our jobs is to teach these self-styled realists that there is a better solution than battling for the world's markets and that is sharing them.

It was this outlook of the old order that I was brought up to believe in and that I did believe in, or at any rate accepted, throughout the eternity of the First World War and for many years after it in spite of all the disillusionment of those years. I belonged to the "civilization" it stood for; I talked only its language. And in the language of that civilization the epithet for a person like me and everyone else who has forsaken it for a wider humanity is "renegade" or, less politely, "swine."

I don't glory in being regarded as a renegade. It is a tragedy to me that there should be such an impenetrable barrier, erected upon traditions of class and privilege, between those who regard it as their right to rule and possess and to maintain the *status quo* and those who seek a juster division of material things among all persons and peoples. It is a tragedy to me that the Machine is operated for the profit of the few and, in war, for the destruction of the masses instead of being operated for the benefit of everyone. I think, too, of the tragic unfulfilment of the sincere creative worker—the artist, poet, composer, craftsman, neglected and despised by this commercialized civilization for their devotion to things of the mind and spirit, on whom and on which true progress and culture depend. And always there is for me the memory of that lost generation to which I belong, adventurous, idealistic, ignorant—the generation that believed everything it was told.

To you, leaders of the old world and your supporters, I would say this in answer to your charge of "renegade": When you have sent Youth into the hell of modern war to defend your lives, your homes and your possessions; when you have spurred Youth on with glowing phrases about Justice, Liberty and a better world, do you imagine that the remnant who return will have forgotten what you told them? Do you think that they will come back the same in body and mind and soul? If you do—and you did after the last great massacre of Youth—it would be a thousand times better for them and for the generations of the future that you should have to undergo the same experience, the same suffering. Then you, too, might have the same dreams, the same desire for that new and less selfish world—Peace, and with it happiness. Life, and with it love. Justice and freedom for all men.

Where Christianity and common sense have failed, perhaps only the bomber can succeed.

v. THE NEW CONSCIOUSNESS

During the last two years of peace I had that opportunity that I mentioned earlier of talking to members of another generation of Youth and of hearing their views upon the world and the leaders they had inherited. To me those discussions were tremendously inspiring, and curious too—as though my own generation had come back, and we were, all of us, young again, and our lives were repeating themselves. Everything was repeating itself. Men who had organized the First Great War were still in power and getting ready for another one. The same ideals that we had fought for were soon going to be held aloft for us to fight for again. The nations were taking sides, manœuvring for position, as they had when we were boys. We seemed to be travelling around a walled-in circular track that passed through darkness to light and light to darkness. It made me think of a kind of underground railroad with all the points, where lines led elsewhere, hidden by huge posters: "Continue round for Justice, Liberty and Democracy." And we were the passengers, being driven once more towards the darkness and apparently just the same as we had been twenty-three or -four years earlier. Outwardly—yes, we were the same. But inwardly we were different. There was not one, even the youngest of these friends of mine, who looked at t iings as I, for instance, had looked at them back in 1914. They believed just as much, if not more, in Justice, Liberty and Democracy, but they did not believe any longer in the possibility of attaining them within that walled-in circular system. Because they had sought for the truth, they had glimpsed it, in spite of the posters. It was this that was so inspiring to me.

They are scattered now, and some of them have already died. Were they representative of Youth as a whole? No, I cannot say that. Youth is naturally progressive, but it is not encouraged to think ahead of its elders, so more often than not it does not think at all. "No politics!" these elders cry (and they have cried it at me). They mean, in fact, no progress; no outlook other than their own; nothing that will upset the maintenance of "civilization" as they know it. "You must fit yourselves for the commercial battle for the world's markets that will follow the war"—this is their message to Youth. *This is their world, remade.*

VI. BATTLE FOR TRUTH

It happened before. Are we going to let it happen again?

"I know. But I've got a wife and family to support, so I don't dare risk doing anything about it. I'd lose my clients . . . I'd lose my customers . . . I'd lose my chance of promotion . . . I'd lose my job."

It *is* happening again, or men wouldn't talk like that. Everywhere those who have worked for a new world have learned the power of the old order to shackle them to the old world. And next time it won't be a capitalist world but a totalitarian one. Society glorified the gangster and the Beer Baron (of whose outlook Nazism is the natural projection), and like the gangster and the Beer Baron, Big Business will group and muscle in and battle for the markets and domination of the earth.

Freedom! Is that the kind of freedom for which we are fighting? For my part I can see no freedom from the terrible economic stranglehold of the old order, no hope of individual liberty and a richer, fuller life for the nobodies after this war, unless we fit ourselves now for the *spiritual* battle on which our future and the very future of humanity depend—the battle for truth.

It is easier to fight for one's country than it is to fight for truth. In our present rôle *as members of a class and nation* we do not and cannot stand for truth (unless it happens to suit our class or nation); it is left to us to do so as individuals, if we dare. And the greater the value to common humanity of the particular truth for which we dare to stand, the greater the likelihood of our having to suffer at the hands of our group.

"If the world hate you, ye know that it hated me before it hated you." It was the world of the high priests and reactionaries that hated Christ. The mob was their tool, easily roused, easily fooled, because it was neither educated to think nor capable of teaching itself to do so.

In this battle for truth there is a fundamental issue of supreme importance that I believe we must force to the front if we sincerely desire a new co-operative system not just for the English-speaking nations alone (which is impossible, anyhow) but for Western civilization as a whole. It is that we acknowledge in our hearts and through our religious and political leaders our share of the guilt for these wars. How large or how small a share posterity will judge; we cannot. What matters is that we have this means of repudiating the hypocrisy of the past and of rallying the forces of good everywhere—the only forces that have the slightest chance of leading "the forward march of the common people in all lands towards their just inheritance."

I believe in the individual and the right of the individual to work out his own salvation. But the individual, however wonderful his own heaven may be, is helpless against world currents of the present magnitude and powerless (except through martyrdom) to change the course of them. Therefore we must find each other and help each other under the leadership of men whom we can trust and with whom we can work out not two separate programmes of behaviour to fit within the old narrow frontiers of our respective nations (as though we were creatures of different species, forced to seek different ends) but a single programme based upon common loyalty to that different way of thinking and living, in which fellowship and creative service replace power and profit as the dominating motives of society.

"No man can serve two masters: for either he will hate the one, and love the other; or else he will hold to the one, and despise the other. Ye cannot serve God and mammon."

Let us begin, then, by translating our present group loyalty into loyalty to our fellow-seekers in all lands, and let us draw faith and inspiration and courage for our struggle as individuals from the martyred yet living Christ of the New Testament. "God is a Spirit: and they that worship him must worship him in spirit and in truth. . . . If ye continue in my word then are you my disciples indeed; And ye shall know the truth, and the truth shall make you free."

Do we need to have hell knocked out of us in order to become conscious of the truth that is within us? I used to think that one could pass on experience and thus save others the cost of it. I'm not so sure, now. I certainly needed the experience of that first great tragedy to teach me that there was something infinitely more worth working for than wealth or power, or any material ambition—and that was happiness. And I needed the experience of the aftermath with all that it brought of personal sorrow and collective disillusionment to teach me that happiness is the finding of love and that love in the ultimate reality, the world of the spirit, is one with truth and beauty, and God. So, during the long years of this war I have learnt the power of the spirit to overcome physical separation and physical loneliness.

In consequence, I see nothing starry-eyed or Utopian in advocating a truer understanding of the meaning and value of love—and I am thinking now of the love of man for woman, woman for man, and of them both for their children—as the cornerstone of the new age, so that there may be the happiness of personal unity on which to build the happiness of international unity, commencing with us, the English-speaking peoples, and radiating outwards to other peoples through the power of the spirit within us.

The isolationist and imperialist may say that I'm prejudiced through being married to an American and having a young daughter who is both British and American

I guess I am!

BIOGRAPHICAL NOTES

The Right Hon. Sir Archibald Sinclair, Bart., K.T., P.C., C.M.G., M.P. Chevalier de la Légion d'Honneur. Served in the Great War, 1914–18; became personal Military Secretary to the Secretary of State for War and Air, 1919–20; in 1921–22 was assistant secretary to the Secretary of State for the Colonies. Chief Liberal Whip, 1930–31; Secretary of State for Scotland, 1931–32; Leader of the Liberal Party in the House of Commons, 1935; Secretary of State for Air, 1940.

Sir Philip Gibbs, K.B.E. Author and Journalist. At early age became a literary Editor of the *Daily Mail, Daily Chronicle,* and *Tribune.* War correspondent in the Balkan Wars and throughout the Great War, 1914–19, on the Western Front for the *Daily Chronicle, Daily Telegraph,* and *New York Times.* Was knighted for his war services; Chevalier de la Légion d'Honneur. Author of many novels and historical works. Vice-Chairman of Charing Cross Hospital.

The Right Hon. Viscount Samuel, P.C., G.C.B., G.B.E., D.C.L. Member of Parliament for Cleveland Division, North Riding, 1912–18; Darwen Division, Lancashire, 1929–35. Appointed Under-Secretary of State for Home Office, 1905; Chancellor of the Duchy of Lancaster with a seat in the Cabinet, 1909; Postmaster-General, 1910; President of Local Government Board, 1914, and again Postmaster-General, 1915; Home Secretary, 1916; Chairman of Select Committee of the House of Commons on National Expenditure, 1917–18; High Commissioner for

Palestine, 1920–25; Leader of the Liberal Party, 1931–35; again Home Secretary, 1931–32; Viscount, 1937. Author of works on Politics and Philosophy.

Harold Callender. For several years European correspondent of the *New York Times.* Well known in the United States and Great Britain for his brilliant articles on the political and economic conditions in many countries. Has lately been in Mexico and other parts of Latin America. Now Washington correspondent of the *New York Times.*

Frank Swinnerton. Author of many novels now famous on both sides of the Atlantic. Also distinguished as a literary critic.

Francis W. Hirst. Biographer of *Adam Smith, Thomas Jefferson* and *John Morley.* Editor of *Economist,* 1907–16. A Governor of the London School of Economics. Author of *Liberty and Tyranny* and of books on Political Economy and Public Finance.

The Right Hon. Sir Percy Harris, Bart., P.C., M.P. Called to the Bar, Middle Temple, 1899; Member of the London County Council, 1907–34; Chief Liberal Whip, 1935, and Vice-Chairman of the British-American Parliamentary Committee. Member of Parliament for the Harborough Division of Leicestershire, 1916–18, and for S.W. Division of Bethnal Green since 1922. Author of *London and Its Government.*

The Right Hon. Lord Davies. President of Aberystwyth University; Chairman of the New Commonwealth Society. He served in the Great War, 1914–16, as Lieut.-Colonel commanding 14th Battalion, Royal Welsh Fusiliers, and was appointed Parliamentary Secretary to Mr. Lloyd George in 1916. Author of a number of books on the problems of international security and federation.

Nora Waln is an American, born in Pennsylvania. She is married to an Englishman and has one daughter who, like herself, was educated at Swarthmore College. Author of two books, the first about China, entitled *The House of Exile,* and the other about Germany, entitled *Reaching for the Stars.* She is now nearing the completion of a third, a book about England. In England, besides keeping her husband's house, she administers the Kappa Kappa Gamma Fraternity Fund for bombed mothers and children, a fund established by United States and Canadian University Women; serves on the China Convoy Committee of the Friends Ambulance Unit, a bridge of friendship organization sponsored jointly by American and British Quakers; and is an American representative to the London headquarters of the Associated Countrywomen of the World, an organization of which Madame Chiang Kai-shek is a member.

Sir Cecil Hurst, G.C.M.G., K.C.B., LL.D. Edinburgh and Cambridge. Called to the Bar, Middle Temple, 1853; K.C., 1913. Assistant Legal Adviser to the Foreign Office, 1902, and Legal Adviser, 1918. Legal Secretary to the Peace Conference at The Hague, 1907; a British delegate to the League of Nations, 1927–29. Elected a Judge of the Permanent Court of International Justice at The Hague, 1929, and President, 1934.

Megan Lloyd George, M.P. for Anglesey since 1929. Vice-President, Liberal Party Organization; Member of the Women's Consultative Committee of the Ministry of Labour; Justice of the Peace for the County of Caernarvon. Also well known as a broadcaster.

Mass-Observation is an independent, scientific, fact-finding body that for the past six years has documented the processes of social change, of political trends, and of public and private opinion in a series of books, bulletins, broadcasts and articles.

Antonia Bell was chosen by the English-Speaking Union for the Walter Hines Page Scholarship as lecturer in the United States, 1941–42. She travelled extensively in the Middle West, California, Texas and the South, lecturing to schools, Rotary and Women's Clubs and other institutions on social conditions in Britain during the war.

Air-Commodore P. F. M. Fellowes, D.S.O., joined the *Britannia* in 1899 and became a pilot in the R.N.A.S. in 1915. He was wounded, shot down and captured in 1918 at Zeebrugge while taking part in a dive-bombing attack on the Lock Gates. Twice mentioned in dispatches and awarded the D.S.O. and bar. In command of an expedition which surveyed and opened the first regular world air route between Cairo and Baghdad. He received the high appreciation of the C.-in-C. and High Commissioner in Turkey for his services in command of the Air Force in the Chanak Crisis, 1922–23. Director of Airship Development, 1924–28; led the Houston Everest Expedition in 1933 and flew over Kanchenjunga. Air A.D.C. to H.M. the King from 1925 to 1929.

Robert Waithman. During the past six years chief correspondent of the *News Chronicle* in the U.S.A. He has written many admirable and revealing dispatches from New York and Washington and has earned a high reputation with his "American Diary," a weekly summary of what America is thinking and doing, and his book, *Report on America*. Before going to the U.S.A. he worked for several years in the Manchester and London offices of the *News Chronicle,* gaining a wide experience of every kind of journalistic work.

Colonel Elliott C. Cutler, Professor of Surgery, Harvard University. Chief Surgeon, Peter Bent Brigham Hospital, Boston, Mass.; formerly Professor of Surgery, Western Reserve University, Cleveland, Ohio, and Chief Surgeon, Lakeside Hospital, Cleveland, Ohio. Previous war service: April 1917–April 1919. Capt.—Major. Distinguished Service Medal. Honorary Degrees: University of Vermont, University of Strasbourg, Royal College of Surgeons.

Ulric Nisbet. Left school at age of seventeen to join the Army on the outbreak of the Great War, August 1914; served in France, Flanders and India; was wounded three times and promoted captain. Has since worked in Burma, England and the U.S.A., writing in spare time, occasionally under pseudonyms. From 1938–40 co-warden of Salcombe, Devon, Youth Hostel with his artist wife, Christine Bacheler Nisbet of Hartford, Conn. In 1941, while warden of the first Ipswich, Suffolk, Youth Centre, he organized a committee of boys and girls to establish regular contact with the Youth of Ipswich, Mass.